YOU DON'T LOSE 'TIL YOU QUIT TRYING

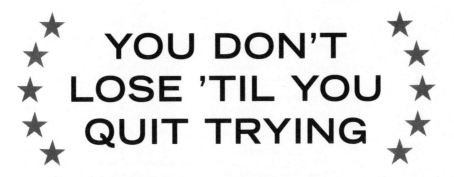

YOU DON'T LOSE 'TIL YOU QUIT TRYING

Lessons on Adversity and
Victory from a Vietnam Veteran
and Medal of Honor Recipient

Sammy Lee Davis

with Caroline Lambert

BERKLEY CALIBER, NEW YORK

BERKLEY
CALIBER

An imprint of Penguin Random House LLC
375 Hudson Street, New York, New York 10014

This book is an original publication of Penguin Random House LLC.

Library of Congress Cataloging-in-Publication Data

Names: Davis, Sammy Lee. | Lambert, Caroline.
Title: You don't lose 'til you quit trying : lessons on adversity and victory
from a Vietnam veteran and Medal of Honor recipient /
Sammy Lee Davis, MOH, with Caroline Lambert.
Other titles: You don't lose until you quit trying
Description: First edition. | New York : Berkley Caliber, 2016.
Identifiers: LCCN 2015047951 (print) | LCCN 2016007810 (ebook) |
ISBN 9780425283035 (hardback) | ISBN 9780698408029 ()
Subjects: LCSH: Davis, Sammy Lee. | Davis, Sammy Lee—Childhood and youth. |
Davis, Sammy Lee—Philosophy. | Vietnam War, 1961–1975—Personal
narratives, American. | Soldiers—United States—Biography |
Heroes—United States—Biography | Medal of Honor—Biography | Vietnam
War, 1961–1975—Veterans. | Veterans—United States—Biography. | Disabled
veterans—United States—Biography. | BISAC: HISTORY / Military /
Veterans. | BIOGRAPHY & AUTOBIOGRAPHY / Military. | BIOGRAPHY &
AUTOBIOGRAPHY / Personal Memoirs.
Classification: LCC DS559.5 .D377 2016 (print) | LCC DS559.5 (ebook) |
DDC 959.704/342092—dc23
LC record available at http://lccn.loc.gov/2015047951

First edition: May 2016

PRINTED IN THE UNITED STATES OF AMERICA

10   9   8   7   6   5   4   3   2   1

Jacket design by George Long.
Jacket photo of the Vietnam Veterans Memorial © f11 photo / Shutterstock.
Interior text design by Kelly Lipovich.

| Penguin |
| Random |
| House |

For my wife, Dixie

You only live once, but if you do it right, once is enough.

—MAE WEST

I am an American; free born and free bred, where I acknowledge no man as my superior, except for his own worth, or as my inferior, except for his own demerit.

—THEODORE ROOSEVELT

Foreword by Gary Sinise

In 1967, Sammy L. Davis was at war.

Like his grandfathers, his father, and his two brothers before him, Sammy was now a US Army soldier. Back then, I was still in grade school and had no idea what Sammy and his fellow brothers in arms were doing so far away in Southeast Asia. I knew nothing of the challenges they faced and the difficulties they'd had when they returned home. It was a little later in life, when I was in my early twenties, that I received a real education from the Vietnam veterans in my wife's family. They told me what it was like to fight there, to lose comrades and friends, and then to return home to a divided nation that had turned its back on them.

Sammy L. Davis was one of those soldiers fighting for his country in the jungles of Vietnam, and Vietnam changed Sammy's life forever: Besides the memory of war that soldiers live with for the rest of their lives, he also received the nation's highest military honor for valor in combat, the Congressional Medal of Honor.

I have had the great pleasure and privilege to get to know Sammy over the years through the Medal of Honor Foundation and our mutual support of today's active-duty service members and of the veterans who have come before them. I am also proud that he is an ambassador of the Gary Sinise Foundation.

He is a kind, gentle man of great strength and faith. A tender warrior who continues to give in service of something greater than himself. Each day, with courage, dignity, and his lifelong devotion to Duty, Honor, Country, Sammy honors all his fallen brothers, those for whom he wears the medal.

His is an extraordinary story. Yet he would be the first to tell you that he was simply an ordinary soldier doing his job. On November 18, 1967, fighting an enemy force of over fifteen hundred with only forty-two fellow soldiers in his artillery unit, he did his job—and more.

About the medal and going to war, in his own very humble words, he says:

I didn't do anything heroic. I did my job. That's what soldiers do. And if there was one of these [medals] given that night, there should be at least forty-two of them. Because if any one of us had not done his job, there would be none of us alive. It sounds silly perhaps to say that I went to war and found out about love. What real love is. You know, I didn't go to war to kill people. I went to war because I loved my daddy, I wanted him to be proud of me. I went to war because I loved my grandpas, and I loved my country. And when I got over there . . . the reason why we fought so hard was because we discovered we loved each other, that we were all we had. And they became brothers. We became brothers. And that's lasted up . . . you know . . . it's been thirty-six years, and those men that I fought with are still my brothers. So I learned about what real love is.

I have learned a great deal from this brave, humble soldier and his giving heart. His story, told in the following pages, will grip you, and move you, and inspire you, and teach you about love, as Sammy has done for me. I love him dearly, and after reading this story, I have no doubt that you will too.

I am grateful that our country has such men and women, who give so much of themselves, so that we can remain free.

And to Sammy, let me simply say: *Thank you, brother.*

Preface

FIRE SUPPORT BASE CUDGEL, MEKONG DELTA, VIETNAM

NOVEMBER 18, 1967

"Hey, Davis! Wake up! Can't keep my eyes open. Talk to me, man! I need to stay awake until my guard's over."

It seems I have only been asleep for minutes.

I sit up and look at my watch. 1:45 a.m. Only fifteen minutes and I will replace Marvin Hart anyway. So I slip on my boots and grab some instant-coffee packets out of my C rations. I find an empty C ration can, dip it in the rice paddy, and fill it with murky water. I light a cloth sandbag and stuff it inside an empty 105mm canister, hang my tin of water on top, and wait for it to boil. One cup of gourmet coffee coming up!

The moon is bright, but the night air is thick. No breeze to cut the heat. It is quiet, except for the guys slapping armies of skeeters

---

all over the encampment. Our unit was airlifted here this morning with four of the six 105mm howitzer artillery guns that make up our Battery C. We have left the other two at our home base in Tan Tru, Long An Province. Our guns glittered in the sun, suspended in the air before the choppers landed. We're here to support the Fifth Battalion, Sixtieth Infantry Regiment. Hart and I work the same howitzer, together with Sergeant James Gant and Delbert Cole, a city boy from Vidor, Texas. This is not my regular gun. My regular howitzer has stayed at Tan Tru. But the unit was short of guys for this operation, so I have volunteered.

We're set up in a bog. There's hardly any solid ground, and our howitzers are on a small patch barely above water. The wheels are in the mud and so are the trails that support the gun carriage. We've bolstered our position with sandbags, but as soon as we started digging, water seeped into our foxholes. We are by a large canal about thirty-three feet wide and ten feet deep that runs north–south, and my gun is closest to the water. In front of us, across the canal, an expanse of tall grass and palm trees runs into a thick jungle. Behind us are open rice paddies, where Battery D has set up three howitzers on aluminum platforms standing on hydraulic legs, but we can't see them. Some infantry guys are also securing the perimeter, but I don't know where they are. This is Fire Support Base Cudgel. We're deep in the Mekong Delta, west of Cai Lay.

"Thanks for sitting with me, Davis," says Hart. He's a country boy like me, but he hails from Oscoda, Michigan.

"No problem," I say, yawning. "I wasn't sleeping that good anyway."

While waiting for my coffee, I try to hang on to the dream I was having a few minutes ago. I've just turned twenty-one, and my sleep was filled with cold beers and the prospect of ladies stateside. I'll finally be able to order drinks with a valid ID. Now, that's something to look forward to.

My thoughts of cold beers are shattered by the sound of a mortar sliding down the tube. Then another. And another. I can hear them clearly, so I know they're real close.

"I didn't know we had any mortars," I tell Hart. "When did they move in?"

Hart pauses. "We don't have any mortars."

Just then, the first round lands and hits our makeshift ammo dump—the area where we have stacked and organized our ammunition. The mortar sets off the ammo like fireworks from hell; this ain't no Fourth of July. Half deaf and blinded by the explosion, we crawl to our foxholes and scream to the other guys to take cover. For the next forty minutes, mortars rain all over us. When they slack off to just a few rounds a minute, we get ready for what we know is coming next: waves of Vietnamese soldiers.

A mortar lands between my foxhole and Hart's and knocks me silly. Hart and Cole probably think it hit me dead center, and they yell for me. But I can't yell back. It takes a few minutes for my head to clear. Then I get up on one elbow and peek over the sandbag. I can't see Hart or Cole, but I see the hole the mortar left no more than a foot away from me.

"Poor Davis caught the sucker dead on!" I hear Cole say.

"Yeah, he didn't have a chance."

I feel my limbs, and everything's still there. "If this nonsense doesn't stop, I'll call my congressman!" I holler to them.

Their heads pop up, faces and helmets covered in mud. Boy, am I happy to see them. They cuss me for a minute. "Thanks guys. I'm okay."

Earlier in the day, our artillery unit fired nonstop from eight in the morning until five in the afternoon to support the Fifth/Sixtieth Infantry. By late afternoon, the enemy broke contact. A Huey chopper landed by our base, and a major got out.

"Your probability of getting hit tonight is a hundred percent," he announced.

So, what's new, I thought. *We've been hit all day by mortar rounds and small-arms fire.* Then the major turned around, stepped back into his chopper, and flew off. In the early evening, a few soldiers wearing South Vietnamese uniforms came walking down the canal and stopped to ask us for cigarettes. They had a good look around, and after they'd walked on, we reported their visit to our captain, who radioed the Vietnamese commander for the zone. When we heard that our South Vietnamese allies had no troops in our area, a chill ran down my spine. That wasn't good. What we didn't know yet was worse: A whole enemy battalion with heavy weapons was on its way in. Fifteen hundred men. They were only two miles away.

So Hart, Cole, myself, and the rest of our unit are now having a taste of the hundred-percent probability. We hear orders being screamed in English from across the river.

"Go kill the GI!"

A bugle signals the charge. As we look across the water, waves of Vietnamese soldiers storm out of the jungle and head straight toward our position. A few wear the collarless black shirt and pants that look like pajamas, typical of the Vietcong insurgents. Many more are in the North Vietnamese Army's khaki uniform and pith helmets. Others wear only T-shirts and shorts. Hundreds of them swarm in the open space only twenty-five meters away. *Oh boy.* There are only forty-two of us kids in Battery C.

Then we hear our mean-ass Sergeant Gant, our crew chief.

"Get up and turn the gun!" he yells.

A twenty-seven-year-old professional soldier from Lansing, Michigan, Sergeant James Gant is old. And worse, Sergeant Gant is mean. When other gun crews are done for the day, he makes us sit back to back in hundred-degree heat and set the time fuses that go on artillery shells with blindfolds. He hands us a fuse, we set it, and if we get it right, he taps our backs so we pass it on. If we get it wrong, he whacks us on the back of the head, and we do it again. To us this is pointless and ridiculous. The Army issues flashlights and fuse setters—which look like big wrenches—so why do this by hand, and blindfolded? Mean old Sergeant Gant also makes us polish every single bullet out of every single clip every single day. He checks clips every evening, and if he finds bullets that do not blind you in the sun, he's all over us. All of us in the battery hate working his gun because he's so strict.

So when mean old Sergeant Gant yells that night, we jump. We pull on our flak jackets and run to our howitzer. To fire at the incoming enemy, we have to move the gun so the spades that are supposed to anchor the gun to the ground are in the creek behind us, and the wheels almost in the canal. The mud is knee deep, the enemy is shooting straight at us, and Sergeant Gant is yelling like crazy. We have a hell of a time turning the two-ton gun into the proper position.

"Beehive, muzzle action!" he shouts. We have to lower the barrel of the howitzer until it is horizontal, so it can fire beehive rounds straight at the enemy coming at us.

Before shooting these rounds filled with thousands of razor-sharp, one-inch darts, soldiers are required to stand upright, be visible to the enemy, and shout, "Beehive, beehive, beehive!" We've quickly learned that it's much more practical to shoot first and then jump up and yell our warning.

I grab a round, set the fuse to muzzle action so the darts are released as soon as the round fires out, and ram the shell home in the breech. Cole fires it. The beehive round thins the North Vietnamese out, but more keep coming.

I step over the gun trails to the assistant-gunner position, while Hart, Cole, and Sergeant Gant get more ammo ready. We load another round, and I fire. Then all hell breaks loose. A rocket-propelled grenade fired at our muzzle blast hits the shield of the howitzer that is eight inches from my head. I am blown into my foxhole facedown. Sergeant Gant is hit straight in the chest and disappears. Darkness falls.

When I wake up, my head hurts, my ears are ringing, and I can't hear a thing. My back and legs burn as if fire ants are crawling all over them. I try to brush them off with one hand, but there are no ants. Instead, my fingers find beehive darts and something warm and sticky. *Blood.* The back of my legs and my lower back are covered in blood. The guys manning the howitzer behind us thought we'd all been killed and fired at our position to push back the enemy trying to take over our artillery piece. I have about thirty beehive rounds buried in my flesh, from my mid thigh all the way to my lower back. Luckily, my flak jacket took the rest, and the darts appear to have missed major organs and blood vessels. I pull off as many fléchettes as I can from my legs and my butt, and I roll over to lie on my back. I look straight up. Pretty blue, white, red, and green lines crisscross the sky.

Wow, I think. *This is just like Christmas.*

★ 1 ★

COUNTRY BOY

The Christmas lights sparkled in the dim light of dawn. All of us kids were sitting on the stairs looking down through the bars of the banister on the big pine tree and all the gifts waiting to be opened. My older brothers, Buddy and Darrell, and my baby sisters, Delilah and Charlene, were there with me. Johnny wasn't born yet, and Charlene was still in diapers, so I was probably no more than six years old. Back then we lived in a big old drafty house a few miles west of West Salem, a village in southeastern Illinois. All the bedrooms were upstairs, and we sat on the stairwell waiting for Mom and Dad to wake up, because we were not allowed to go downstairs before they did. I remember being so excited, trying to figure out what treasures were hidden inside those bright paper wrappings. When Mom and Dad finally woke up and told us we could go, we raced downstairs and tore into the presents. It smelled like Christmas, the scent of pine mixed with candle wax and cold roast.

The evening before, we had sat around the big dining table for our usual Christmas meal with the family. A few of Dad's six brothers and sisters had come over. Uncle Bruce and Aunt Mary—as well as their kids, Jimmy and Harriet—had driven down the 170 miles or so from Indianapolis, which was a very long drive in those days. Uncle Jess, my dad's younger brother, was there as well with his wife, Arlene. He was still in the Marine Corps back then, and he came wearing his uniform. This is my earliest Christmas memory, and all these years later, my heart grows warm thinking about it.

I come from small-town America. Like my dad before me and his dad before him, I lived most of my life in eastern Illinois and western Indiana. This is home. To me, those very rural parts of the country are where America's heartland lies, and they played a big part in making me who I am today. Growing up there, life was about family, neighbors, and country. It was about hard work, and stretching every dollar. The Wabash River, which runs between Illinois and Indiana, seems to be our family's North Star, the center of gravity that keeps pulling us back. We've moved up, down, and across its waters. Like most people in my family, I've traveled the country and even the world at one time or another, but home keeps calling me back, and I have always returned. When all is said and done, I am a farm boy from the Midwest. This is who I've always been, and who I'll always be.

Robert Houston Davis, my dad, was the fifth of seven children. His father was a carpenter from eastern Illinois who had gotten into the oil business in the early days of the twentieth century. Back then, oil derricks were made out of wood, and before Dad was born,

Grandpa Davis was offered a job building rigs in Oklahoma. I believe Sun Oil Company was drilling oil over there. So the family moved to Enid, Oklahoma. Grandpa and Dad's older brothers and sisters always talked about how they'd walked behind the wagon when they moved down there. Grandpa Davis took to drilling oil wells real well, I guess, and he was transferred back to southeastern Illinois when oilfields were first developed in the Hardinville area around 1911. Thanks to oil discoveries and new technology, Illinois had become the third largest oil-producing state in the country by then. When the oilfield where Grandpa was working started to falter a little bit, the family moved to Detroit. The factories were getting real big over there and offered a lot of employment. The family didn't last very long in Detroit, however. Grandpa evidently became disenchanted with big city life, and soon after Dad was born—in 1917, I believe—the family moved back to rural Illinois. That's where Dad grew up, and where he lived most of his life.

Times were real hard during the Great Depression, and in 1938, Dad joined the Civilian Conservation Corps. The CCC was set up by the Roosevelt administration to create jobs for unemployed single young men. My dad and other youngsters from the Hardinville area were sent to Burley, Idaho, to plant pine trees and dig ditches. He used to talk fondly of the mountains and how beautiful it was over there. Although the CCC wasn't part of the military, officers ran the camps and everything was organized in regiments, so Dad always said it was good training for what was coming. When World War II broke out, he went straight into the military.

He met Mom when he was stationed at the Sheppard Air Force Base in Texas. In 1945, Bonnie Chloe Helle was driving from Dayton, Ohio, to San Francisco, California, with her aunt Margaret.

They overnighted in Wichita Falls, Texas. Mom always loved to dance, and she and Margaret must have gone to a dance hall where Dad happened to be with a bunch of other soldiers. They danced and they talked. Mom convinced her aunt to stay for a few more days so she could get to know Bob better, and that was that. Margaret drove on to San Francisco, but Mom stayed in Texas and married Dad. Their favorite song later became Ernest Tubb's "Waltz Across Texas." I guess it brought back good memories.

Mom was also from small-town Illinois. Unlike Dad, she didn't have any brothers and sisters. Her father, John Henry Helle, was long on wives—he married seven times—but short on children. Grandpa Helle was born in the United States soon after his parents left Germany to seek a better life in America. He felt American through and through but still spoke German and passed some of it on to Mom. He and Grandma Ora Lea married when they were very young, and Mom was born in 1923 in Illinois. The marriage did not work. Grandma Ora Lea remarried, and I was named after her second husband, Samuel Wolmer. They stayed in Illinois, but I didn't get to know them much growing up, because for some reason, it was Grandpa Helle's sister Margaret who raised Mom. As far as Mom was concerned, Margaret Helle was her mother. Grandpa Helle moved to Dayton, Ohio, where he lived all of my life. But unlike Ora Lea, I got to know him real well, because he often came and visited us wherever we lived, bringing whatever wife was current at the time. None of them left a big impression on me, except for Louise. I believe she lasted the longest of his seven wives. Louise was a portly lady and was real nice to us kids. She was like a real grandma. Unfortunately, she didn't last either. She died before Grandpa had a chance to divorce her.

After Dad and Mom got married, Dad was transferred to Wright-Patterson Air Force Base near Dayton, Ohio. That's where I was born in 1946. Then Dad left the military, and we moved to Indianapolis. Dad worked as a Polar ice deliveryman for a bit, until he and Mom started running a restaurant in Poseyville, a very small town in southwestern Indiana. The restaurant was a two-story brick building next to a railroad track. My very earliest memory, and I don't really know how old I was, is of Mom sitting on the outside steps of the restaurant, watching me play in the cinders from the railroad. Trains were running on coal back then, and I can still smell it. We lived above the restaurant, and there was a big grate on the floor right above the grill to heat the upstairs apartment. At naptime, I remember lying on that grate, looking down and watching Mom fix hamburgers or whatever it was she was cooking on the grill. She would talk to me through the grate, trying to convince me to go to sleep. I can't have been more than two years old.

When Dad got a job working on the Illinois oilfields, like his dad had done before him, the drive from Poseyville was too long, so we moved across the state line. We first lived just east of Parkersburg, Illinois, right by Lincoln and Sylvia Judge's farm. Every family in the area did some farming, and part of the fun of growing up was how much we helped one another. We all did what we could for one another. When the threshing machine came to town, all the neighbors got together and everybody threshed every one else's wheat. The machine looked like a locomotive, with a firebox and a big old steam engine that ran on coal. It had to be filled with water from the local ponds, with two men operating the big hand pump. When it blew its whistle, all the farmers along the road got their wheat onto wagons and brought it out for threshing.

When I was four years old, Dad put me up in the cab of the threshing machine, and looking down, I was just about tall enough to see all the moving parts of the steam engine. It was real neat, and I felt like a grown-up. The threshing machine traveled at the neck-breaking speed of about a mile an hour, so I got to stand up there for a long time. It smelled like coal, and I could hear the stones on the road going up to the Judges' farm being crunched under the weight of the big steel wheels. When I wasn't on the threshing machine, Lincoln Judge would always let me ride Salt and Pepper, the black and white horses that pulled his wagon. Holding the reins, their big knobs rubbing against the palms of my hands, I felt like a king on top of those horses.

I was reminded of those days when I later joined the Boy Scouts. Besides the usual camping and fishing, being part of the Scouts meant helping out local dairy farmers, tending cows and cleaning stalls with pitchforks. It was real hard work, but the camaraderie was awesome. It also reinforced the idea of service to others that Mom and Dad drilled into us at home.

By the time I started school, we had moved near West Salem, just a few miles down from Parkersburg. We still did some farming, and we always had hogs and rabbits and chickens. Sometimes cows for milk. With Dad working in the oilfield and Mom cooking, cleaning, and looking after the babies and the vegetable garden, it was my older brothers' and my job to look after the animals. I learned a few good life lessons looking after those pigs and cows. I first learned that Dad meant what he said and said what he meant. I must have been about five years old, and our sow had just had piglets. I wanted to play with those baby pigs so bad. "Son, don't go into the hog lot," Dad warned me. But I was too curious. I crawled under the lumber board fence and went over to where the pigs were. As I came closer, the mama pig started squealing real loud. The next thing I knew, I was in the air flapping my legs, lifted by the collar of my shirt, and the sow was charging against Dad's legs. He had to jump over the fence real quick, and he was not happy. "I told you not to go in there," he said. "That hog would have eaten you up!" He took off his belt and gave me a memorable spanking. That's the only spanking I remember ever getting from Dad, but it convinced me that, from then on, I should probably do as he said.

I also learned about never giving up. When I was nine or ten years old, one of our calves kept on getting out of the pen. That calf was probably four or five hundred pounds, and I was still little for my age. I was in charge of the animals, so I had to bring the calf back inside the fence. I'd put the rope on its neck like I was supposed to and try to lead it back, but that cow would just take off and drag me through the mud. Mom was standing on the side of the hill, watching. "You don't lose 'til you quit trying, Sammy!" she kept telling me. I'd get up and try again, and I'd still be dragged right, left, and center through cow dung. I finally had an idea. I placed the rope around the calf's neck, pulled up one of its legs, and wrapped the rope around the foot and back up around its neck. Once the cow had only three working legs, I easily walked it back inside the pen, and there were no more mud baths for me. From then on, whenever the cow got out, that was the first thing I did, and it worked every time. You don't lose 'til you quit trying.

I used that same trick on a hog. One day the mama pig got out of the pen with all of her new babies. It was summertime and she liked the water, so she ran down to the creek by our house. I got her back up by tying one of her legs up like I did with the calf. But then I had to get the little babies. *Oh boy.* These piglets were running everywhere, and it was a big litter. As I tried to wrangle them, it seemed like there were fifty of them, even though I know there couldn't have been that many. And there was my mom, standing on the side of the hill. "You don't lose 'til you quit trying, Sammy!"

I lost count of how many times Mom and Dad said that to us growing up. It was one of the things that motivated us kids to keep on rolling. It had become a family refrain. I think it actually came from Grandpa Helle. He certainly took his own advice to heart when it came to marriage, but I also remember him saying it to Mom whenever life was being unkind. With six kids and money always short, times were often hard. Dad had to work lots of different jobs. He was a very good machinist and only had to take one look at anything mechanical to know how to fix it. So he could always get a job, but one department or another always ended up closing down, and he had to look for something new.

In the early spring of 1956, Dad no longer had a job. He had been a driller on the oilfields of southeastern Illinois, but more and more rigs were being shut down. He might have been able to work as a regular roughneck on some of the remaining rigs, but he preferred the drilling job. Dad's nephew Bud Hammond had moved to Texas, and he was working for his father-in-law. His wife's daddy was a superintendent with a construction company that installed cracking units in oil refineries. Cracking units break down crude oil and convert it into gasoline. There was demand for the newer catalytic cracking units that could extract gasoline quicker and cheaper than the old thermal ones. So Dad got a job in the construction industry, and we moved to Houston, Texas.

The trouble was it took only six months to install a cracking unit, and then Dad had to move on to another refinery. So every six months we packed up and moved. Dad's job took us all across the oil belt down south, where the big refineries were. From Houston, we moved to Comer, Georgia. Then it was Shreveport, Louisiana, before we headed back to Texas. We spent six months in Odessa, and then we were in La Porte, right next to Houston again. All this moving around shattered me. Every six months I had to get used to a new place, and by the time I'd made really good friends, we'd move away and I had to say good-bye. Every six months I was in a new school. When I left Illinois, I had graduated from the sixth grade, but when we first got to Houston, I was told that I wasn't old enough for the seventh grade in Texas. My birthday wasn't until November, after the start of the school year. So I was held back a year. I felt defeated. I had just left my home and my friends in Illinois, and I was forced to repeat a grade. I gave up on school and went fishing instead. I ended up flunking that year and had to repeat it one more time. Leaving Illinois put me back two years in school. I'd quit trying, and I lost big time.

At the time, all this moving around was really tough for a shy kid like me, but looking back on it now, I know it helped form my character. I learned to make new friends easily—some of whom I never saw again, and others to whom I'm still real close. I learned to feel at home wherever I was, and I got to see a lot of the country. I learned to adapt. All that was to help me greatly when I later joined the military.

Those years are a bit of a blur now. We moved so often that all the places where we lived blend together in my mind. But one of the highlights of those years took place when I was in Zavala Elementary School in Odessa, Texas. Andy Devine, a comic with a funny voice, came to perform for all the kids at school. Andy Devine was very big back then. He had appeared in many radio shows and movies, especially Westerns, but had become real famous playing Jingles in *The Adventures of Wild Bill Hickok* on television and radio. He also hosted *Andy's Gang*, a kids' TV show with a frog. When Andy Devine came to our school, several hundred of us were in the auditorium. Mr. Devine was on stage sitting on some kind of barrel or keg, all dressed up in his chaps and cowboy hat. After he'd talked to us for half an hour or so, he said, "I'm gonna need someone to come up and help me with my stage props," and pointed at me. There were many of us, and I was one of the smallest kids in school, so I couldn't quite believe he had picked me. "Yes, you son," he said. "Come on up here!" So I came up on stage and helped him with his number. I remember handing him a cane and something that looked like a grass skirt, but I no longer recall what they were for. Then I got to go backstage and visit with him for a while. I thought Andy Devine was a very nice guy.

Then we moved to the Houston area again. I actually have some real good memories of La Porte, Texas. It was very pretty. We lived right on the Gulf, a block and a half from the water, and I got to go fishing almost every day. I got a job selling *Grit*, which in those days was a big, thick newspaper popular all across rural America. *Grit*—claiming to be "America's Greatest Family Newspaper"— had something for everyone. It carried some news pages, fashion features, and recipes. There were also some funnies, crossword puzzles, and serialized stories. Newsboys like me sold the weekly newspaper door to door for a dime, carrying a white canvas bag with *Grit* written on it in big red letters. I made four cents on every copy I sold, which was pretty good money.

I also got my driver's license in La Porte when I was only thirteen and a half. By then I had a bicycle, but I convinced Dad that if I had a motorcycle, I could expand my newspaper sales. In Texas, the rule was that you could get a learner's permit at age thirteen if you had a job. I already knew how to drive. I'd learned to maneuver our old John Deere tractor back in Illinois when I was about five years old. It had a long hand clutch sticking out from the floor, and Dad had showed me how to snap it into gear. By the time I was seven, he was letting me drive our 1946 Chevy on country roads. Learning to drive these bumpy and muddy roads from an early age served me well in Vietnam, and my enduring taste for motorcycles and cars was born on those roads. Once I got my Texas learner's permit, I bought myself a Sears Allstate 175cc with the money I had already made and a loan from Dad. Man, did that work well. With all the extra newspapers I was selling, I paid for that twenty-five-dollar motorcycle real quick, and I was happy as a clam driving it.

In 1959, Dad finished installing the cracking unit in La Porte, Texas. Mom had had enough. "Bob," she said, "I followed you all over the United States. My mama's getting older, and I want to go spend some time with her in California." She meant her aunt Margaret, who after raising her had gotten married and lived in San Francisco. So we loaded everything we could get in trailers and hauled out west. The first three months, we lived with Grandma Margaret and her husband, Forrest Rainey, in San Francisco. They lived in a big apartment building at 150 Laguna Street, right off Market, the big diagonal thoroughfare that cuts through the city. We and other kids in that neighborhood made the most of the city's unbelievable hills. Grandma kept some old roller skates from her youth, and the ball bearing was really good. I unscrewed the wheels from the bottom of the shoes and put them on a flat board. The board was long and wide enough that I could sit down and lean. It was like a sled on wheels basically, and it worked great. Pretty soon, eight or ten of us had those sit-on skateboards, and we zipped down the hills at full speed. It was awesome.

Apart from speeding down the hills, those weeks in San Francisco were tough. For us, who had lived out in the countryside all our lives, being cooped up in an apartment on the eleventh floor was terrible. There was no grass nearby, no place to play besides the street. After a couple months, Dad decided it wasn't working out for our family. He got a job as a machinist for Diamond Walnut Growers in Stockton, about eighty miles east of San Francisco in the San Joaquin Valley. We settled in French Camp, a small town just outside of Stockton, where we finally stayed put for six years. After working for Diamond Walnuts for a couple of years, Dad got a better job at a company mining asbestos in the same area. It paid really good money, but he didn't realize that job would cost him his lungs—and eventually his life.

Only a few hundred people lived in French Camp proper back then. Agriculture was very big, with all kinds of vegetables, fruits, and nuts being grown in the area, but the town itself didn't offer much besides a gas station, a little grocery store, and several bars. French Camp was a rough little town. All the farm workers came in to party or drown their sorrows in the local bars. The place turned severely wild on weekends or during the off-season, when there wasn't much fruit or vegetables to pick. I would probably have turned into a hoodlum if I had lived there longer than I did.

Yet there are three of us Medal of Honor recipients from French Camp, California, population four hundred souls or so. How about that? We all lived there at the same time, but the three of us didn't know one another back then. I guess as kids, a few years made a big difference in who we ran with. It wasn't until years later, sitting in a bar in Washington, DC, after some Medal of Honor event, that we became aware of that unusual coincidence. We couldn't believe it, and we talked about the people we knew. Delbert Jennings was about the same age as my big brothers, Buddy and Darrell, and he remembered them. Rick Pittman is just a year or two younger than me, but he knew my baby brother, John.

I finished the seventh and eighth grades in French Camp and went to high school in Manteca, a town just south of us. I started off riding the bus, but soon drove myself to school—before anyone else even had a driver's license. When we moved to California, Dad went down to the DMV office to turn in his Texas driver's license and get a California one. I went along with him. I reckoned that, since I was going to get a job, I would be allowed to drive, just like I had in Texas. I didn't know that I was supposed to be sixteen to do that in California. When we got to the desk, Dad laid his driver's license on the counter, and I laid mine right beside his. They wrote Dad's out, and then without blinking, they wrote mine out too. I guess they didn't pay attention to my age, and that's how I got a California driver's license at fourteen.

I first bought myself a motorcycle, which I drove when I was still in the eighth grade. Later I got an old 1947 Chevy Fleetwood for ten dollars. It was my very first car, and to me it was the most beautiful thing in the world. The only problem was it had a cracked head. It leaked water like an open faucet and ran on one cylinder. I think that's why Dad let me have it: he knew I couldn't go very far or very fast with it. I always had to carry a five-gallon water can in the trunk.

That car sure was thirsty, and I had to pour twenty gallons of water in it to drive the ten miles or so from home to Manteca High School. Before I left, I would fill up the can with water, put it in the trunk, fill the radiator up, and start driving. I knew where I could stop between home and school to fill the radiator again. Water was free, and even though I was not about to break any speed records, that old Chevy ran fine just on that one cylinder. It was pretty cool being able to drive my own car to school. There weren't many freshmen able to do that.

I wasn't a good student. Mom and Dad's rule was that I had to pass. So I passed. Barely. I didn't apply myself much, and got Cs and Ds doing absolutely no homework. I used to write out my papers standing in front of the teachers just before handing them in, which infuriated them terribly. But who has time for homework when there is so much fun to be had? I certainly hadn't. I had too many other irons in the fire. I played football. I really enjoyed it, but I wasn't anything outstanding. I was also on the school swim team. More important, I wanted to be popular with girls. Looking back now, I was painfully shy. I had lots of friends who were girls, but I didn't always have the gumption to turn them into girlfriends. Regardless, I figured that to have any chance with the ladies, I needed money in my pocket. I had to have a decent car, and the insurance and gas that went with it. To support my habit, I worked jobs after school. All that left no time for homework.

One of my first jobs in California was to mow our neighbor's yard. There was this sweet old lady named Gertrude living by us. When I finished cutting her lawn, she would invite me in for cookies and milk. One day I was sitting at her dining room table and the closet right in front of me was open. In it was an old guitar. When

I asked her about it, Gertrude told me the guitar was her late husband's. Gertrude played the fiddle, and they used to travel up and down California together, singing and playing in clubs. "Would you like to hold it?" she asked.

I was a teenager, and like most boys my age, music was a big part of my life. I listened to country-western mostly. I was particularly fond of Hank Williams, Jimmie Rodgers, and of course, Johnny Cash. I also went to a nearby Pentecostal church most Sundays just for the music. I had gone to Sunday school growing up, but I had never heard anything like this. Those churchgoers sure knew how to praise the Lord with good rhythm and lots of clapping, and I found it really uplifting. Music was also a family tradition. Mom always had the radio on and tuned to some country oldies station. When I was maybe three years old, she used to go listen to Dixie Belle, a bluegrass singer from Kentucky. She dressed me up in cowboy boots, little blue jeans, chaps, and a cowboy hat, and stood me up on the stage by Dixie Belle. Music was also big on the Davis side. Whenever we had family reunions, my dad and his brothers all played the harmonica together and the little kids danced. They all had learned from Grandpa Davis and used to reminisce over old tunes from the 1930s. They've all been gone a long time now, but I still have my uncle Boo's French harp. When I was growing up, harmonicas were too expensive to allow kids to mess around with, so when I lived in California, I still had not learned how to play. I didn't know yet that I would learn to play the harmonica in Vietnam, and that music would see me through very hard times over there.

So when our neighbor Gertrude offered to let me play her husband's guitar, she didn't have to ask twice. There were only four or five strings left on it, but she showed me a couple chords. Every week when I went to mow her yard, I played the guitar a bit. After a while, she put six brand-new strings on it, and I kept strumming. At the end of the summer, she asked me if I wanted to take the guitar home with me. Boy, was I happy. That was my first guitar, and I named it Old Gertie after that sweet lady. I asked Randall Wayne Basie, a boy who lived around the corner from us, to teach me how to play properly. Wayne was a couple years younger than me, but we were good friends. He was a real good player, and that kid could sing too. He used to come over to our house with his guitar, and we all loved listening to him. I still remember one of his songs, something he wrote about his collie dog Queenie. It was such a beautiful song. I wish I could remember the exact words. Then his mother got divorced and remarried a guy in Idaho. Wayne moved away and I never saw him again. But every time I see or hear Randy Travis, the famous country music singer, I think of Randall Wayne Basie, who sounded and looked a bit like him. As for Old Gertie, I still have it, and it still plays real well.

Besides mowing Gertrude's yard, I always worked jobs after school or in the summer. One winter I worked for a guy down the road from us who had his own septic-sucker company. In those days, almost everyone had septic tanks. I drove the big vacuum truck and crawled in the tanks to clean them up. I can't say that was pleasant, but it put money in my pocket. During a couple summers, my older brother Buddy got me a job working with him at the St. Francis Yacht Club on Tinsley Island, out in the Sacramento–San Joaquin Delta. I also worked as a lumberjack when school got out after my junior year. I was working for a construction company building a road around Big Bear Lake, up in the San Bernardino

Mountains of Southern California. Billy Pete Lawson, a friend of my brother Darrell, was the superintendent, and he got me the job. We first had to clear the trees to make way for bulldozers. I used to climb up the big ponderosa and jeffrey pines with a chainsaw strapped to my back to cut them down into forty-foot sections. These were majestic trees, close to two hundred feet tall, with thick trunks. I built strong arms and legs working those trees. We used to sleep in big tents up in the mountains. I often thought of Dad and his days in the CCC planting pines in Idaho.

One day, the superintendent came to me and said, "Sam, how would you like to be a powder monkey?" Powder monkeys were the guys blasting the tree stumps, and they were shorthanded. I'd always liked blowing things up. As a kid, I used to play with fire-crackers a lot. We had cherry bombs, these exploding fireworks that were so popular back then. They've been banned for a long time now, but they were awesome. They were made out of round paper globes filled with powder, with sawdust or string glued onto them. They were usually a pinkish red color with a green fuse coming out of a little bitty hole, and they looked like cherries. I'm sure I made some poor decisions at times, but I was always careful and never seriously tore anything up. I wasn't the kind of kid that blew up mailboxes and other nonsense like that. I used to blow up tin cans with my brothers or with my friends. We'd fill big cans with water, drop a cherry bomb in it, and put another can on top. We pulled the cherry bomb out of the small hole on the top and then we'd light the fuse. Man, it totally sealed that thing and would propel it out of sight. Luckily, we never caught any can shrapnel. We did all kinds of neat things, experimenting with strings of fireworks, setting off delayed rounds with long fuses, always thinking, *Gee, I wonder what this would do?* Back then, we could get fuse for pennies. We used to put on our own little shows with bottle rockets and firecrackers.

So when Billy Pete asked me whether I wanted to become a powder monkey, I said yes. It seemed like good fun to me. I learned to make powder, mixing dynamite and fertilizer. I made good use of that knowledge later in life—except on one occasion after I came back from Vietnam, when my taste for explosives cost us several windows and a few good dinner plates.

Lumberjacking was hard work. Most of the time, I was working six-twelves: six days a week, twelve hours a day. But I was making big bucks. Three dollars and ten cents an hour. In fact, I was making more money than Dad was. I was driving a cool motorcycle— a 1962 Harley-Davidson that I had bought brand new some time before—and a beautiful 1953 Buick Roadmaster. It was a very nice, big baby blue car with a metallic blue top. I was just happy as heck. Until one Friday night in July 1965. I had a bit of time off, so I drove back home from the San Bernardino Mountains. It was a long drive, and I got home late in the evening. I was going to drive back the next day, until Dad dropped a bomb.

"Son, we're moving back to Indiana," he said. Dad had had enough of California and was ready to go home. Grandma Margaret was doing well, and he figured it was time to go.

For a second or two, I was speechless. "But Dad . . . I don't want to go!"

"We'll be leaving on Monday morning," he said. "And you're coming with us."

I was devastated. I was having the time of my life that summer. I had a good job paying good money, and I didn't want to call Billy

Pete Lawson to tell him I wouldn't be coming back to Big Bear Lake. I was looking forward to my senior year at Manteca High and to graduating there. I had real good friends and dreaded saying good-bye again. I didn't want to let go of my beautiful Buick and my prized Harley. But we needed money for the trip, and I had to help drive Mom's 1953 Oldsmobile and the pickup truck pulling Dad's sixteen-foot fishing boat back to Indiana. So I had to sell both my car and my motorcycle over the weekend for a fraction of what I'd paid for them. It broke my heart.

There was something even worse than all of this though. My older brothers, Buddy and Darrell, decided they would stay in California. It had been hard enough to be apart for several years when they'd been in the military, but eventually we had reunited in French Camp. Although they no longer lived with us by then, they lived close by and I saw them all the time. We were very close, and the idea of being once again far away from them filled me with dread. I feared the family would never be whole again.

As it turns out, I was right.

★ 2 ★

DON'T YOU LEAVE YOUR LITTLE BROTHER!

Growing up in a big family made me who I am today. And no one shaped me more than my three brothers and two sisters. With six kids at home and much work to do, Mom taught us that part of our job was to take care of one another. "Now, don't you leave your little brother!" she said over and over. Being in the middle of the brood as I was, I got to be that little brother for a while, until it was my turn to look after the younger ones. Sure, we teased one another, as all brothers and sisters do. But they also taught me plenty. The truth is, we would have died before letting anything bad happen to one another. I learned early on that a shared experience forges a bond as strong as blood, and throughout my life, I've longed to find that connection again. I wish I still had pictures of those days, when we were kids and carefree. Before life stole two of my brothers well before their time.

I learned a lot from my two big brothers. Hubert Houston—we all called him Buddy or Bud—was ten years older than I was. Next was Darrell Dean, who was three years younger than Buddy. Wherever they went, I tagged along. "C'mon, Sam!" they'd say. "You know we can't leave you!" It always made me feel good that they'd come and find me.

We were country kids through and through. Across the road from our house a few miles from West Salem, Illinois, was one of those really big, forty-acre woods full of squirrels. When we were not working in the vegetable garden and taking care of our animals, Buddy, Darrell, and I spent most of our time out in those woods playing in the mud and dirt or by the ponds and creeks that were all around us. We dug caves into the sides of hills, shoring them up with logs. Down at the bottom of our hill was a creek. We'd go down and sit for hours with our fishing poles waiting for the bluegills to bite. Buddy showed me how to set the pole and clean our catches before bringing them home for dinner. He also taught me to run a stick through a fish and roast it real good over a campfire.

In the summertime, when that creek was pretty full, it formed a nice big pool by the road. We'd go splashing in there or in one of the many neighboring ponds. One hot summer afternoon—I was maybe five or six years old—we walked to a pond on the next hill, where we always met the neighbor boys. I couldn't swim yet, so my brothers told me to sit it out. They were all climbing up a big old maple tree, walking out on a limb hanging over the water and diving headfirst. I was lying by a willow tree, watching them have fun for the better part of an hour, when I noticed a branch going straight over the pond. I looked up, and then looked at the boys having fun, and then looked up again. *If my brothers can do it, then I can do it*, I thought. I waited until they were distracted, and I climbed up that tree. I walked along the branch stretching toward the pond, hanging on to a limb above. Before I could reach the water, I heard a loud *crack*, and the branch broke right under me. I fell about seven or eight feet and landed flat on my back on the hard ground. It knocked the breath out of me, and I probably passed out for a few seconds, because when I opened my eyes, all I could see were faces. My brothers and the neighbor boys were all looking down on me.

"Breathe," Buddy said. "Breathe real shallow. You're okay. Get your breath."

I took in small breaths, panting like a dog. And sure enough, soon I was back on my feet. I hadn't broken anything.

"Don't tell Mom!" my brothers pleaded. I didn't tell her for a very long time. But after that day, my brothers didn't let me go near the big Mason pond north of our house. I had just scared them out of their wits, and they were not yet ready to take any chances. They still took me with them—"Don't leave your brother!" my mom still told them—but they locked me up in the rabbit cages every time they went swimming so I wouldn't get into trouble or get hurt again. As boys, that was the best they could think of to protect me. I cried and cried and threatened to tell Mom, but I kept my mouth shut when they said they'd never take me with them again if I ratted them out. I wanted to be with my brothers, even if they didn't let me swim. I had too much fun running through the woods, looking for arrowheads, and doing all the things that country boys do. So much of the stuff we did as kids I never told Mom about. If I ever see her again after I'm gone, I'll have a lot to answer for. "*Mein Gott im Himmel*," she's probably saying from heaven, shaking her head.

Not too long after my dive from that willow tree, Buddy and

Darrell were once again heading for the Mason pond. It was hot as hell on fire, and the thought of being locked up in a rabbit cage again sent me kicking and screaming. "Teach me how to swim, then!" I pleaded. Buddy looked at me, thought for a few seconds, and with a tilt of his head, signaled that I could come along. I ran to my brothers before they could change their minds. When we were by the pond, Buddy turned to me. "Are you ready to learn, Sammy?" I nodded. Then he picked me up and threw me in the water. "Now swim!" he said.

I first swallowed a big gulp of muddy water and started kicking and flapping my arms to keep my head above water. "Kick with your legs, and paddle like a dog!" Buddy shouted. "Yeah, that's it!" Darrell echoed. "Keep going!" They stood close by, ready to get me if I went under. By the end of the afternoon, I could float and move around well enough. Over the following few weeks, I observed my brothers and the neighbors to learn the strokes, and tried to do as they did. "Use your legs more! Stretch your arms!" my brothers instructed. Before long, I could swim properly, and my rabbit-cage days were over.

With two older brothers, I smartened up quickly. There was an old well where the lane leading down from our house and the road intersected. It still had good water, and as we waited for the school bus early in the morning, my brothers would have a drink of water with a tin cup hooked on a string. One morning, Darrell held out his hand. Buddy put two or three little black round pills in his palm, and Darrell took a shot of water from the well. Then Buddy took a few of those little bitty pills himself. After a day or two watching that routine, I was real curious. "What are they?" I asked.

"Well, Sammy, those are smart pills," Buddy said.

"Smart pills? Really?"

Buddy nodded.

I had just started kindergarten, my first year at school. Smart pills seemed like an excellent idea. "I'd like to have some of those, please."

Buddy gave me a couple. I put them in my mouth and washed them down with that cool sweet water from the well.

After two or three days of smart-pill treatment, Darrell and I were busy cleaning the rabbit cages. "You know," I said to Darrell, "those rabbit droppings look just like those smart pills that y'all been feeding me."

Darrell burst out laughing. "Wow," he said. "These pills really work! Because that's what they were, and look, you're getting smarter already!"

Although my big brothers never missed a chance to tease me, they were always there when I needed help. In West Salem, we lived about three miles from school. Whenever the school bus broke down, we'd have to walk there, and the distance was more than my short little legs could handle. Whenever I was tired, Bud and Darrell took turns carrying me on their shoulders all the way to school and then back home. I've also lost count of the number of times they covered for me, taking the blame when I played in the creek instead of picking beans or radishes in the garden as I was supposed to.

When we were not horsing around swimming, fishing, and digging caves—or eating rabbit poop—we did a lot of trapping and hunting. With six kids at home, money was always tight. We grew vegetables in the garden, had a cow for milk, and we also raised pigs, rabbits, and some chickens. Hunting and fishing put extra food on the table. It sure was fun to scout the woods by our house with traps or guns, following animal trails. But to us it was no sport. Dad always called it "making meat."

We laid traps to catch raccoons, beavers, and foxes. We ate the raccoons and skinned the foxes to sell their furs. A few times we caught several skunks by mistake. In those days, we could sell a whole skunk for about a quarter, but we could get a whole extra dollar if we skinned it out. A dollar was pretty big money, but after I skinned a couple and almost choked on the stink, I quickly learned that it wasn't worth it.

I was four or five years old when I handled my first rifle. Dad was setting up at the back of the house to shoot tin cans off the fence. He showed me how to load the little .22 rifle single shot, how to pull the hammer back, and cock it. He also showed me how to handle it safely.

Dad gave me my first lesson, but I owe my shooting skills to Buddy and Darrell. My big brothers and I spent much of our time hunting squirrels, and they'd correct how I handled the firearm, showing me how to shoot it properly. It wasn't until I was eight years old or so that I got to carry a shotgun though. Dad handed me the family .410 and said, "Okay son, you ready to go rabbit hunting with us?"

Rabbit hunting was a big family tradition. My brothers; Dad; my uncles Bruce, Mel, and Jess; and my cousins would all get together, and there'd be maybe fifteen or eighteen of us. I had been walking with them from the time I was maybe five, but up to that point, my job had been to carry rabbits. I would tie the legs of the dead rabbits onto sticks and sling them onto my belt loops until I had rabbits all the way around me. You couldn't fit more than five rabbits that way, so all of us little kids were the rabbit carriers.

Was I ready to go hunting proper? "Oh, yes, Dad, I am," I said. Man, did I feel good. I was with the big boys now. Everybody lined up, and off we went. We walked in silence next to one another, dead leaves crackling under our feet. The rule was that everyone shot only the rabbits that got up in front of them. When a pair of long ears scampered ahead of me, I brought the shotgun to my shoulder and took a deep breath. With the scent of wet earth in my nostrils, I pulled the trigger. The rabbit rolled across the ground, and I exhaled. My chest just about burst with pride. I had just hit the mark in front of the whole family, and all this practice shooting squirrels with my brothers had paid off. I ran to collect my prize. But when I picked it up, I saw its dead eyes and blood-soaked fur, and my heart grew heavy. A few seconds before, that rabbit had been alive, and I wondered whether it had suffered because of me.

When I was ten years old, my world turned upside down. Buddy had finished high school and decided to enlist in the Navy. Soon, he would be gone for four years, and the thought of his absence weighed on my mind. One evening, as we were having dinner, Buddy carefully placed his fork down on the table and cleared his throat.

"I need to know where my mother is," he said, his eyes glued to his empty plate.

I was astonished. First, it wasn't like Buddy to speak up at dinner unless spoken to. He had always been kind of shy, a boy of few words. But more important, Mom was right there, sitting in front of him. What was he talking about? I looked at Mom, but she didn't look at me. I looked at Darrell, waiting for him to run into the conversation as he always did—whether asked or not—and make a good joke out of it. "Hey, Bud," he'd laugh. "Are you off your rocker?" But for once, Darrell kept quiet.

Dad was silent for a moment but his jaw hardened. "What for?"

"My birth certificate. I don't have it. And the Navy wants it," Buddy said, still staring at his plate.

Over the next few days, I grilled Buddy. What was going on? I also asked Mom. This is how I found out that Dad had been married before, and that Buddy, Darrell, and I were in fact half brothers. I was also pretty shocked to find out that I had another brother who didn't live with us. I vaguely remembered Bobby from when I was maybe two or three years old, but had not seen him for many years. He was five years older than me, and I had always assumed that he was my cousin, because he lived with my aunt Dorothy—one of Dad's sisters—and her husband Mark.

I know very little of Dad's first wife. I was told she had some problems and was mentally unstable, but I never heard the whole story. In any case, the three boys' mother was unable to care for them when the marriage collapsed. As for Dad, he had been in the military at Sheppard Air Force Base in Wichita Falls, Texas, and couldn't take care of three young boys. So Buddy, Darrell, and Bobby had gone to live with Grandpa and Grandma Davis in Illinois.

If Bobby was my brother, I couldn't understand why he wasn't raised with us. It turns out that Aunt Dorothy and Uncle Mark thought they could not have children. So they came to Grandpa and Grandma Davis's house, and took in the youngest, Bobby. As far as I know, they never legally adopted him, but they raised him as their own. When I asked Buddy about him, he said he missed his little brother. But he understood, I guess.

When Mom met Dad during that pit stop on her way to California, she didn't know any of that. Dad didn't say a word about his sons until they got together and moved to Wright-Patterson Air Force base near Dayton, Ohio. That's when Dad brought her up to speed on what his life had entailed up to that point—including three young boys, two of whom still lived with his parents. If Mom ever felt surprised or blindsided, she graciously took it all in her stride. She had a real big heart, our mom, and maybe the fact that she'd been brought up by a woman who wasn't her biological mother played a part as well. In any case, she loved Buddy and Darrell like her own sons. The feeling was mutual. They called her Mom, and as far as I could tell, they loved her every bit as much as I did.

If Mom was very much their mother, I was very much their brother. Buddy and Darrell never gave me cause to suspect anything different growing up. So if I was more than a little surprised when I realized we were not full blood brothers, I quickly got over it. By the time I found out, it made no difference to me, or to them. All those days hunting, fishing, and swimming in ponds, all that time teasing me and carrying me on their shoulders had forged an unbreakable bond. We didn't give a rat's ass about biology or what our birth certificates might have said. We shared a life and would have done anything for one another. We were brothers, and that was all there was to it.

Shortly thereafter, Buddy joined the Navy, and just like that, he was gone. We moved to Texas when Dad's work on the oilfields dried up, and a few months later, Darrell decided to enlist in the Army. Within less than a year, I found myself in a strange land that didn't feel like home, and in the even stranger position of being the big brother. I had lost my running buddies, with whom I did every-thing and went everywhere, the brothers I looked up to. Our house felt eerily empty to me without Darrell's jokes and Buddy's quiet presence. I kept fishing and hunting and doing all the things they had taught me, but I missed them big-time and felt lost.

Left to my own devices, I still had a few lessons to learn. Our first Christmas in Texas, I got my own BB gun as a present. It was a powerful little Daisy, the kind that you had to pump to cock, and I could hardly wait to try it. We lived in this little bitty settlement right on the Gulf of Mexico and had all these robins in our yard. Armed with my brand-new Christmas present, I went out and shot four or five robins. I picked up the dead birds by the legs and ran back into the house. Dad looked at them, each shot right through the head.

"Good job, son. I'm proud of you," he said. "How do you want your mother to cook them?"

I stopped in my tracks. Cook them? Who'd ever heard of eating robins?

"What's the rule?" Dad said.

"You don't kill anything you don't eat," I mumbled. My brothers had taught me to skin and gut squirrels, rabbits, and fish, so they'd be ready to cook by the time we brought them home. Every single thing we'd ever fished or hunted had ended up on our dinner table.

"Correct. So how do you want your mother to fix them?"

I swallowed hard. "Fried, I guess."

I ate all of them robins until the very last. As every bone of those birds crunched under my teeth, the rule I had heard all my life finally sunk in. I never shot another robin.

With Buddy and Darrell gone, I had a job to do. I was ten years old, and I had become the big brother. John Forrest—Johnny to us—had just been born, and was too young still for me to recruit, but I had two little sisters. It was my turn to take care of Delilah and Charlene, teach them what I knew, and rule the roost.

I took them roaming the fields that stretched around our house in Texas whenever I could. I took them to play in a little fort I had built out of dead limbs with my buddy Mickey, who lived across the field from us. I thought it looked just like the forts in the movies, and I was real proud of it. The girls were too young to stay out at night, but I camped out there many a night, grilling fish over little campfires.

I tried to show them what Bud and Darrell had showed me. How to handle a BB gun. How to follow game trails and identify the best fishing spots. Buffalo Bayou was right there by us, and I took them fishing for big carp and bluegill. I repeated what I had been told so many times before. "See the log over there? That's a good place for the fish to hide," I'd say, or: "See where that branch is hanging over the water? Now, the fish will be hiding under that, because they like the darkness." I still loved swimming, and most summer days, we'd head to the Gulf of Mexico.

Although they turned out to be pretty good shots, Delilah and Charlene were never big on hunting. They came along on a couple of family hunts but didn't care to do it again. As they grew up, they were no longer interested in running around the woods with their brother but developed a taste for a different kind of hunting. They were not old enough to date yet when they grew an eye for boys. "Do you know that Jimmy who's in your class?" they'd ask me. "Why don't you make him a friend and bring him to the house or something?" Whenever they had their eyes on a good guy, I would bring him by the house and let the girls talk to him. But some of these boys they'd mention I knew for a fact were up to no good. I didn't particularly want them messing with my baby sisters, so I never brought them home and refused to drive my sisters to any party where I knew they would be. Delilah and Charlene were not happy, but I'd make it up by taking them dancing or to the drive-in.

With my sisters pursuing other interests, I took Johnny hunting and fishing. He was ten years younger than me, and I once again passed on what I had learned. "Don't you leave your little brother!" Mom was still saying. Except now, she was talking to me. Johnny would not have let me go anywhere without him. "What about me?" he'd always ask. In any case, I was happy to take him with me. Johnny was the kind of kid who brought sunshine everywhere he went. He made us all laugh with his jokes and his easy grin. He had a talent for happiness, and it was fun to be around him and watch him grow up. I used to take him swimming, carrying him on my back across choppy rivers so the current wouldn't take him. I can still feel his arms around my neck and hear his laugh in my ear.

By then, we had moved to California, and Buddy and Darrell had finished their service. After four years in the Navy, Buddy had been discharged in San Diego. He bought a car and drove north to French Camp and got his own place. Darrell had spent three years in the Army, and he moved back home with us for a few months until he found a job and got on his own feet.

Some things had changed. We were older, and although I was still their little brother, we each had grown into our own lives during those years apart. Buddy and Darrell had also picked up new habits during their service. They smoked considerably and always seemed to carry a beer in their hands or, as the day progressed, some stronger stuff. They'd become more unpredictable, losing their tempers at the slightest provocation. Any sudden noise made them jump out of their skin. Buddy, who'd never been a big talker, withdrew further into silence.

At the same time, some things we picked up as if we'd never been apart. There wasn't much opportunity to hunt rabbits in California, but pheasants were phenomenal out in the many islands where the Sacramento River and the San Joaquin River meet in an inland delta. The delta is a maze of waterways encircling patches of fertile land, and it was a hunting and fishing paradise. There were lots of asparagus fields out there, and the little red berries that grew on the asparagus ferns attracted unbelievable numbers of pheasants. Darrell, Buddy, and I went back to hunting together. Sometimes I'd get to take some schoolmates, like Larry McCurdy, Gary Hall, or the Reynolds twins. We'd dress up nice and warm, and load up our pickup truck when it was still dark. I rode in the back with my buddies as daylight broke. Riding out in the open, sitting on the truck bed with the cold morning wind cutting our cheeks was the best thing in the world. After an hour or so, we'd get out, and all of us walked down to go hunt pheasants, our boots squishing in the fertile sediment and our eyes scanning the pure blue sky that reflected in the water all around us.

My brothers and I also reunited over fishing. We would go up to the Sacramento River and catch big striped bass. We also fished for trout up in the mountains. Just being out there was reward enough, and then we'd catch a trout too, as a bonus. We called them pocket trout, because they were just big enough to fit in our pockets.

Over the summers of 1963 and 1964, I got to spend considerable time with Buddy. He was working as a caretaker for the St. Francis Yacht Club, and he hired me as his assistant during school break.

The club was based in San Francisco but had an outpost on Tinsley Island, a thirty-eight-acre patch of land in the Sacramento–San Joaquin Delta, just west of Stockton. A lighthouse brought up from the coast and grafted onto the island had been turned into a fancy clubhouse, with eight or ten bedrooms and a formal dining room that could sit twenty people. Some of the club members stayed there in the summer.

The clubhouse also had a small kitchen, and Buddy taught me the basics of cooking—which I put to good use just a few years later in Vietnam. I learned how to grill hamburgers, hot dogs, or steaks and bake potatoes in tinfoil. Simple stuff like that. As we peeled buckets of potatoes or flipped burgers on the big outside grill, we'd talk about his birth mom. He showed me letters she had written. You could tell from her writing she had some problems, and at times, she was not coherent. In the evening, when our work was done, Buddy and I also played a lot of guitar together. Darrell was never much of a musician, but Bud loved country music, and I guess that's where I got my taste for it. Even today, more than fifty years later, every country tune I hear still reminds me of him.

Buddy also showed me how to drive boats. Part of the job was to bring the club's sixty- or seventy-foot yachts into Stockton to fuel them up. But the yacht owners and their insurance companies were real nervous having a sixteen-year-old with no captain's license drive their big yachts. The license involved a stiff written test and a practical, so although I'd been a Sea Scout in Stockton, I still had a lot to learn. There were green and red buoys of different shapes and numbers delineating the navigating channels for those who knew how to read them. Bud and I spent hours maneuvering the yachts around the club and into Stockton, and he'd quiz me over and over.

"If you're going around that green buoy, and the buoy is a marker nine, what does that mean?" It's been long enough now that I've forgotten most of it. At the time, I enjoyed having Bud guide me through the intricacies of river navigation. I got my license.

It was hard work, but I had a lot of fun. I got to swim plenty, scrubbing the pool with a big brush and cleaning the filter. I became friends with Allen, whose dad piloted the big ships into Stockton's harbor and was a member of the St. Francis Club. Allen and his family would come out and stay in the lighthouse for a week or so in the summertime. They brought a beautiful old runabout boat whose original propeller system had been replaced by a Jacuzzi water jet. Nobody had ever seen one like that before, and Allen and I spent a lot of time test-driving it. I learned to water ski behind that steady jet boat, which could go forty miles an hour pulling one skier or eight skiers or no skier at all.

In the evening, as soon as Buddy and I got everything squared away, I could go waterskiing before it got dark. Whenever he could, he would come as well. At that time of day, with the sun barely above the horizon, the water would get totally flat, and we routinely pushed the envelope. Another family with a club membership usually stayed on the island with two of their four daughters, Cindy and Cathy. Their runabout boat—named the *Four Cs* after their four daughters—was a real hot rod, running on a Ford 409 engine. That runabout would scream. We used to ski at a hundred miles an hour along a canal used for irrigation that ran three miles in a straight line, then made a U-turn, and skied back three miles until we merged into the main channel.

One evening, we had pulled out of the long end of the canal into the waterway and were running the few miles back toward Tinsley

Island. I was waterskiing, and one of the girls was driving. We were running sixty or seventy miles an hour, but the water was real nice and I signaled that I could take some more speed. The 409 roared, and within seconds we were running a hundred miles an hour going down the main channel. I felt the skin of my face crawl toward my ears and wings grow on my back. Then I spotted a tugboat and a barge coming toward us, pushing three big waves in front of them. Surely the girls were going to slow down.

They didn't.

When the runabout boat hit the first wave, it took off and the rope that was pulling me grew slack. I held my arms up in the air trying to pull it taut, but just when the slack was yanked out of that rope, I hit that first wave at a hundred miles an hour. I took a gigantic tumble, flew through the air, and rolled like a ball on top of the water to the riverbank—and right into thick blackberry bushes. I lay there for a while, unable to get up or call out. I heard the boat slowly coming past, its engine bobbing. "I know he's here someplace," the girls said. "It looked like he went in right here." Finally, I was able to call out, and they came to get me. When they saw me, they turned pale: the blackberry thorns had torn me up, and I looked as if I had been run through a meat grinder. It looked bad, but miraculously, I wasn't really hurt. Mary McCarthy, who ran Tinsley Island with her husband, Pat, and was like a mama to Buddy and me, brought me into the lighthouse. Once she cleaned me all up and checked me out, there were only a few places that required Band-Aids. The girls apologized profusely: they hadn't seen the waves, they said. After that, we decided to control the speed. At least for a little while.

When the summer ended and I was back at school, I didn't get to see much of Buddy. Darrell was always at the house, even after he moved out. But Buddy stayed on Tinsley Island most of the time. At first, he'd come stay with us on Friday night or have dinner on Saturday whenever he was in French Camp for a night or two. But after a while, he'd call for me to meet him somewhere in town, and he only stopped by the house to see Mom when Dad was at work. Even when we were kids, an invisible fracture ran between Buddy and Dad. I'm not sure why exactly. But as Buddy got older, the fracture widened into an open rift, and they were unable to bridge it.

In 1965, at the end of the summer, the family was ready to leave California and move back to Indiana. I had just completed my junior year in high school. At first Darrell stayed in California but soon joined us so he could stay close to the family. Buddy didn't. Before we left French Camp, he came by the house to say good-bye. I was hoping that, in time, he would change his mind and follow us.

I never saw him again.

★3★

IN FLANDERS FIELDS

When we left California, we first landed in Hardinville, Illinois. We stayed with relatives for at least a month while Dad drove around looking for work. One day, he came back and said he had found a job at Diamond Chain, a company making bicycle chains in Indianapolis. So we moved to Waverly, a small town just south of Indianapolis. I didn't have a car, I didn't have a job, and I didn't have any money. It was back to square one.

I went to high school in neighboring Mooresville for my senior year and got a job as a cook at Big M bowling alley. There weren't a whole lot of jobs for high school seniors that would pay a whole lot of money. I grilled hot dogs and hamburgers at the snack bar and sold homemade pies and cakes by the slice. I worked there after school, from five p.m. until midnight, six nights a week. That didn't leave much time for anything else, and I dropped out of football.

There was a TV in the lounge at the bowling alley, and one

evening, I watched President Lyndon Johnson hang a medal on a wide ribbon around Roger Donlon's neck. American military assistance to South Vietnam had been on the rise since the early 1960s, but after one of our destroyers clashed with a North Vietnamese vessel in the Gulf of Tonkin in August 1964, US involvement escalated rapidly. Captain Donlon, a commanding officer in the Special Forces, was the first to be awarded a Medal of Honor during what had become the Vietnam War.

I didn't know much about the Medal of Honor. Dad and his brothers sometimes talked about it, and I had read a small blurb in an encyclopedia. I knew it was the highest military distinction any soldier could receive, a medal honoring valor and selfless courage awarded to those putting their lives on the line above and beyond the call of duty. To me, it was the medal of heroes.

As I watched the black-and-white TV footage of the ceremony at the White House, a voice-over explained that a reinforced Vietcong battalion had attacked the captain's camp near some place I'd never heard of called Nam Dong. With wounds in the stomach, leg, shoulder, and face, Captain Donlon evacuated his injured men, administered first aid, and then crawled from position to position to direct firing operations and keep everyone's spirits up. The camp held, and the enemy retreated.

I was starstruck. Only some serious hero possessed that kind of courage and fortitude. Captain Donlon looked so tall and straight and proud, shaking the president's hand in his crisp uniform. I wanted to be like him. I decided that, once I'd graduated from high school, I would enlist. In my family, being American meant that you had to serve your country for a few years. Then you could come home and go on with your life. Nobody had ever become a career soldier, but both my grandpas, my dad, my uncle, and my big brothers had all served in the armed forces. Our country's history is such that each of them had fought in a war or been involved in some serious crisis.

My dad's dad, Bruce Davis, fought in the Spanish-American War in 1898. He didn't talk much about it, but on occasion, I'd hear him mention it to Dad or Uncle Jess, Dad's younger brother. One of the things he always said was that he had been up the *real* San Juan Hill with Teddy Roosevelt—who incidentally was awarded a Medal of Honor more than a hundred years later for his actions during that offensive. That battle was the bloodiest of the war in Cuba. American troops suffered heavy casualties trying to take the hill from the Spanish forces that fired at them from the ridge, but in the end they prevailed. The Spaniards still used muskets—these long muzzle-loading guns—and Grandpa Davis was shot through the hip by a musket ball. The .58 caliber lead ball gave him a bad limp for the rest of his life, and as a child, I thought all grandpas walked like that. There must be some truth to that, because I'm a grandpa myself now, and sure enough, I walk with a limp too.

Because of his injury, Grandpa Davis walked with a cane. He had chopped it himself out of some tree, and on the side, he had carved a skull where a knob or a burl had been. That skull was not very big, maybe the size of a thumbnail. But it left a big impression on me, because its eyes were two tiny shining stones that looked like diamonds. He said the skull helped him remember all of the men that he'd served with. Grandpa Davis got to live until he was ninety-three years old. He's long gone now, but I still have his cane. Every time I look at it, I think of him and all the men who fought on the *real* San Juan Hill so many years ago.

My mama's daddy, John Henry Helle, served as well. He was an artilleryman in World War I and fought in the battlefields that stretched from western Belgium to northern France, an area known as Flanders. Just like my other grandpa, he didn't talk about it much. That war—which pitched an alliance led by France, Great Britain, and Russia against Germany, Austria-Hungary, and Turkey—was one of the greatest reapers in history, killing close to 10 million soldiers and wounding another 20 million. For years, the western front across France and Belgium barely moved, with troops on both sides bogged down in muddy trenches and killing each other in great numbers. On the wall of my home hangs a big, framed poster from 1917. It's a list of all the men from Fulton County, Illinois, who were serving in World War I at the time. My grandpa's name is on it. When the United States joined the Allied war effort that year, John Helle went to Europe to fight the country of his ancestors. As far as he was concerned, he was 100 percent American.

I never heard Grandpa Helle say anything about the men who died. What he talked about were horses. In those days, horses pulled caissons, those two-wheel carts carrying artillery units and ammunition, and they strained all day to move them through the mud. "Those beautiful animals, they served us so well," he'd say, his eyes filled with tears. "They'd give their lives for us, and then they'd lie in the mud, gasping for air, and we had to shoot them." The Germans used mustard gas against their enemies, and gas masks just didn't fit the horses as well as they fit people. The gas burned the horses' lungs real bad, until they had to be put out of their misery. After I got older and went to Vietnam, I came to understand that he was talking about more than horses. Now I'm certain that he was crying for the men whom he'd served with, because the same thing would have happened to them. Mustard gas would have burned their bodies, and if they hadn't put on their gas masks quickly enough, if they'd gotten just one big huff of mustard gas, their lungs would have blistered and filled with fluids until they drowned.

Dad served during World War II. He did not serve overseas. He was first stationed at Sheppard Air Force base in Wichita Falls, Texas, where he trained as a mechanic for gliders. For some reason, he spoke a little bit of German and was transferred to the Wright-Patterson Air Force base near Dayton, Ohio—where I was born—to guard German prisoners of war. From 1943 until after the end of the war, two hundred to four hundred German prisoners were held there. Little is known about these POWs, but they painted big green monsters on the wall of their mess hall, and that mural is still there today.

Dad didn't speak a whole lot about it, but we had one picture of him standing in front of a jail with German POWs. The Germans were behind bars wearing civilian clothing, and Dad was in military uniform. When I was little, it was astonishing to me that, except for their attire, the Germans looked very much like Dad. Maybe I expected the enemy to have big horns or something, but they just looked like regular folks. I haven't seen that picture for fifty years probably, but I still see it as clearly as if it were in front of me.

Dad's older brother, Bruce—Uncle Boo to us—didn't join the military. The fingers on his right hand had been cut off and sewn back on, but they no longer worked, so he wasn't fit for service. But Jesse James Davis, Dad's youngest brother, served during the Korean War. Uncle Jess was in the Marine Corps for four years, I believe, based out of San Diego. When I was a small boy, I thought he had been a soldier all his life, because he always wore his uniform when he came to visit us. I don't know much about Uncle Jess's service, because he never spoke of it. What I know for sure is that he evidently understood a whole lot about what combat does to a young man's soul, because he helped me and some of my Vietnam buddies a great deal after we came back home all broken.

My eldest brother, Buddy, enlisted in the Navy and served four years on the USS *Dixie*. The USS *Dixie* was a destroyer tender, a support ship repairing and supplying warships. Buddy was based out of San Diego but went on tours to the Western Pacific to support the Seventh Fleet. Buddy got front row seats during the second Taiwan Strait Crisis in 1958, when communist China shelled Taiwanese troops on some islands in the Formosa Strait. American vessels helped protect the supply lines to the islands. Buddy once told me that he dove off to save a man who had sunk almost to the bottom. He went hand over hand down the big anchor chain to get deep enough to swim over to him and bring him back up, but it was too late. The sailor had already drowned. Buddy only spoke of his service when no one else was around.

So did my other brother. Darrell was in the Army during the Berlin Crisis in 1961. After World War II, Germany was split, its eastern part occupied by Soviet troops, and a western section under the control of the Allied forces. The Americans, the French, the British, and the Russians also occupied different parts of Berlin. In the 1950s, many East Germans wanted to flee Soviet domination, and after the borders were closed, they could still slip into West Berlin and escape to freedom. That made the East German and Soviet authorities very unhappy. In August 1961, East German troops sealed off the western section of Berlin and started building a big wall almost a hundred miles long around it. Tensions escalated until American and Soviet tanks faced off on each side of the wall, and each side backed down. Darrell told me that, during those tense few months, he was driving one of the trucks trying to bring supplies to East Berlin. East German guards posted on the Berlin Wall would not let them through and pointed their rifles at him every day, shouting, "Today, GI, you die!"

Then the Vietnam War came along, and it was my turn. I didn't give it a second thought. The America I knew didn't question the war or dodge its duty. The America I knew answered the call. Distant grumblings against our involvement in Vietnam hardly filtered through to the world I lived in. In May 1966, some of my friends told me they'd been drafted, and a couple of others wanted to join. It was a good time for me to go as well. So I drove from Mooresville, Indiana, to the Army recruiting station in Indianapolis with four buddies. I was nineteen years old and still in high school.

I wanted to join the Marine Corps. I thought of Uncle Jess. My older brother Buddy had been in the Navy and passed on his love of ships to me. I had really enjoyed working at the St. Francis Yacht Club with him when we lived in California, and I had fond memories of my days as a Sea Scout. But in 1966, I hadn't heard much about the Navy in Vietnam. Most of the action seemed to happen on land, and joining the Marine Corps felt like a good compromise. I would still be in the Navy, but I'd do my job where it was most needed.

My buddies and I stood in line for an hour, but we were going nowhere fast. The recruitment line for the Army was moving much faster. So my buddies and I talked among ourselves for a while and decided to step over to the other line. That's how I got to join the Army for three years and volunteered to go to Vietnam. It's funny how that little decision changed the course of my life. Just moving from one queue to another. Everything happens for a purpose, I guess.

I didn't have to report back to Indianapolis until September 28, 1966. That was the earliest date available. So I graduated high school in June and spent the summer working in the oil fields of Illinois. I made big dollars—$1.10 an hour—and big muscles. In September, I drove back to Indianapolis to start my three years in the military. Back in May, my friends and I had enlisted in the "buddy system," which was supposed to keep us together through basic training and our first assignment. That sounded good on paper, and the recruiter had done a good marketing job on us. Unfortunately, the system didn't work very well in practice: we were shipped to different locations from the get-go.

From Indianapolis, I was sent on a bus to Fort Leonard Wood in Missouri. The reception station was so overcrowded that we ended up waiting in line for what felt like days. It was rainy and cold, and we were given blankets while we were still waiting. Fort Leonard Wood wasn't prepared for such an influx. The food was terrible and there weren't enough beds. Some of us had to sleep outside. The ground was all muddy, so I slept on top of a brick wall for three nights. Every evening we got dry blankets, and within a few minutes they were soaking wet. We were still in our civilian clothing. I finally did get a military uniform, and my clothes were shipped home in a bag. When Mom opened up the package, shoes, pants, everything was mildewed and totally ruined.

Sleeping out in the rain, a lot of us got sick with pneumonia. So we had to line up, and a medic came through and shot penicillin in our arms with what looked like an air gun. I felt I had been shot in the arm with a real gun. Within a few minutes, my throat started closing up and I was flapping on the ground. That's how I found out that I was allergic to penicillin. Or maybe they gave me way too much of it. In any case, I was shipped to the infirmary pronto and got to spend the night in a dry cot on the floor. After three nights in the rain, that felt like the Ritz.

I spent twelve days at Fort Leonard Wood. This was my first contact with the Army, and I wasn't impressed. Not one bit. This was a long way from what I had pictured when I enlisted. To relieve overcrowding, some of us were transferred to Fort Jackson in South Carolina for basic training. We left Missouri in the late evening, and after a night and most of the next day in the Greyhound bus contracted by the Army, we finally arrived at our destination. Some of the guys were not awake yet, even though it was in the afternoon. A drill instructor jumped right on the bus. "Get your butts off that bus and fall in line, you useless maggots!" The veins in his neck looked like they were about to pop out, and his face was all red. He promised us right there that he was going to make men out of us. He was very convincing, and we all rushed out of the bus.

We were first assigned to our barracks. After a shower and getting squared away in what was going to be our home for eight weeks, we had supper in the mess hall. Drill sergeants kept yelling at us the whole time. At nine thirty that night, we went to our bunks, our ears still ringing from all the screaming. The next morning, we were up at four thirty.

On the first day, we were given green uniforms and fatigues, belts, caps, and black leather boots. We also picked up our toilet kits, skivvies, sheets, blankets, and pillowcases, and the drill instructors showed us how everything was to be folded and put away. Our hair was clipped off to just the skin. Mine was already pretty short, so it didn't bother me that much, but some kids had beautiful long hair, and they totally freaked out. By the end of the day, I was no longer Sammy. I had become Private Davis, squad number RA16947771. I bet that anyone who's been through basic training still remembers the number they got.

Every morning at four thirty a.m. sharp, the drill sergeant came through our barrack and rattled his club against the metal railing of our beds as he walked down. *Bang bang bang bang bang.* "Wake up, you lazy maggots! Where do you think you are? Summer camp?" That was our wake-up call, as the bugle played reveille. That sure made you feel like a soldier. We made our bunks and got our pistol belts and helmet liners. We'd all file outside, where it was still pitch-dark, and started the day running and doing PT—physical training—until chow at seven thirty a.m. After breakfast, we fell into company formation and marched to the drill grounds, where we worked out until eleven a.m. Then it was platoon drill until lunch. At one p.m., we fell back in line and marched to a different drill ground for more PT. We came back at four thirty p.m., and our corporal gave us drill ceremony and more PT, or we'd fall in line again for rifle or grenade class. Once we were done with training, we still had to mop, wax, buff, and wash our barracks until after nine p.m., when we got to shave and take a much-needed shower. By then, we finally got to hit the sack. I was so beat by then that all I could think of was sleep. But I still needed to find time to spit shine my shoes and fix my footlocker. The next day, we'd do it all over again. We hardly had time to breathe. The days were hard and long and the nights very short. "I'm very tired, a little hungry and extremely disgusted with my life," I wrote home.

We ran, we jumped, we low-crawled, and we hung from horizontal ladders. Anything that involved muscling up. It was hard, but I didn't mind PT too much. The drill sergeants first evaluated what kind of shape we were in and then every day for eight weeks pushed us to the limit. And every day, we got just a little bit better, a little bit quicker, a little bit stronger. There was an obstacle course that we had to go through, and there was a time limit. If we failed, we got our butts kicked, and the drill instructors yelled in our faces. But if we managed to do it faster, then they always tried to reward us a little bit with things that were important to us at the time, like eating chow at the front of the line or something. It felt real good to go through the forty-yard low crawl in less than thirty-six seconds, or to move through seventy-six horizontal bars in under a minute.

Doing all this on a few hours of sleep every night was very tough. But hard as it was, the physical part of basic training was easier for me than for most of the other guys. I had spent the summer working twelve to fifteen hours a day, six days a week in the oil fields. I had been a rod tailer, pulling up strings of thirty-feet sucker rods attached to the oil pumps that needed fixing. We brought up the steel rods that ran two or three thousand feet down into the well and laid them down. When the pump sitting at the bottom of the well was repaired, we put everything right back in and went on to the next one. It was real physical work, so I was in excellent shape. But for some of the kids who had spent most of their time behind a desk or at the library, PT was exceptionally challenging. We had to run up this big sand hill all the time. Running in sand is extremely difficult, but running in sand uphill is even harder. The sand gives under your feet, and you keep slipping down. They had us broken down into small groups of fifteen or twenty, and if the whole squad didn't succeed, we all got punished. So we latched arms and those do push-ups. Push-ups were the currency of punishment during basic training. Our drill instructors dispensed push-ups according to an elaborate scale of penalties. Something wrong at the foot of the bed? Ten push-ups. A pillow not situated just right? Twenty push-ups. On bad days, I was doing maybe a couple hundred push-ups. On other days, maybe forty or fifty. During our morning PT, we all did twenty or thirty just to get started. Then the extras kept piling up during the day. If I didn't throw a hand grenade far enough, the drill sergeant would shout, "Drop and give me ten, Davis!" I'd do my ten push-ups, then get another hand grenade and try it again. And again. I did a whole lot of push-ups over my M14. We had to disassemble our standard-issue rifles and lay all the parts out on a sheet until the sergeant gave us the signal. "Reassemble!" he'd bark. We each had to put our weapon back together in so many seconds and make sure it functioned properly. I'd been shooting guns pretty much all my life, so I was very familiar with weapons. But my big fingers were not well suited to handle the little bitty parts and pieces. Sometimes I'd drop them and lose a second or two. I got to do a lot of extra push-ups over those M14s.

At the time, I thought that was all really stupid. "I don't think a person could hate something as much as I do this," I wrote Mom shortly after I got to Fort Jackson. "They try to make mindless bodies out of you. All during your life you're taught to think for yourself, and all of a sudden, you can't even wiggle your toes unless you're told." Now I understand they were trying to teach us obedience and to follow orders—and muscle us up in the process. I eventually got used to it. It was real hard to fall in line, but I adapted.

My drill sergeant was Francisco Quinones. We thought he was the meanest person alive. He picked on us and pushed us until we could go no further, and then pushed us some more. He barked in our faces all the time, encouraging us, as he put it, to get our heads out of our rears. I can still see him running backward, facing us as we moved forward. "If any of you low-down miserable punks think that you can run backwards with me, you're more than welcome to try!" he told us in the first few days. I was feeling strong. So I turned around and ran backward with him. All I can say is that he didn't particularly care for it.

There was an acting corporal—a real tall blond-haired kid by the name of Lochmueller—who helped me a great deal to understand the point of all this and accept it. He had just completed basic training himself and wanted to be a DI—a drill instructor. So he was there to help teach us. The drill sergeants never told us why we had to do what we did. They just told us to do it. Corporal Lochmueller, on the other hand, would tell us the reason why we had to do the low crawl in under so many seconds. If we couldn't do it real quick in the jungle in Vietnam, we were not going to survive. He was hard on us, but he also reminded us why we were there and what was at stake. More sweat in training, less blood in combat. He was the meanest, nicest guy you could ever hope to meet.

We also trained in a gas chamber. The drill instructors told us the Vietcong might use different types of gas on our troops, and we had to be ready. We got sprayed with riot gas and pepper gas. That was no fun at all. Everybody was crying, laughing, and barfing all at the same time. I thought of Grandpa Helle in Flanders, and knowing what could happen if I didn't reach my mask in time scared the hell out of me. Luckily I never had to use that knowledge in Vietnam.

Thinking of home kept me going. "Everything I do, I do for you,"

I wrote Mom during boot camp. "When we are running and I want to drop out, I say no, Mom's pushing me all the way. Anything I do, you're right behind me giving me courage, strength and hope."

Working that hard and being nineteen years old, I was always hungry. We had plenty of food, but all the meat and potatoes, eggs, oatmeal, and grits I wolfed down during these eight weeks never seemed to fill my stomach. When we were out on bivouac or trucking in the bush during the day, we ate C rations. This was our first experience with C rats, and most guys hated them. I thought they worked great. Everything we needed came in green tin cans with brown packets, all packed in a box. We didn't have to keep them cold or keep them hot, and they probably could have kept for a hundred years. The cans could even be used as a stove. With a little bit of Tabasco sauce, they tasted good—but I suppose with hot sauce, pretty much anything does. The main course was typically turkey, pork, beef, or chicken of one kind or another, or else ham and beans. We also had crackers, peanut butter, and gum. Because we never knew what we were going to get, there was a lot of trading going on. The guys who didn't like the chopped ham and eggs swapped with the guys who didn't care for the turkey loaf or whatever. The ham-and–lima beans meal was particularly unpopular for some reason. So was the Beanie Weenie—beans with frankfurters in tomato sauce. I admit the little hot dogs didn't taste all that great, but at least they added a bit of grease to the beans.

The brown pack had salt, sugar, instant coffee, and other essentials like toilet paper—and, of course, cigarettes. C rations had four cigarettes with a meal, and those of us who didn't smoke didn't get a smoke break. So I started smoking with everybody else, and once I started, I couldn't stop. It took me decades and the love of a good once in a while, just so I could read about my old life and hold a little piece of home in my hands.

Friendships were built according to the alphabet. That's how everything worked in boot camp, how bunks were assigned, how we stood in line for chow, and how we trained. So naturally, I got to know my fellow Ds pretty well, as well as the Bs, Es, and Fs. Two or three bunks from mine was Johnston Dunlop. At twenty-five or twenty-six years old, he was older than most of us. He had prior experience in the military, but because he had been out for a year or two, he had to do basic training again. He had already gone through it and done it all, and he would show us all kinds of tricks. He taught us how to wax the barrack floor to make it shine like a mirror, and our floor was always perfect. He showed me how to reassemble the M14 quicker—and saved me a few push-ups.

Johnston wore the big black-framed glasses issued by the Army and spoke with a funny accent. At first, I thought everyone in his hometown of Auburn, New York, talked that way. But Johnston turned out to be from Scotland, and stuck to his guns when it came to pronunciation. "*I* am not the one with a speaking problem, my friend," he used to tell us. "*You* are." He taught me and my Southern drawl how to speak like a Scot.

A few weeks into boot camp, Drill Sergeant Quinones took me aside. "Private Davis, how would you like to be acting corporal?" he said. I stood a bit straighter and said I would be honored. I didn't get more money or anything, but I was in charge of eleven guys and had to tell them what to do. The job didn't really make me too many friends, but it sure made me feel better. A few weeks later, when I was getting ready to leave Fort Jackson at the end of basic training, Sergeant Quinones called me into his little office in our barracks.

"Sit down, Davis," he said. I did as I was told. He reached under his bed and pulled out a bottle of Jack Daniel's. "I'd like to share a drink with you," he said. I thought it was another test, because we were not supposed to have alcohol or drink in the barracks. So I thanked him and said I didn't care for any. He smiled, and with a twinkle in his eye, he said, "Sammy, I would like you to have a sip with me." I was blown away. That was nothing like the drill sergeant I knew. I thanked him and took a swig of whiskey. Then he told me that the reason he had been so hard on me and a handful of other guys over the previous eight weeks was because he knew we had more capability than most of the men in the squadron. "I wanted you to be the very best you could be," he added.

I realized there and then that I owed a whole lot to Sergeant Quinones. Although he was Puerto Rican and looked nothing like my dad, he reminded me so much of him. Like Dad, he patted me on the back if I did something good, but kicked me in the butt—or rather, make me drop and give him ten—if I did something he didn't like. He was always in my face, pushing me very hard every single day to always be better and go further. He never let me give up. He truly cared about the troops that he was training. Later in Vietnam, I often thought of him and how lucky I had been to have him as my drill sergeant. When I lived through a war, firing howitzers night and day on little to no sleep and staring death in the eye, I came to appreciate how and why basic training made sense. The intense physical training, the discipline, the long days, the relentless push to go beyond our limits. Basic training prepared me well for what was to come. I don't think I would have made it back home if it hadn't been for Sergeant Quinones.

When the military asked me who I wanted to invite for my Medal of Honor presentation after I came back from Vietnam, I gave his name right away. After the ceremony, he came up to me and shook my hand. Then he turned around and walked away. Unfortunately, I did not get to see him or speak to him after that. But he did come. Six or seven years later, I tried to find him again. I talked to somebody who knew him down at Fort Jackson, but I was told he'd moved on. I asked the military to try to find him, but they said they couldn't locate him.

On December 2, 1966, I graduated from basic training. I said good-bye to my buddies and left Fort Jackson. Johnston Dunlop went straight to Vietnam, where I didn't yet know I would get to see him again. I reported to Fort Sill in Oklahoma to become an artilleryman.

After the mild humidity of South Carolina, I nearly froze to death during my eight weeks in Oklahoma. "It sure is cold, wet and nasty here," I wrote in one of my first letters. It was the dead of winter, and a sharp, icy wind blew across the plains and cut right through us as we learned to operate the big howitzer guns. Apart from the arctic conditions, artillery training was definitely less intense than basic training. We had a lot of brand-new things to learn, but it was far less physical. We were taught how to position artillery guns and make sure they were all shooting at the same point. We learned about powder and how to read maps. We went out on maneuvers and bivouacs, and learned to drive all sorts of Army trucks. We were taught to handle M60 and M50 machine guns, and learned to operate M79 grenade launchers and the 3.5-inch bazooka. I enjoyed night ops, when our artillery fire illuminated the dark sky. It sure was pretty.

Unlike in basic training, we also got most weekends off. We

headed to town in Lawton. We drank as much beer as we could and visited the go-go girls at the Bamboo Lounge. Then we would get into a taxicab and drive back to Fort Sill. Our barracks were also right across the street from a beer garden, and every evening we went over and drank a little foam. Of course, we were not supposed to, but it was right there, and we figured we should make the best of it. I bought myself a real pretty guitar for $22.50. It didn't play as nice as my old Gertie at home, but it helped take my mind off things a great deal.

In some respects, life wasn't that much better though. From acting corporal, I was once again a plain old private, and it was rough. "Boy I don't think I'll shut my eyes once while I'm home," I wrote. "Just living life while I can. Because you sure can't in the Army." Just before I went home for a few days over Christmas, I was on KP duty, which meant working in the kitchen. Kitchen patrol involved mostly cleaning and peeling potatoes, and I remember mopping the mess hall and washing what felt like hundreds of dishes right before I left. The very first evening after I came back from leave, I was lying on my bunk, trying to get some shut-eye after the long Greyhound ride. It had been so hard to leave everyone and everything I loved in Indiana and head back to Fort Sill, and I was feeling pretty sorry for myself. The sergeant came to my bunk and said, "Davis, you're on KP!" I pointed out that I couldn't be, because I had just worked in the kitchen before Christmas. He showed me the KP roster, and it said Davis. Someone had forgotten to update it, but it didn't matter. Orders were orders. The next morning at three thirty a.m., I headed back to the kitchen, cursing in silence. "I guess I'll stay a follower the rest of my service time. Three long, long, hard years," I reflected in one of my letters. "They say you learn a lot in the Army and you grow up a lot. But I'm not too sure. You sure learn a lot about hating things, you just get sick of everything around you." On some days, turning in at night was about the only thing I could really look forward to. And that always was disappointing, because I had to wake up in the morning.

I still missed home like crazy. "A guy really never knows how much he loves his parents until he's out of reach from them," I wrote from Fort Sill. "Then you sit and realize you won't have each other forever and that every second of each day is so precious. You know you're not going to be able to have them for three whole years, and it kind of hurts to know that some day, the people you love most will be gone." I seriously wondered whether I should get married right out of training. I was thinking about a few girls at home—well, one in particular. At least I was training in artillery with three of my buddies from Fort Jackson, so I wasn't too lonely. But there sure were mean guys stationed at Fort Sill as well, and most days, I got to use a little hand-to-hand combat on someone.

Our good old civilian lives felt like years away. The Army took over everything we did or thought about. "How do you get into a foxhole?" I used to ask my buddies in training. Without exception, they all went through the correct method of digging a defensive fighting position. Not one of them remembered that all you have to do is lift its tail.

Shortly after I arrived at Fort Sill, I had been told that, because of a back condition and the operation I'd had on some infected teeth during boot camp, I could no longer train to be airborne. My back was sore from a fall I took during my final PT test. A doctor at Fort Sill told me that, when one of my back muscles tired, it caused a bone to move out of place. I was disappointed, but I figured there were plenty of other ways to serve. We had to write down on some form where we wanted to go after our eight weeks: Europe, Alaska, Hawaii, Korea—or, of course, Vietnam. In reality, the Army sent us wherever it suited them: 90 percent of the previous cycle of trainees had been shipped to Vietnam. The other 10 percent were sent to Germany or Korea, and very few got to be stationed in the United States. I hardly knew anything about Vietnam: it was little more than a sliver of a country on the other side of the globe. But I had enlisted to serve my country, and this was where I was needed. So I picked Vietnam. Unsurprisingly, I got my wish. A couple weeks before the end of artillery training, I was told this was where I was headed. I felt well prepared, not realizing that nothing can really prepare you for war. I just hoped that I'd be shipped with some of the cool guys I'd befriended at Fort Sill.

On February 13, after eight weeks of advanced individual training, I graduated and went home. I had a thirty-day leave, and it felt like Christmas. After several months of military life, I was anxious to spend time with the family. I was also looking forward to seeing my girlfriend. As it turned out, she'd been thinking of getting married as well, but not with me: she had met another fellow while I was away and, unbeknownst to me, had moved on. I was a bit miffed, but I was too happy to be home to let it spoil my spirit. During those thirty days before I left for Vietnam, I drove to northern Illinois to see my grandma. Dad also took us to see some of his relatives. As the date of my leaving for Vietnam was getting close, I grew more and more anxious. I didn't want to say good-bye.

The night before I left, we had a big dinner at home. Mom invited the few pals who hadn't joined the military yet and were still around, together with their families. All my brothers and sisters were there, except for Buddy, who was still somewhere in California. Everybody patted me on the back and wished me good luck.

When I said good-bye to Grandpa Helle, he gave me a piece of paper. On it was the last stanza of "In Flanders Fields," a poem penned by a Canadian physician who'd fought in World War I:

Take up our quarrel with the foe:
To you from failing hands we throw
The torch; be yours to hold it high.
If ye break faith with us who die
We shall not sleep, though poppies grow
In Flanders fields.

When I first read it, I sort of understood it. But it wasn't until I served in Vietnam that it truly touched me. It wasn't until I went to war that I fully understood the sacrifice of those who had fought before me. I carried that piece of paper in my wallet for years, and now I keep it in my Medal of Honor box.

The next morning, it was time to go. My uncle Bruce came to pick me up to drive me to the airport in Indianapolis. Dad just gave me a hug, and told me to go do my job. He didn't tell me he loved me, but he didn't have to. I knew he did. Mom burst into tears, which made me cry too. Tears rolled down my cheeks as I kissed my baby sisters and little brother. Luckily, I could always count on Johnny to lighten up the mood. He whacked me on the head, pointing out that my leaving for Vietnam had one obvious upside. "Now I finally get to have your bedroom!"

I first flew to San Francisco. A couple of days later, on March 3, 1967, I boarded a plane for Vietnam.

★ 4 ★

WELCOME TO VIETNAM

The civilian aircraft contracted to transport us to Vietnam stopped in the Philippines for maybe five or six hours, and then we took off again for the last leg to Vietnam. There were several of us on that plane who had been together at Fort Sill, but loneliness crept into my heart. As we flew over the Pacific Ocean, it suddenly hit me: it was going to be a very long year.

I was twenty years old. Looking back on it now, I was a kid, eager and naïve. I was keen to serve my country and to apply all the things I'd been taught in boot camp and at Fort Sill. I had a job to do, and I was ready to do it. At the same time, I felt uneasy. What would it be like being under enemy fire? Living in the jungle? Would I make Mom and Dad proud? I had never fought a war before. Heck, I had never even traveled outside the United States or been away from home for more than a few weeks. I was headed to a foreign land, thousands of miles from everything and everyone I knew, and I was leaving for one year. Twelve whole months without sitting at the dinner table with Mom, Dad, and my baby sisters and brother. Three hundred and sixty-five days without hunting and fishing with my brothers and uncles, without having a good laugh with my buddies from home, and without taking a girl out on a date. As much as I tried to imagine what it would be like, I had no idea.

And then, there was the real clincher: I wasn't all that certain I would be coming back home.

Just before two a.m., we approached Tan Son Nhut airbase, just outside of Saigon. As the aircraft prepared to land, I heard explosions and saw flashes of lights through the window. When I realized mortars were hitting the airstrip, all the blood drained from my face and rushed down to my feet. I wasn't on Vietnamese soil yet, and I was already being shot at. *Holy crap, what am I doing here?* Luckily, we made it to the ground in one piece. The crew opened the door and, my heart still pounding, I took a deep breath and walked out of the cool and clean American Airlines aircraft. I might as well have stepped straight into a sewer. It was the middle of the night, but the heat and humidity were unbelievable. So was the stench of mold and rot. I will never forget that smell. Never. And every Vietnam veteran I've talked to remembers it as well. By the time I stepped onto the tarmac, sweat was trickling down my back. I was a long way from home.

Buses took us to the reception station at the Ninetieth Replacement Battalion, where all of us cherries—new guys fresh off the plane—were to be processed before being shipped to our units throughout Vietnam. The battalion was located at Long Binh, a sprawling base about twenty miles northwest of Saigon. Many other units and the command headquarters for the US Army in Vietnam were there as well. About forty thousand soldiers were stationed at Long Binh, making it the largest military base in Vietnam. It was nothing like the Vietnam I had imagined or seen on TV. I was expecting to land in the jungle. I hadn't pictured a military base with restaurants, bars, nightclubs, or a bowling alley—let alone a swimming pool and a golf driving range. For good measure, there was also a jail.

Long Binh was also home to the largest ammunition and explosives depot in the country. Everything coming into Vietnam was stockpiled there, in what we called the ammo dump, before being dispatched. Ammo and explosives were stacked into dozens of neat pads covered with tarps and hemmed in by dirt dikes. Those pads stretched for miles, and roads ran between them for trucks to deliver or pick up ammunition. From the sky, it looked like a giant grid.

I was supposed to stay at Long Binh for a few days, just enough time to get processed and acclimatized to the heat and humidity. My original orders were to join the Twenty-third Field Artillery Group, right on the DMZ, the demilitarized zone separating North and South Vietnam. I never made it there. On my third evening at the Ninetieth Replacement, I was hanging out in the compound where all newbies like me had been parked, killing time, when I felt the air being sucked out of my lungs. I saw the explosion, its shockwaves moving through the air, before I heard it. A second later, there was a massive *bang* some distance from us, and artillery rounds came raining down on us. I'm talking big, fat high-explosive shells, the kind that can flatten pretty much anything in a heartbeat. Then I heard several other loud explosions down the road. We ran around like rabbits, seeking cover from the hail of metal. At first, I thought this was enemy fire. But something was off: the rounds were hitting the ground with a thud, and then nothing. They didn't explode. I realized they had no fuses. These projectiles were not being fired: they were flying from our own ammunition depot, a mile or so from us. The Vietcong had managed to sneak across the ten-foot-tall fence into the perimeter and blow up several ammo pads, sending stock-piled artillery rounds and unexploded bombs flying all over the area.

I don't remember anyone getting seriously hurt, but it scared the poop out of me. *This is life in Vietnam. This is what it's like.* A week before, I'd been home with Mom and Dad, hanging out with my friends, driving my car down good old American country roads. Over three short days, I had dodged mortars aboard an aircraft and almost been flattened by artillery duds, courtesy of Charlie. Wel-come to Vietnam.

How was I going to survive one whole year of this? "Try to be good," I wrote to my baby sisters a few days in. "I'm telling you girls this now, because you never know, I might not make it to tell you to your face." It wasn't until a bit later that someone who had been at Long Binh a while told me that it wasn't like that all the time. Thank goodness. My new life sure was no picnic. But during the few months I spent at Long Binh, this sort of incident didn't happen every day.

Nobody had thought that Charlie could mess with the depot. It had a big fence around it and airplanes flying over with spotlights. The enemy infiltration sent shockwaves across the chain of com-mand, and a decision was made to ramp up security. Following the attack, about a hundred among us being processed at the Ninetieth Replacement were pulled in and informed that our initial orders had been struck. Instead of manning big howitzer guns for the Twenty-third Field Artillery, my job was to be a pad guard at the Long Binh ammunition depot until further notice. A dozen guys I knew from Fort Sill had been reassigned with me. All the others moved on, and most of them I never got to see again.

I moved to the Third Ordnance Battalion encampment less than a mile down the road, right across from the depot. There weren't enough barracks to accommodate the new guards, so we put up tents. Here I was, sleeping next to a cooler full of Cokes in a base as big as a city, with a beer garden and an Olympic-size swimming pool down the road. Sure, I was sharing that tent with fifty other guys, and the humidity was so bad that condensation from the tent roof dripped onto our faces at night; nothing was ever dry. But even with the mortars and the ammo dump explosion, this was a five-star accommodation compared to sleeping rough in the jungle with mosquitoes and leeches. There was even a TV—although all it ever showed were military programs. *This isn't too bad*, I thought.

During these first few weeks, I was pretty green. A few days in, our sergeant lined up the rookies who had just landed in Vietnam. The FNGs, as we were known—a moniker far too rude to spell out here, but that every Vietnam veteran probably remembers. "We need a hundred and fifty men for an essential mission!" he barked. I was keen to do my job, and with that many men working at it, I thought it would be okay. I stepped forward. Soon, there were enough of us. "Congratulations, gentlemen! You're on honey bucket detail!" he told us.

Honey bucket detail? What the hell was that? Some code name?

It was code all right. I was in for a surprise, and it wasn't a good one. We were marched to the latrines, and it slowly dawned on me that the "essential mission" was not going to be what I had in mind.

Our latrines were wooden boxes with a hole on top and no bottom, carefully positioned over fifty-five-gallon drums cut in half. The job was to pull the drums full of poop, pour fuel in, set the mix on fire, and stir. I couldn't believe I had just volunteered to burn poop—mountains of it. Those smart pills my brothers had fed me as a kid evidently hadn't worked too well after all. But I had cleaned septic tanks back in California, so I thought I was prepared. I wasn't. The stink of burning feces was something else, and I wasn't used to the heat and humidity yet. I threw up. "Well, guess I will never volunteer for anything else in the Army," I told Mom in a letter. Honey bucket detail. A sweet name for a real stinker.

After a week or two, I started getting used to the smell and to the heat. I realized early on that, during the dry season, all I had to do if I got too hot was pour a bucket of water over my head. And when the rains started in April and didn't stop for several months, we were always wet anyway. When I wasn't burning feces, my job was to patrol the ammunition depot. Trucks picked us up from our camp late in the afternoon and took us to the ammo dump down the road for our night patrols. Teams of two were typically assigned to secure a few ammo pads in twelve-hour shifts. Normally, one guy walked around the pad, and the other stayed in a foxhole. After an hour or two, we'd switch position.

When nothing happened, those shifts were endless. Hours stretched ahead of us like molasses. So getting assigned to the pads that had the neat blow-up stuff was a real treat. After patrolling the pads, the guy whose turn it was to sit in the foxhole would kill time getting a close look at bombs and grenades, or playing with the TNT and C-4 explosives. We had unlimited access to virtually every explosive device on the face of the planet. You name it, it was all there.

We'd take everything apart, look at how it worked, and put it back together. It was a giant playground for kids like us. I thought I had a pretty good knowledge of ammo and knew a thing or two about explosives from my job as a powder monkey in California. I learned a whole lot more patrolling those pads.

We were playing, but we were also watching. My third night at Long Binh had made it clear that the ammo dump was a good target for the enemy. The Vietcong kept probing the perimeter a couple of times a week. They were trying to steal ammunition or destroy it. Some of the probing was not real serious. They shot at us, and we shot back at them. They'd come in and fire a few rounds from a distance. We figured they were just checking us out and making sure we were awake. Other times, attacks were far more serious. They tried to infiltrate the perimeter again. We were also mortared four or five times during my time at Long Binh, and some kids got shrapnel wounds. I don't remember anybody getting killed though.

During the first few weeks, I would often hear shots being fired or see flares going off in the distance. I shot at some dark things here and there, but I don't think I hit them. Nothing I could recognize as people. When the trucks came to pick us up at seven o'clock in the morning to go back to our compound, I couldn't wait to hear the other guys' stories about what had gone down during the night.

One night I was sitting in my foxhole by one of the ammo pads near the fence when I heard a *zing zing*. It wasn't very loud, but the night was quiet, so I heard it clearly. I realized this was the sound that concertina wire makes when it is being pulled. I looked hard toward the big tall fence and saw a dark shape. I pulled a flare to get a better look at what was going on. When the flare went off, a hail of automatic fire came my way. Luckily, I wasn't hit. With the flare lighting up the perimeter, I saw someone crawling through the wire wearing the typical Vietcong shirt and pants that looked like black pajamas. I pulled the trigger of my M14 and shot back at him. He dropped his AK-47 and stopped moving. He looked dead.

Relief made me giddy. I had almost been killed, but I was still in one piece. I'd done my job better than he had. I silently thanked my brothers Buddy and Darrell, who had taught me how to shoot accurately. Blood still pounding in my ears, I came out of my foxhole, carefully walked to the fence, and pulled the enemy through to my side. His eyes were open and his face was frozen in disbelief as if death had taken him by surprise. He looked so young, probably about my age, and he didn't have anything that could identify him. I wondered whether he had a family. I remembered that old photo of my dad with the German POWs who looked like regular people. In that moment, I felt real stupid and then great sorrow seeped into my heart. For the first time, I had killed someone. Someone just like me. The only reason it was him lying there and not me was because I was a better shot. Or maybe I'd just had better luck.

Some of the other guys, alerted by the fire, had come in. We dragged the Vietcong kid over to the bunkers, and a jeep came over to pick him up. I don't know what happened to the body. When we came back to our camp the next morning after our shift, he was not there. But I still see his eyes. That's what stays with you forever. The look in their eyes.

After that night, I was on edge. Sometime in April, I heard a suspicious noise during one of my shifts. I grabbed a flare to see what was going on and to alert the other guards. I popped it, but it didn't propel. I found out the hard way that explosives are not all play. The flare exploded in my hand, and the bright light blinded me. I was burned pretty bad: the skin of my palm peeled off and stuck to the flare canister. The medics gave me some pills that kept me dozing off for a few days, but I was lucky. The third-degree burns on my hand healed well and my eyes fully recovered.

We had to watch out for all kinds of unwanted visitors, and I had a few more scares. A little while later, during another of my night shifts, I heard gunfire down the fence some distance away. From the amount of bullets being fired, my pad buddy and I thought a really big attack was going on. The *rattatttattt* of semiautomatic weapons kept getting closer and closer, so we got ready for the enemy to get to us. I was down in my foxhole, and all I could see were the bullets fired from other positions ricocheting up. When the gunfire reached us, I stood up and saw a dark shape crawling real fast right along the fence. I fired, and the shape dropped right in front of me. An infantry lieutenant in a roving patrol jeep came rolling in, pulling up just in front of my pad.

"It's just a pig," I told him. It had been hit several times, but the full metal jacket rounds had made just little bitty holes in it.

"Help me load it up in the jeep," the Lieutenant said.

I did. Then I thought of the C rations we ate on patrol night after night. My mouth watered and my stomach growled at the thought of cutting out that hog and roasting it up. "Sir, do I get to keep the pig?"

"We'll see," he said. "This is evidence of tonight's incident, and we may have to keep it."

The following morning, when we were relieved from our shift and went back to the camp, the truck drove right past the infantry unit. The lieutenant was standing by a makeshift fire and was busy roasting my "evidence" on a spit. He just gave us a big old grin. I didn't get to taste a single bite of that pig. That was a real bummer.

As a country boy, I was used to all kind of wildlife. But Vietnam was a whole new ballgame. Besides the occasional pig, badass snakes were crawling all over the ammo dump, and several guys got seriously bitten. We also saw a black panther lounging on top of ammo piles at night. It startled the hell out of us a few times, so we got used to shining our light up to make sure that black cat was nowhere near before checking for footprints or other evidence of enemy activity.

We were supposed to sleep during the day after our night shift, and we had one night off every eight days. But life was too short for sleeping. Whenever we had a free night—or sometimes right after our shift—we'd shower, put on clean clothes, and catch a Vietnamese pedal cab into town. Situated next to Long Binh, Bien Hoa was a bustle of bicycles and motorbikes zigzagging among three-wheelers and old French cars. It was like nothing I knew. Under the thin varnish of modernity, I could just about sense a way of life that seemed as old as the ages. For every kid on a motorbike there was an old peasant in a cone hat carrying water on his shoulders. For every car, a cow pulling a wooden cart. Few streets were paved, and the rice paddies never felt very far.

In Bien Hoa, anything and everything was for sale. Televisions, radios, and all kinds of electronics. Stuff we didn't even know we wanted until we saw it. We just had to say what we were after, and someone would guide us down some small alley to a shop. *Lai dây! Lai dây!* Come over here! I sent money home as much as I could to help out Mom and Dad, and with all the temptations Bien Hoa offered, I was always broke. I borrowed money from time to time, and a buddy named Larry Holden helped me out with twenty dollars one night. When we left Long Binh, Larry and I shipped to different units and I lost track of him before I had a chance to give him his money back. I don't know what happened to him. Some others guys told me he got killed in Vietnam, but I haven't found his name in the list of casualties. That I never paid him back still weighs heavy on my heart.

One day, I saw a guitar in a music shop window. I instantly fell in love. It was one of the most beautiful guitars I'd ever seen, and I couldn't believe it was for sale. I tried it, and it played real well. I went back to look at it two or three times, until I could no longer resist. I had to have it. After much talking, I bought it for two hundred dollars. That was a small fortune back then, but I figured I might as well enjoy myself while I could.

It was worth every dollar. Playing the guitar entertained me when I was bored, and warmed my heart when I was homesick. I strummed at Long Binh, and one of the guys had a TEAC tape recorder that could engineer all kinds of sound effects. I played "Walk Don't Run" by the Ventures—a popular tune in the mid-1960s—and he recorded the guitar riff with echoes and other fancy stuff. Our mess hall was in a tent, and when we got a brand-new brick-and-mortar one, I got to play at the grand opening. It was really neat. I also took my guitar to town and played Beatles songs with locals in bars and on back porches. I've never been much of a singer, but these guys were great. I played and they sang.

We went into Bien Hoa seeking what typical twenty-year-old boys were after. We hung out, drank beer, and spent the little money we had. We visited the ladies. Then we'd go back to Long Binh and nap for a few hours before our night shift at the ammo dump. The circumstances we found ourselves in brought us all together: Farm boys and city slickers. Enlisted and draftees. Blacks and whites. There was a large contingent from Puerto Rico, and most of them were a bit older than me. I spent my time with guys from all over the country and from all walks of life. Even though I had moved around a lot, my horizons now broadened a whole lot more.

In town, I met guys from other units and from other countries. Some Australian soldiers were stationed near Bien Hoa as well, and I had an awesome time listening to their stories over cold beers. They were really cool guys, easygoing and fun to be with. They called me "mate" and talked with funny accents about the beaches in Sydney or the red sands of central Australia. It sounded exotic and beautiful, and I longed to travel over there and see it all for myself.

One day, I bumped into Johnston Dunlop, my old buddy from basic training. I couldn't believe it. By then he was a sergeant in a long-range reconnaissance patrol with the Ninth Infantry Division. I do not remember why he was in Bien Hoa that day, but I sure was happy to see him. We stayed in touch, and I was to see a lot more of him when I transferred to the Mekong Delta.

Bien Hoa was not all fun though, and I was quickly reminded that the war was never far. We had to go through some rough areas on our way to town. We were not allowed to take our weapons with us: alcohol and guns usually don't mix too well. Local hoodlums— or maybe they were Vietcong—realized that they could stop pedicabs and extort a small ransom. Most of the time it was very little money, nothing worth getting shot for, so we'd usually pay up. One day, those guys got carried away and demanded several dollars. One of us thought that was way too much and started arguing. He tried to grab the Vietnamese guy's gun. We heard a shot, and a red stain spread on our buddy's chest. Then it was mayhem. Everybody started screaming, and the Vietnamese ran away. We rushed back to Long Binh, but our guy was dead.

I didn't know that poor kid real well, but it was the first time I lost one of my buddies. That sent a chill through my heart. I was stunned. For some dumb reason, I thought going to town was okay, that both sides saw it as some kind of truce. I guess I was still new to Vietnam and thought we could take time off from the war. Never again would I let my guard down. We could all get killed any second of any day. After that day, we were allowed to carry a weapon, and one of us had to stay sober to look after the others. It usually worked pretty good—although some guys were much better keeping off the sauce than others.

I was really homesick. I missed my family. I missed my old life. I missed my country. It all seemed so far away and so long ago. Everything and everyone was foreign in Vietnam, and even at Long Binh, war was everywhere. "You sure do a lot of thinking over here," I told Mom in a letter. "Sometimes I just feel like cracking up and crying, it gets so bad, but I always manage to say to myself, I'm over here for Mom, Dad and the kids, and then it don't seem half so bad."

I wasn't the only one wishing I could go home: I still chuckle thinking about that kid named Jim, who marched into the orderly room one day and told the captain he was quitting. He ended up in the stockade for his trouble. I wrote home almost every day, and asked pretty much everyone I knew to write me letters. Best case, mail took between nine and twelve days to travel in each direction, and sometimes it would get backed up. I wouldn't receive letters for a while, and then they'd arrive all bundled. Mail was the only connection to loved ones. I tried my best to sound reassuring. "I don't want you to worry about me Mommy, cause I worry about you worrying, and then we're both all messed up," I wrote. "You know I'll be all right." All of us who were reassigned to the Third Ordnance were allowed to take one complimentary picture to send home. To show that we were okay and living the good life, some of us took identical snapshots of each other in full gear, holding our M14 rifles and smoking a big fat cigar in front of sandbags. I still have that picture. We passed the cigar along when it was our turn: we only had one.

Every day, a sergeant brought the mail and called out our names whenever there was something for us. Receiving a letter felt like Christmas. For a few minutes, I could slip back into my old life, and I was still part of a sane, familiar world. That normal world, where people went about their lives working hard, paying their bills, and going fishing. It felt good to read about people I knew and about all the mundane things that made up a normal existence back home. I asked Mom about her garden, and I wished I could be back there, picking lettuce and radishes for her. I asked about fishing and about my brother Johnny's new colt.

One letter brought a real piece of home to me. Sandy, a former girlfriend from California, told me in one of her letters that Larry McCurdy was serving in an engineer company with an address that looked a bit like mine. Larry was my best friend back in French Camp. He used to live a block from our house, and we'd gotten into our fair share of trouble together. I asked around and found out that his unit was down the road from me. I couldn't believe my luck. I went over there as soon as I could. It didn't take me long to find him, and just as I was walking over to him, he turned around. "Sammy Davis!" he yelled when he saw me. It felt real good to see a familiar face, someone with whom I shared so much history. From then on, hardly a day went by that we didn't do something together. We visited each other whenever we could. We went to town and partied together. We hadn't seen each other in a couple years, but he was pretty much the same old crazy Larry. Even Vietnam failed to take all the mischief out of him: one evening, he climbed on top of a flagpole at the base. I guess after one too many beers, a lot of stupid things seem like good ideas. He fell off and broke his leg pretty bad. That didn't get him a medical discharge or an early trip back home, but he walked with a limp for the rest of his life.

I got pulled to do other jobs besides guarding ammunition. Sometimes we were sent out on ambush squads at night, or "bush-whacker patrols." A few times, I also got to ride on gun jeeps securing truck convoys. And whenever I could, I moonlighted as a "door gunner" manning M60 machine guns mounted on the sides of Huey helicopters. I had met some guys from the 118th Assault Helicopter Company—known as the Thunderbirds—based in Bien Hoa. I found out that they sometimes needed volunteers from other units to be door gunners. That sounded much more interesting than guarding ammo pads, so I offered to help out. They checked that I knew how to operate an M60, and tried me out on a few short flights. On my very first mission, we flew to some old French fort about an hour away toward the Mekong Delta. I don't know why we went there exactly—it wasn't my job to know—but I think it had to do with collecting some document or paperwork. Pretty routine stuff, nothing hair-raising. We landed on the airstrip, and

I stayed with the helicopter while the captain went off to do whatever he was there to do. After about half an hour, he was all done, and we headed back to the Bien Hoa airfield.

I sat by the open door of the chopper and looked down. Emerald green rice paddies stretched below us as far as I could see. It reminded me of eastern Arkansas, with all the rice growing right by the Mississippi River. We were flying up pretty high, but I could see people working in the rice paddies down below. Nobody shot at us. It was so beautiful and peaceful that it took my breath away. For the first time since I'd arrived in Vietnam, I felt cool fresh air on my face. I was hooked. Over the following few weeks, I volunteered as a door gunner whenever I had a chance. I was on guard duty or bushwhacker patrol at night and was sometimes door gunning during the day. That didn't leave much time for sleeping, but I wouldn't have missed these flights for the world. Door gunning was much better than lying on my cot in a hundred-degree heat. Looking back, I don't know how I made it on so little sleep.

There was one big downside. Door gunners used to say that their life expectancy after takeoff was thirty minutes—and less than thirty seconds when under fire in a "hot" landing zone. I don't know if those numbers are accurate, but it sure was dangerous work. Door gunners fired at the enemy from an open door, and that left them pretty exposed. The enemy targeted the guys doing all the damage sitting by the machine guns. I quickly understood why the chopper unit was shorthanded: the job wasn't too popular.

I loved it though. I really enjoyed flying and seeing the country from the air. The adrenaline rush made me feel more alive. We were at our most vulnerable when dropping off or picking up troops, and we had to move real quick. At times, everything looked quiet, and then a hail of bullets would hit the helicopter from out of nowhere. The Vietcong really knew how to make themselves invisible. When we came under attack, my job was to keep the enemy down as much as possible with my M60 so they wouldn't fire back at the chopper or at the troops. As a door gunner, I never saw the face of the enemy. Shooting at people from a distance is one thing. But as I found out over the following few months, it's a whole different story to look them in the eye and kill them.

Mostly, I went on reconnaissance missions, trying to locate enemy positions and movements. Once in a while, our job was to take down specific targets. I instinctively knew when to start firing to hit the mark, taking into account the speed and the movement of the helicopter. With an M60 firing 550 rounds per minute, a door gunner spraying too widely or too soon quickly wastes a lot of firepower. And the last thing I wanted was to run out of ammo during a surprise attack.

During one of those recon missions, we sighted three elephants close to the Cambodian border, along with twenty-five or thirty people on foot. Besides being packed to the hilt, there was something peculiar about these elephants: they were pink. We called it in.

Orders came back on the radio. "Take them down!"

The pilot asked for confirmation.

"Take them down, dammit! These elephants are Vietcong trucks!"

We realized why they were pink. They had been rolling in red dirt, and red dirt was from up north. The elephants were moving enemy cargo along the Ho Chi Minh trail that ran from North to

South Vietnam through Laos and Cambodia. That trail was a major route for supplying equipment, food, and troops to the Vietcong and the North Vietnamese Army operating in the south.

By the time we flew back over them, the elephants had been off-loaded and stood alone on the trail. Their handlers had vanished into the jungle. As the chopper approached, I used the M60 to take them down. I felt terrible killing these poor animals. I remembered my dad's rule: you eat what you kill. I thought of these robins I had shot with my BB gun as a boy and how Dad made sure I ate them all. I couldn't eat the elephant, but we alerted a nearby village. The villagers butchered the meat, cooked what they were going to eat that day, and dried the rest.

So killing these poor animals wasn't a total waste in the end. But almost fifty years later, it still bothers me. I realize feeling bad for dead elephants when so many people were getting killed every day—some of them because of me—probably sounds strange. It is odd, the things that go through your mind during a war, the things that really get to you. With so much fighting and so much death going on, any collateral damage—even if they were animals—became almost too much to bear. I eventually came to terms with shooting people who wanted to kill me, but butchering elephants that had nothing against me felt entirely different.

In early May, two months after I landed in Vietnam, I was still at Long Binh and without new orders. Door gunning was way better than guarding ammo pads, and I wanted to transfer to the helicopter unit permanently. The first step was to pass a pretty stiff physical test. Candidates had to be in excellent shape, hear well, and have perfect vision. A big part of the job is to be the eyes and ears of the crew, and search the ground for signs of enemy presence and movement. No point being a door gunner if you can't see what you're supposed to shoot or evaluate distances properly. I went down to the 118th Assault Helicopter Company, and my test was scheduled for mid-May. I can't remember whether I flunked the physical or whether the company just decided to select someone else. Whatever it was, I didn't make it to the 118th.

I was bummed out about missing out on door gunning, but as it turned out, it didn't really matter. A few days later, I finally got my new orders. I was assigned to an artillery unit in the Ninth Infantry Division, together with some of the other guys who had been pulled to guard the ammo pads. The Ninth Infantry was head-quartered in Camp Bearcat, about twenty miles northeast of Saigon. I shipped my guitar home before heading out. I was sad to part with it, but where I was going was no place for a nice guitar. I gave it to a high school buddy of mine, but unfortunately, he died before I came back. I asked his parents about it, but they didn't know where it was. I didn't have the heart to press any further, so I never played that guitar again.

At Bearcat, the first order of business was to become familiar with the M16 rifle. All our training back home had been with the older M14, and that's what I had been issued when I arrived in Vietnam. The military was transitioning to the newer rifle. The M16 and its ammo were much lighter and more effective in close combat. The military thought that it was much better suited to the new kind of war we were fighting in Vietnam, where we usually fired at such close range we could look our enemy in the eye. The M16 had some serious problems though. The early version didn't do too well in the wet and mud of Vietnam, and it jammed pretty often. That made it unreliable in combat.

I spent a few days firing an M16, taking it apart, cleaning it, and putting it back together again. Then we were sent out to the jungle to learn how to execute an ambush properly. Helicopters dropped us off, and we moved into position just before it got dark. We set up along a trail through the jungle. I sat in the dark, holding very still, trying to make myself as small as possible, waiting for the bad guys to come walking down the trail. Then I felt something, a presence. It's a hard thing to describe, but I could have sworn somebody was watching me. A foul smell was floating in the air, like rotting meat.

I turned my head slowly and looked to my right.

Nothing.

Slowly, I looked to my left.

Nothing.

Still crouching, I turned around. It was dark, and I couldn't see much through the heavy vegetation. Then I saw a pair of big glowing eyes about four feet away and heard some heavy breathing. As I looked harder, I realized those eyes belonged to a tiger. Boy, I'd never realized how unbelievably large these cats were. I was petrified. I had come to Vietnam to fight for freedom, and here I was, about to turn into tiger chow. The tiger was moving toward me, taking its time, getting closer and closer. I had to do something. I stood up real quick and was getting ready to shoot my brand-new M16. Then, out of the blue, the tiger changed course and disappeared. One second it was there, and then it was gone. I spent the rest of the night wondering whether it was still circling, waiting for the right moment to pounce. Daylight finally broke, we were extracted from the jungle, and I never saw that tiger again—or any other actually. But that was a harrowing experience, and that cat still shows up in my dreams from time to time.

During one of our next training patrols, we were walking back to Bearcat when we heard a helicopter flying over us. We were in the trees, maybe three or four hundred yards from the dirt berm that surrounded the encampment. I looked up, and some white stuff got straight into my eyes. I instantly felt as if they were on fire. The helicopter was spraying Agent Orange—a defoliant widely used to clear vegetation in Vietnam—all around the camp to kill the vegetation and improve visibility for the guards that secured the perimeter. That way, it was much harder for the bad guys to creep up undetected. After I got sprayed, everything was blurry for several days. I could make out light and shapes but couldn't see well enough to recognize faces. It scared the hell out of me. I went out on other training exercises almost blind. I was told to keep washing my eyes, so I washed and washed, but it didn't do much good. Eventually, I went to see the medic and told him what had happened. He shook his head, rinsed my eyes out with some liquid, and gave me some eyedrops that helped ease the burn.

At Long Binh, we had been told that Agent Orange wouldn't hurt us. During our shifts, we sprayed a lot of it with little individual backpack pumps to keep the ammo pads clear, and the area outside the perimeter was being sprayed from the air. We'd sat through an orientation seminar one afternoon on what Agent Orange was and how it worked. I remember watching a little movie of some guy from the chemical company that manufactured it: he said it was perfectly safe and drank water that supposedly contained the defoliant.

So once my eyes recovered a few days after I got sprayed, I didn't think much of it. There were still some little white blisters on my skin, but I had more pressing concerns on my mind: I still had to make it through another nine months in Vietnam. Once our induction into the Ninth Infantry Division was over, we all split to join our new units. Together with a couple of other guys, I'd been assigned to Battery C of the Second Battalion, Fourth Artillery, Ninth Infantry Division, based out of Tan Tru, Long An province.

I said my good-byes to the guys who had been at Long Binh with me and headed to the Mekong Delta.

★5★

WAR IN THE LAND OF DRAGONS

At the end of May, I joined Battery C of the Second Battalion, Fourth Artillery, Ninth Infantry Division. From Bearcat, I headed to Tan An, Long An province, where our artillery unit was headquartered and resupplied. Then I boarded a truck for the last ten-mile stretch to Battery C's base camp in Tan Tru. The three other artillery batteries in the battalion—A, B, and D—were in other camps set up a few miles apart, so we could cover each other in case one battery was in trouble. After a very bumpy ride on a real bad dirt road, I got out of the truck—and landed in mud up to my knees. I had arrived at Tan Tru.

Compared to Long Binh, or even Bearcat, Tan Tru was beyond the boondocks. No more beer garden or swimming pool, no more golf driving range, no more military store. No more civilian cars, paved roads, and bars. This was the Vietnam of the jungle, mosquitoes, and mud, some godforsaken place that barely showed on a map. This was the Vietnam of the evening news, where young men with their whole lives ahead of them died every day.

Our camp was built next to a little bitty village and a river shaped like the outline of a big old pair of testicles. We were set up in the middle of rice paddies. . . . I arrived during the rainy season, and the place was a bog, with mud and water up to a Texan's belly button. Our tents and bunkers were set up on top of fifty-five-gallon oil drums. Bulldozers had dug out, stacked up, and flattened dirt platforms where our battery's six howitzer guns and the fire direction center—or FDC—were set up. Perforated metal walkways held up by iron stakes connected the guns, the FDC, and the mess hall. Each gun crew slept in bunkers next to their gun, the walls and metal roof padded with several rows of sandbags that stood between us and the mortars that the Vietcong regularly fired our way. The whole camp only had two small generators, and one was powering the fire direction center. With practically no electricity and clouds often covering up the moon and the stars, the nights were unbelievably dark.

I felt really isolated. Our artillery camp was home to 110 guys or so, including gun crews and support personnel, and I didn't know anyone besides a few buddies who had been at Long Binh with me. Battery C was a closely knit unit. The guys had all trained together stateside before taking a boat to Vietnam and shipping out to the Delta. Some had rotated to other units, others had been injured, and we were the replacements. Next to us was the much larger camp for the Second Battalion, Sixtieth Infantry. We were there to provide fire support for their operations, but we didn't know them too well. We pretty much kept to ourselves, and they did the same. In any case, these guys were often out on operations, sometimes for days. When they came back all muddy and exhausted, all they could do was crash and hope to get some shut-eye time through the noise of our artillery fire.

Luckily, my first few days at Tan Tru were real busy, and I had no time to think about how lonely I was. The forward observer—one of the artillery guys embedded with the infantry—kept calling our fire direction center on the radio to request fire support. We worked the guns nonstop and brought a lot of smoke on Charlie's tail. I had been bored mindless guarding ammo pads at Long Binh, where most nights nothing happened. I was happy with the change of pace.

In any case, loneliness was the least of my problems. Life at Tan Tru made me realize real quick how relatively easy I'd had it at Long Binh. The bad guys kept us on our toes, probing the perimeter or firing mortars, usually at night. Even when Charlie wasn't trying to flatten us out, we couldn't get much sleep. We worked in shifts to guard the camp. The infantry was in charge of securing the perimeter, but us artillery guys were often roped in to help out. There were small bunkers all around our camp looking out, and we sat there with M60 machine guns for hours, looking out for enemy activity. In our section of the perimeter, flocks of ducks often hung out. I'm not sure why they liked that spot, but we sure were glad to have them. Any noise or movement made them quack and waddle off, and they became like our guard dogs, alerting us when we needed to keep our eyes open extra wide.

Most of all, fire missions kept us busy, day or night. The calls would come through the radio at the fire direction center, and these guys then had to figure out from the grid coordinates what each gun needed to do. They had to take into account weather conditions and apply all kinds of corrections. Within a minute, they called the guns on the phone with instructions, so we knew where to direct our fire, how to angle the howitzer, how much charge we needed to put in, and what fire pattern to follow. So in each gun crew, one of us had to sit by the phone at all times in case a fire mission came in. When nothing happened, sitting by a silent phone in the middle of the night trying to keep your eyes open after a long day was no small thing. But when fire missions came in, there was no time to breathe. Sometimes, I was hanging out by the FDC when the calls came in on the radio. We could hear what the infantry was going through. The sound of mortars and fire, the screams, and a voice yelling, "We need fire cover *now*! Please, *please*!" Those voices coming through the radio still haunt me. The urgency, the fear, and the desperation clutched my heart. I quickly took to sleeping with my pants and my boots on so I could jump out of my cot, run to the howitzer, and do my job without wasting any time. Sometimes fire missions came one after the other, lasting for days. We were always shorthanded. Back at Fort Sill, I had trained on the howitzer gun as part of an eight-man crew. At Tan Tru, we were lucky if we had four men on a gun. Most of the time, there were only two or three men available.

When requests for fire support went silent, we went from being scared out of our wits to being bored stiff. There was no middle ground. When not working the guns, we sat around cleaning our equipment and catching up on never-ending details. We shoveled dirt to fill mud holes around the camp. We polished our bullets and filled sandbags and waited for something to happen. We played with bugs by pitching rhinoceros beetles against each other in our steel pots. We took the liners out of our helmets to make them nice and sleek, and the beetles would joust, trying to flip each other over with the big horns that stuck out of their foreheads. Minutes felt like hours, and hours felt like days. It should have felt good to have a little bit of peace and quiet. But we were always on alert, and we could never truly relax. Sometimes it was just easier to be in the middle of it, adrenaline pumping with no time to think.

Having time to think was usually no good. I worried about people back home and about all the things I wished I'd done differently. "I know I've really messed up a lot back home," I wrote shortly after I joined my unit. "I only hope when I return that I can straighten them out. I really am all messed up Mom." Downtime also made me real homesick. I wrote home as much as I could, but after I arrived at Tan Tru, I received no letters for a good long while. Loneliness and heartache weighed on my mind real heavy. "I'd just like to lay my head on your shoulder and cry for a while," I told Mom in a letter. "I think that would help a lot. Over here I don't get nobody that I can sit and talk to, and it sure helps if you do have someone to talk to." I kept writing, but it turns out that Mom and Dad were not receiving my letters either. They had moved from Indiana to Robinson, Illinois, at about the same time I'd left Long Binh. I guess, with all these changes, our mail got messed up. Mom later said she got no letter from me for sixty-three days. I don't believe it was nearly that long. But whatever the exact number of days was, she evidently became concerned and went down to the Red Cross office in Martinsville, Illinois, to find out what was what.

One early morning I was on perimeter guard. The sun hadn't come up yet, but the sky was getting light and I could see the pink clouds of dawn. Daybreak always felt good because it meant I had made it through another night. The enemy was less likely to attack us during daylight. I was enjoying the moment when I heard the slurping noise of somebody wading through the mud. It had been a quiet night, but someone was coming, and at first, I thought it was outside our perimeter. I looked hard across the seventy-five yards or so we had cleared out around the camp. I didn't see anything. So I looked inside our perimeter line, and sure enough I saw someone walking straight toward me. By then it was light enough that I could see the silhouette of a GI with a helmet. *Thank goodness*, I thought. It was one of us. When he got closer, I recognized my captain. Judging by the look on his face, he was not happy. This wasn't good. I was sitting on sandbags that had turned to mud and trying to think of what I'd done wrong.

"Private Davis," he said.

"Yes, sir!"

"You haven't been writing home to your mother."

I almost fell over. Of all the things he could have told me, he was on my tail for that? I was so amazed—and relieved—that I didn't even tell him that I had in fact been writing home.

"I don't care what you write about," he said, "but you will write home to your mother. Every day."

The Red Cross had contacted the Pentagon, and the Pentagon had gone down the chain of command all the way to my captain with a list of all the bad boys in the unit who had not been writing home and needed a good talking to. After a while, the mail connection got sorted out, and letters and packages started coming my way. Writing home wasn't easy, though. I didn't have much time to spare, and the writing material always got wet. The paper we carried in our pouches just turned into spitballs, and some guys even took C ration boxes apart to turn them into postcards. Besides the poor writing material, finding something to write about was a real brain squeeze. I didn't want to write about what was really going on and get Mom all worried, but I didn't want to lie either. That didn't leave much.

So I wrote about the local fish, and asked if Dad and Johnny had caught anything good. I kept counting the days I had left in country and wrote the numbers down. I wrote about the future. "I was thinking the other day what I could do when I get out of the Army," I said. "I don't want to become a bum. Not for a few years at least." I wrote about the letters I'd received and the ones I'd written. I asked Mom if she was getting the money I kept sending her. Mostly, I asked about everyone I knew back home—particularly girls. "I'll be so glad to see an American girl I'll probably run around like an idiot for a week after I get home." Sometimes I wrote only a line or two just to say I was okay. "Hi, just a note to tell ya I ain't zapped yet."

At the mail call one day in July, the sergeant was standing on an ammo platform pallet, and there was a package at his feet. I saw my name on it and got real excited. I thought that Mom had sent me some of her famous oatmeal raisin cookies. The package was big enough for maybe ten or fifteen of them, and my mouth started watering thinking about those cookies. When the sergeant finally called my name and handed me my package, I backed away from the other guys to unwrap it. I was going to share, but I wanted to make darn sure I got to eat the first one. When I got the plain brown wrapper off, there were no cookies. Instead, I found a harmonica.

On the box, Mom had written a note. "Son, I hope this helps you be not quite so bored." At least Mom was no longer worried. In fact, she thought I was bored. My stomach was disappointed, but I was happy to have something to take my mind off things. Since I'd shipped my guitar back home, I'd played no music, and I missed it. A harmonica was handy. I could carry it everywhere in my pocket, and play wherever I was. From then on, I never parted with it.

There was only one snag: I didn't know how to play it. Dad played the harmonica—as did all his brothers and Grandpa Davis—but growing up, us kids were not allowed to mess with their instruments. They were too expensive for us to play with. When I learned to play the guitar in California, I was happy with that and never thought I'd need to play the harp. After Mom sent it to me, I blew in it and practiced any chance I got, sitting in foxholes or manning the radio.

I had some encouragement. After I'd bumped into Johnston Dunlop, my buddy from basic training, we'd stayed in touch and he knew I'd transferred to the Ninth Infantry Division. When I was in Tan Tru, we got to see each other often. Johnston was with the Ninth Infantry Division as well, but he had volunteered to be part of the long-range reconnaissance patrol—the LRRP, known as "Lurp." Lurps were the eyes and ears of the Army. Small elite teams of four to six men, they patrolled deep into enemy-held territory to gather intelligence on North Vietnamese or Vietcong positions. That intelligence was used to inform troop movement or air and artillery strikes. Lurps also set up ambushes. Once they were extracted from a mission, they'd sometimes be dropped off at artillery camps or firebases, and that's mostly how I got to see Johnston. We'd hear on the radio that he and his crew of three or four guys were coming in, and they'd show up, camouflage paint all over their faces and arms. We thought Tan Tru was the end of the world, but to the Lurps who'd just spent several days being silent and invisible deep in the jungle, this was civilization and safety. Those guys were quite something.

Shortly after I got my package in the mail, Johnston was dropped off at Tan Tru and heard that I had a harmonica. As always, he came to see me.

"Sammy my boy," he said in his funny accent, "play 'Shenandoah' for me on that thingmey." Johnston hailed from Auburn, New York, but when he spoke, he was first and foremost a Scot.

"I can't," I told him. What I meant was I couldn't play the harmonica.

Johnston thought I didn't know that particular tune, and looked at me in disbelief through his big black-rimmed glasses. "Everyone knows 'Shenandoah'!" he said. He hummed the famous tune.

We were friends, but by then he was a sergeant and I was a plain old private. There was only one appropriate response. "Yes, sir," I said.

I blew into my new harp, but what came out sounded nothing like "Shenandoah." So I kept at it. After a couple weeks, the tune I was trying to play became clearer. Whenever Johnston came in, he found out where my foxhole was. He'd come and sit with me and say, "Play it, Sam," like in the movie *Casablanca*. It was our joke. Except I didn't play "As Time Goes By." Over and over again, I played "Shenandoah." That's the only thing he ever wanted to hear.

Before he joined the military, Johnston had studied just outside of Washington, DC. I don't remember what college it was, but he told me it was about seventy miles from the Shenandoah Valley. He felt that his fellow students did not share the depth of patriotism he carried in his heart, and I guess he found it difficult at times. Whenever it became too much for him, rather than get into a fight, he would get in his car and drive to the Shenandoah Valley. There was a bluff right where the river made a big horseshoe. He'd walk through the woods to that bluff and sit on a rock that was right on the edge. He used to tell me that he looked down right into the river and watched the trout swim in the stream. There was always a cool gentle breeze carrying a whiff of pine. He said that just sitting there would help him calm down and "get his karma right." It would give him hope and fortitude, and then he could drive back to his college.

"When you play 'Shenandoah,'" he explained, "I am back on that rock, and it heals my heart and renews my soul."

In Vietnam, Johnston's heart sure needed a lot of healing. So I played the harmonica for him as we sat side by side in a foxhole. I don't remember ever seeing him sleep. He sat there with me at night, sometimes for hours. He'd get heavy lidded, but he never closed his eyes completely and went to sleep. After a while, he'd start stirring and would open his eyes fully. He'd thank me, get up, and gather his crew. Then they'd be gone again.

After I got back home, I found out that Johnston Dunlop never came back from Vietnam. On April 16, 1968, shortly after he'd extended his tour, he and his team ambushed a heavily armed enemy platoon along a main Vietcong supply route. They inflicted a lot of damage to that platoon, but when one of the GIs got wounded, Johnston ran to help him and was shot in the legs. He continued to fire and crawled the last stretch while still shouting commands to his men. The US soldier was dead, and Johnston was shot again while pulling his body back. The Lurp team was extracted, but

Johnston died of his wounds. He was awarded the Distinguished Service Cross posthumously.

Shortly after I'd arrived at Tan Tru, I, together with a couple other guys who had some experience cooking or baking, had been pulled from the guns and reassigned to the kitchen. I had my old jobs flipping burgers at the St. Francis Yacht Club and the Big M bowling alley to thank for that. I moved from the gun bunkers into the tent by the kitchen. Underneath its canvas roof, the heat was less stifling at night, but there were no sandbags to protect us against mortars. The gun crews being so shorthanded, I still helped with the guns whenever I could.

We didn't have freezers and relied on big coolers and blocks of ice. Nothing kept for very long in the hundred-degree heat, and the camp had to be resupplied pretty much every day. At first, the ration-run detail—which involved going to Tan An to resupply—rotated among all the guys. But the guns were already shorthanded, so it was decided that the mess hall crew would do it themselves. I was volunteered to drive ration trucks to Tan An to pick up food, ice, ammo, and whatever other supplies we needed. So almost every day for three months, I drove the ten miles or so to Tan An with a 2.5-ton truck. The rainy season was in full swing, and the dirt road was no longer a road. It was all mud, knee-deep or deeper in some places, with mortar and rocket holes.

Driving to Tan An was a daily game of Russian roulette. The enemy knew this road was our lifeline, and they made it as hard as possible for us to get resupplied. They planted land mines and homemade booby traps to try to blow us up. If we were not exactly sitting ducks driving that stretch, we certainly were very slow-moving ones. Most drivers were city kids and could only drive at ten or twelve miles an hour in that mud. At that speed, the land mines tripped by the front wheels would go off right under the driver's cab, inflicting maximum damage. We wrecked a lot of trucks on that stretch, and we lost good men too. We called it Thunder Road because of all the explosions.

I had been driving mean country roads since I was a kid. Raised on farms, I could navigate badass dirt and mud tracks better than most—although nothing quite prepares you to do that with people determined to kill you. And still, the truck would often get stuck in the mud up to its headlights—sometimes before I'd even left the camp—and a tank or a five-ton truck had to come and wrench us out. Some days, that happened several times on one run. But I figured that if I could drive twenty to twenty-five miles an hour, land mines and other booby traps would explode farther back, keeping me and my legs safe. That system worked pretty good. I tripped my fair share of land mines with my front wheels and blew off the back set of duals on the big ten-wheeler trucks. Every booby trap that exploded scared the crap out of me, but I didn't get badly hurt. There were a few times when they blew me up bad and I had to be pulled out. But whenever I could, I kept driving, dragging the back of the truck through the mud all the way back to our camp. I can still see the first sergeant looking at me and shaking his head. I wrecked several trucks that way. But at least I brought the rations back, and I kept my legs.

Sometimes, the bad guys were waiting on us. There was a sharp turn on that road, right next to some dense foliage. That was the perfect setup for ambushes: I had to slow down to a crawl to take that turn, and the trees provided cover for the enemy. Every time I got near that bend, my heart jumped out of my chest. The best I could do was drive as fast as I could. We came under fire more times than I can count by that turn. The Vietcong were set up on each side of the road, and I kept wondering how they managed to shoot at us without shooting each other. The infantry, which also had to use that road to resupply, sent patrols ahead of time to clear the area and regularly got caught in firefights. But we still got ambushed. We had to get out of the truck, establish a perimeter, and shoot our way out of trouble. The infantry usually sent two jeeps with us mounted with an M79—a grenade-launcher—and an M60 machine gun. I had two or three guys with me on the truck, and we all carried our M16 rifles. But all that firepower didn't feel like much when we were out in the open, ambushed by ten or twelve guys hiding in the jungle. Sometimes, when the road got too bad, we went to Tan An by river barge. But it took much longer, and the barges got ambushed as well.

During one of the runs, we got hit at that turn, and I had to get out of the truck. One of the Second/Sixtieth Infantry guys from our jeep escort got hit not far from me. He was screaming, and I crawled to his position. By the time I got there, he was in real bad shape. He'd been shot in the chest and was making gurgling sounds, struggling to breathe. I didn't know what to do, so I held him in my arms. He looked me straight in the eye, but it was as if in his mind he was real far away. "Mama, Mama," he managed to whisper. I could swear he was really seeing his mom. Then, within a second, he was gone. I didn't even know him, but my heart filled with grief. He was a kid not old enough to vote or buy himself a beer, and he'd died so far away from home on a hellish road in the middle of nowhere. Soon his mama would hear the worst news of her life. I laid him flat on the ground and put his helmet over his face. The enemy was still firing at us from the trees, so I picked up my M16. We gave it all we had and managed to push them back. They broke contact, and we made it back to our camp. It has been over forty-five years now, and I still think of that soldier who died in my arms calling for his mom.

Whenever I could, I joined the infantry to drive to Tan An. Because their camp was much bigger than ours, their ration runs involved convoys of eight or ten trucks. They had guys clearing land mines ahead of the convoy. I became friendly with Smitty, one of the infantry guys doing the runs. One day in July, I got ready for another run with the infantry. I was up by five a.m. and went over to the Second/Sixtieth Infantry camp to have breakfast, get the required vouchers, and sort out the paperwork to pick up rations. It was a beautiful morning. The sky was very blue and I remember the sun coming up over the trees. It was already pretty hot. I got into one of the trucks with an infantry guy, Reed "LaRue" Street— he believed being called LaRue would raise his standing with the ladies—and we drove the truck up to the barricade blocking the road to Tan An. The mine-sweeping crew hadn't started clearing the road yet, so we got out of the truck and waited behind a jeep with a recoilless rifle mounted on it. Smitty was driving the jeep, and in the back were three South Vietnamese soldiers—we called them "Arvins," which stood for ARVNs, the acronym for the Army of the Republic of Viet Nam. While the land mine sweepers were doing their job, Smitty, Reed, and I were shooting the breeze, bull-shitting about the ladies in Tan An. Reed and I were leaning against the truck, and Smitty had one arm resting on the breech of the recoilless rifle.

All of a sudden, there was a tremendous explosion. I hit the dirt. *Damn, incoming rounds,* I first thought. I tried to figure out where the gunfire was coming from. Then I realized I had blood splattered all over me. I checked myself, but I wasn't hurt. Reed was lying next to me and looked fine as well. I waited for a few seconds, and when I realized that no more rounds were coming in, I stood up to see what was happening. People were running to our position.

"What on earth just happened?" I asked Reed.

"Hell knows!" he said.

Then I saw blood and pieces of flesh all over the side of the truck. "Where the hell is Smitty?" I yelled.

I frantically started looking for him, scanning the rice paddy that stretched out on both sides of the road, until I noticed legs sticking out on the south side of the road, about thirty yards out. *Smitty.* I ran out there, hoping he was just unconscious. When I got to him, I saw that his left arm and his head had been blown off, and his chest hollowed out. Only his right arm and his legs were still attached to his body. My eyes saw it, but I couldn't wrap my head around it. It made no sense. This couldn't be him. He'd been right there by us a minute earlier. Suddenly it hit me, and I understood. One of the Arvins had hit the fire button on the recoilless rifle, and Smitty had been caught in the back blast. I reached down and picked up what was left of him, and carried his mutilated body back to the truck, his only arm hanging over my arm. I kept looking down at him. I couldn't take my eyes off his empty chest. I wanted to howl, but no sound came out of my mouth.

After laying him down by the truck, I marched over to the jeeps.

I was moving in a daze, like it was all a bad dream. The Arvins were just sitting there as if nothing had happened.

"What have you done?" I yelled.

They just looked at me and said nothing. Something deep inside me snapped, and rage came flooding in. I lost it. I grabbed two of them by the throat, screaming. I'm not sure if I was trying to make them talk or to break their necks. Maybe both. Some guy managed to pull me off them. The third Arvin, seeing me being so crazy mad, began blabbing away.

"Gun go off! Off!" he shrieked. "It was accident!"

I'll never know exactly why or how it happened. I never even knew Smitty's full name. To everyone at the camp, I was just Dave, and he was Smitty. But I'll always remember looking down on him while I was carrying him back to the truck.

It's astonishing how your brothers can be standing next to you one second, joking and in perfect health, and a second later they're lying in the dirt with limbs blown off or big holes in their bodies. One second. That's how quick life goes. This is a lesson I have never forgotten. No matter how good you think life is, it can all be taken in a heartbeat. It can all change; it can all be gone. So I try to appreciate every moment.

It is one thing to lose a brother in combat, but another entirely to see him killed by accident. It's so random and pointless. But it's always a risk. Sometimes during a fire mission, we'd load a shell in our howitzer, set the powder bags in the canister behind it, and pull the lanyard to fire. We'd hear a *ping*, but the gun wouldn't go off. We'd pull again, and it wouldn't work. Maybe the powder was a bit wet. Maybe it was something else. But we couldn't just sit there and stop firing. So one guy had to open the bridge of the gun, and another took the canister out and turned it upside down to drop the powder bags on the ground real quick, hoping the charge wouldn't explode in our faces or blow our hands off. During my time at Tan Tru, we once received a batch of defective fuses. The fuse is the piece that screws on the shell and is supposed to delay the explosion so the round blows up when it reaches the intended target. With a bad fuse, the round exploded when it was still in the gun, blowing up the tube of the howitzer and sending shrapnel all over the area.

Somehow, we got used to all that. Like we got used to operating on very little sleep, eating out of cans, and living in the dark. Sometimes supplying the camp required creativity. One day, and I don't remember how, our battery got hold of a movie and a projector. We needed electricity to power the projector, and our camp hardly had any. The infantry camp next to us was much bigger and better equipped and had several generators. Our first sergeant mused over how nice it would be if we could borrow one of the infantry generators. That was all the encouragement we needed. That night, I sneaked into to the infantry camp with another guy from my unit and we unplugged one of their generators. Some of their lights went out, and we ran back to the artillery side with the generator, which luckily was mounted on wheels. We crossed the footbridge between the two camps and hid our loot. The next evening, we sure enjoyed watching Alan Ladd and his bright blue eyes staring down the bad guys from his cowboy horse. We hadn't watched a real movie in weeks, and that was a big treat. That same night, we took the generator back and plugged it in. The infantry was mystified but relieved: they thought the Vietcong had snatched their electricity.

We got tired of having too little juice. We'd seen that the battalion communication center in Tan An had big generators. On one of the drives, the guys who were with me went in. After a few minutes, they came out of the communication center and loaded one of the generators on the truck. I assumed we'd finally been given one, and I was real excited. We drove back to Tan Tru, and the generator was installed. Boy, it sure felt good to come out of the dark ages. The following week, I got called into Captain Schaible's orderly room with the guys who'd been on the ration run with me. It had come to the captain's attention that one generator was missing from the battalion inventory at Tan An and had evidently been taken without proper authorization. The serial number of the missing generator matched the number on the unit we'd brought back. The guys standing next to me looked uneasy. They confessed that they'd made up some story about picking up a generator for offsite maintenance. They'd even had the guys at Tan An help to carry it out to our truck and load it up. I thought that was genius. The captain probably didn't think so, but by then, I guess he was happy to have the extra electricity, like everyone else. The serial number was mysteriously scraped off the power unit, and we got to keep it.

Once in a while—not often—we got too much of a good thing. Ice was real hard to get, but one day, we had extra. The coolers were full, and we didn't know what to do with the leftover. Everybody was always complaining about the heat, so together with Bill Few, another guy who worked in the kitchen, I carried the ice blocks to the showers. The showers were fifty-gallon barrels sitting on platforms with a faucet at the bottom. Whenever we had time to wash, which was not too often, we carried water to the shower blocks, climbed up the ladders on the side of the drums, poured the water in, and stood under the tap. Those drums got holes in them on a regular basis, and whenever that happened, we had to scramble to find another one somewhere. That day, Bill and I dumped the ice into the barrels, and sat ourselves just outside the showers, waiting. A few guys went in, and sure enough, after a few seconds we heard some serious cussing. One of the guys even came running out of the block. All he had on him was a bar of soap.

In September, a bunch of guys went home, and I transferred back to the guns. No more sweating over the stove, no more loading and offloading the trucks, and no more ration runs. To be honest, I was relieved. The ambushes and booby traps had taken their toll on me, and I was ready for a change. "A month at a stretch is all right," I wrote home. "But for four solid months and seeing the things I did. Wow. Wonder I ain't nuts." It had been over seven months since I'd graduated from Fort Sill, where I'd become an artilleryman. After guarding ammunition and driving trucks into mud holes, I finally had a chance to do full-time what I'd been trained for. Being a gunman was tough, but at least it was a new kind of tough. We often had fire missions back-to-back or had a taste of the enemy's own fire. Always being short of men, the hours were long and sleep very short. We were on alert twenty-four hours a day, seven days a week. I got used to dozing off a couple hours at a time—and almost fifty years later, I still can't sleep any different.

Each howitzer was under the command of a gun sergeant. The gun sergeants taught us how to act and react in combat situations, how to take care of our equipment, clean our M16 and 105mm howitzers between fire missions, and make sure the powder and the ammo were ready at all times. They took new kids fresh off the plane and turned them into real soldiers. We'd been trained stateside, but we were not adequately prepared for the reality on the ground. This was a whole new kind of war, with no front line and no recognizable

Army, and we had to learn real fast. I kept my ears and eyes open and tried to do what the more experienced guys did and what my gun sergeant told me to do. I learned a whole lot from them.

No gun sergeant was more feared than Sergeant Gant. All of us working the guns reckoned that James Gant, a twenty-seven-year-old professional soldier from Lansing, Michigan, was just old and mean. When other gun crews were done for the day, whoever was on his gun didn't quit working; they set time fuses blindfolded and polished bullets. He wasn't my regular gun sergeant, but I sometimes filled in for someone in his crew. All of us in the battery hated working his gun because he was so strict. But the truth is we could fire our guns with our eyes closed and without thinking, and our M16s— which back then were notoriously unreliable in the mud and humidity of Vietnam—didn't jam nearly as often as the other guys'. We didn't realize then how all that would end up saving our lives.

Being part of a gun crew created a very strong and special bond. We were like the fingers of one hand. We spent our lives next to each other. We worked the gun together, we ate together, and we shared a bunker. Each of us was a small but essential part of a whole bigger than all of us. Our lives and the lives of others depended on every single one of us doing his job. We faced death together and relied on each other to survive. I had enlisted to serve my country, but deep into the Mekong Delta, America was very far away, a concept too abstract and distant to hold on to on a daily basis. I realized that, in the heat of battle, I wasn't fighting for my country. I fought for the guys next to me. We were brothers. I was prepared to die for them, and they were prepared to die for me. There is nothing stronger than that. Nothing. So it was a paradox that we were also real careful not to get too close or share anything too personal. It was self-preservation. I'd learned the hard way how heartbreaking it was making friends and then seeing them die. I also got news of buddies back home who didn't make it. Brock Elliott, one of my pals from Manteca High back in California, was taken as a casualty. "It doesn't seem possible," I told Mom in a letter. "He was such a good kid. Top athlete, A student, but I guess that don't make much difference over here."

Most of the time, we fired from our home base of Tan Tru. But our howitzers had an effective firing range of about seven miles, so when the infantry needed us farther out, we set up a fire-support base out in the jungle. At times, we were out for several days. We trucked out whenever we could or we were airlifted. We'd strap our howitzers and mesh bags of 105mm ammo in slings attached to the big double-bladed Chinook helicopters that carried us out to the middle of nowhere to support infantry operations. It was quite something, watching those big guns suspended in the air, shining in the sun. Being dropped off and picked up was always a gamble, and we never knew whether the enemy was watching. We jumped out of the choppers as quickly as we could and established the firebase. We assembled everything and started firing. We dug out foxholes and filled sandbags. We patrolled the area around the drop-off to secure our position. Sometimes the area had been sprayed with Agent Orange to kill the vegetation and improve visibility. We ate and slept on the ground—if we slept at all—with no roof over our heads to protect us. We'd been issued air mattresses to stay out of the mud and water while sleeping, but they were useless. God knows whose bright idea that was. Most of the time, they had holes in them and offered little padding.

In most areas of the delta, finding solid ground to support the howitzers was real difficult, especially during the rainy season. As soon as we started digging foxholes, water would come up, and we'd be wading in the mud. When sheets of rain fell from the sky, we couldn't see past a few yards in front of us. We were always wet. Most of the time, that was good, because it was so hot. But I remember one operation when we'd been in water for three days straight. It was two or three o'clock in the morning, and we were shaking from the cold. We were convinced that the earth's axis had shifted, and we expected the water to turn into ice. We checked the temperature with the fire direction center. The FDC always knew what temperature it was, because it affected how much powder we had to use.

The captain told us it was 51 degrees. Now, 51 degrees is cold for Vietnam, but it is nowhere near freezing. That wasn't possible. Surely the captain had read the temperature wrong. We sure were about to freeze to death. It turns out that after several days sitting in water like we were in a bathtub, we had hypothermia. The captain laughed and said, "No, it's really fifty-one degrees." He evidently wasn't as wet as we were.

Being in the water so much, we had to watch out for big, fat leeches. They kept appearing behind my knees and around my waist. I'd never seen leeches so big. Then I got used to burning them off with the tip of a lit cigarette. All that water also brought mosquitoes, and mosquitoes brought diseases. Malaria severely weakened US troops in Vietnam. I took my pills every day, and luckily, I was never sick.

When the season turned dry later in the year, we had other problems. The ground got so hard in some places that the metal trails on the back of the howitzers could not dig in and hold the guns. Without anything to keep them in place, they kept scooting back fifteen or twenty feet every time we fired, and we had to pull them back into position. We had to dig holes for the trails, but even with a pickax, it was real difficult with the ground being so hard. So we dug little bitty holes, put C-4 explosives in them and set them off to make the holes bigger. I learned to handle C-4 and how much of it to use to dig the right-sized hole. I was a powder monkey all over again.

Out in the jungle, we worked eighteen to twenty hours a day or more. We survived on our C rations, but eating mediocre canned food three times a day got old quickly. I was hungry all the time. Mom sent me packages with my favorite cookies and fruitcakes, but they didn't last long. So I did my own supplementation. Whenever I could, I fished with the lines Uncle Jess had sent me—or with grenades if I didn't have much time. Sometimes we'd come across old French plantations. They were abandoned, but the trees still produced good fruit, and I picked bananas and pineapples. One day, I saw our Vietnamese scout roasting meat over a makeshift fire. I knew what it was: I had seen him club a big rat and skin it. The Vietnamese were generally really kind and polite, and they often offered to share their food. Most of the time I wasn't too sure what they were eating, so I'd normally play it safe. "Thank you, but I'm really full," I usually lied. That day, all I'd had was a sad can of beans, and my belly was growling. Cooking on a stick, that rat looked like the squirrels I used to roast as a kid, and it smelled darn good too. Our scout must have seen the look on my face, and he asked me whether I'd like to try a piece. That day, he didn't have to ask twice. I was ready to give anything that didn't come out of a C rat box a try. He tore off one of the front legs and handed it to me.

It didn't have much meat on it. I thought I'd put it in my mouth, roll it around a bit, and if it tasted real bad, I'd spit it out when he wasn't looking. I put it in my mouth and rolled it around. Man, that rat tasted so good. I ate the whole leg in a flash, and pulled the bones out of my mouth. He tore off another piece, and we shared the rat.

From then on, I baited rats with cans of chopped ham and eggs from our C rations. Those particular meals tasted terrible, but rats loved them. At times, there were three or four rats fighting over a can of ham and eggs, and I could get them all with one twelve-gauge round. I had skinned and roasted squirrels all the time as a kid, and rats were no different. I did the same with monkeys. Most of the time, I didn't even have to use much bait. When we ate our C rations on the job, we typically left garbage lying around. Rats came to eat leftovers, and everything else came to eat the rats.

I've lost count of how many times, when sleeping in foxholes in the jungle, I felt something crawling against my arm or my leg and realized it was a cobra trying to give me a big hug. These snakes were everywhere, and we had to get rid of them with machetes. Once I came across a large cobra in the mess hall tent at Tan Tru. I was so startled that I instinctively swatted it off. Luckily, I had a knife in my hand, and I cut its head off. The only good thing about these snakes is they had good white tenderloin meat on their backs. So I added snake to my menu. I ended up eating pretty much the same things the Vietnamese ate.

Whether we were at Tan Tru or out in the jungle, one of the hardest things was that our enemy was often invisible. We never knew where they were or when they'd come out. There was a Vietnamese graveyard in one of the rice paddies near Tan Tru, and there were always fresh piles of dirt there. At first that didn't seem too unusual: people were dying all the time and were getting buried. I can't remember now how exactly we figured it out, but the Vietcong had been digging tunnels under the cemetery. The tunnels were heading straight to the infantry ammo dump. They were discovered before anything bad happened, thank goodness, but it was astonishing to me. That was right under our noses. How had they managed to do that for so long without us knowing?

The Vietcong were also hiding in plain sight, and often we didn't even know who the enemy was. Who among the villagers' friendly faces wanted us dead? Who was with us, and who was against us? There was this Vietnamese barber in the tiny village near our camp. We had someone at Tan Tru cutting our hair, but it was good to get out of the camp once in a while. The barber just had a regular chair under a big old tree, and he would cut our hair for something like thirty cents. He was very friendly and spoke excellent English, and he always talked to us, asking questions while we sat on his chair getting our hair cut. This went on for months. One night, the enemy launched a sapper attack on Tan Tru. The next morning, we found our barber tangled in the concertina wire on the infantry side of the compound. We realized that he was Vietcong and had been gathering information about where we were going and what we were doing. He'd asked seemingly harmless questions of this GI, and then of that GI, then put it all together and used it against us.

Their intelligence-gathering capacity was phenomenal. They always seemed to know what we were up to—sometimes before we did ourselves. When we trucked out on a fire mission, some ladies in cone hats were already by the side of the dirt road waiting for us, trying to sell us all kinds of stuff. Some of them came to our camp every day to do laundry or cleaning. Some days they didn't show up, and sure enough, we'd get hit that day. We couldn't even trust the kids. They used to come into our camp, all friendly and with smiles on their little faces, often begging for food or trying to sell us something. After a while, we realized that they were walking between our guns, and the following night we'd get mortared. We watched them more closely, and we became aware that they were putting one foot right in front of the other, measuring the distance to figure out the exact position of our guns. So we quit letting them come into the compound.

At the same time, I felt for them. Looking back on it now, these villagers were in a rough spot, feeling the squeeze from both sides. Some of them had hard choices to make, and they sometimes sided with the Vietcong to save their lives or their families. They were already dirt poor, and the war was destroying their lives. They were just trying to survive and make the best of it. Some of them were so desperate that they picked through our garbage to get scraps of food. The captain had told us that we should not let them have it. So we stopped dumping our garbage on the ground and built a little dock to throw it in the nearby river. But the kids waded out in the water with buckets on their heads and came right to where we dumped the scraps and tried to catch what they could. It broke our hearts. We didn't want to feed the enemy, but here were those little kids who were hungry. When we had a pail that looked like it had good stuff in it, we tried to dump it in the kids' buckets. I think they knew that we were trying to help them. At least I hope so.

We did whatever we could. When we went through villages, we often walked by tiny kids of two or three years old wearing rags and with sores all over their bodies. Most of us were from big families with baby brothers and sisters, and we hated to see these little bitty fellows in such bad shape. We asked our medic how we could help. "Best you can do is give them a bar of soap," he said. I asked Mom to send me some supplies, and I carried a washcloth and some Ivory soap. When we came through a village for the first time, the kids were understandably standoffish and pretty frightened. We'd ask the village chief if we could wash the children. And if he said yes, we'd set ourselves up with a bucket of water. We'd try our basic Vietnamese on the kids, and they'd answer with the little bit of English they knew. But most of it was sign language. The next time we would go through that village, the kids often waited for us. When I was doing the ration runs, I also got to feed and wash a bunch of kids in Tan An while waiting for the barge to take me back to Tan Tru. I got to know a few of them real good. Lam, Bear, Mao, and Chin. When I didn't know their names, I just called them baby-san, and they called me pappy-san or same-same. While I was washing those kids, I could almost forget the war. I remembered why I was there and why I was fighting. Even today, whenever the ghosts of the men I killed or the buddies who died next to me come to haunt me, I try to remember these kids with big smiles on their faces.

Days stretched into weeks, and weeks into months. I kept counting the days until I could go back home, but it was hard to believe I would ever leave Vietnam. I felt I had been at Tan Tru for a very long time. As time went by, home slipped further and further away. My old life no longer seemed real, but instead like something I'd dreamed about. I held on to anything and everything that reminded me of home. Whenever I could, I fished. As long as I could sit for a bit with a fishing line in my hand, I was no longer in the middle of a war but back home with my big brothers. I could drop a line anywhere in the rice paddies. I caught some minnows and deep-fried them. The "memories make up your life. You look forward to each hour of rest because you can relive these memories." Getting news from home reminded me of who I was, and that there were people out there who loved me and thought about me.

It's real hard in these days of the Internet and cell phones and Skype to explain how isolated we were. How far and lonely I felt without a few lines from home, without reading familiar handwriting. My heart sank every time the mail came in and there was nothing for me. When I visit schools today, kids look at me as if I'm talking about life on Mars. "Why didn't you just text them?" they ask.

But life back home was moving on without me. Some of my friends were getting married and having babies. I was holding on to the dream of love with some of the girls I had dated, but they moved on. Now I understand, but at the time, it tore me apart. There was one in particular, a friend of my sisters' who stayed with our neighbors. She was a beautiful young lady, and I was head over heels in love with her. The truth is we weren't that close, but I believed we would get married and have a good life together after Vietnam. I hung on to that pipe dream as hard and as long as I could, and it gave me hope. She didn't write very much, and I kept asking my mother and sisters about her. Then I found out she'd gotten pregnant. My hopes shattered in a million little pieces, along with my heart. "Boy, girls sure are a lot of trouble, aren't they," I reflected in one letter.

I was changing as well. In some ways, I was still the same old Sammy, a kid who couldn't believe he was about to turn twenty-one. "I sure used to look forward to that day," I wrote as my birthday was getting near. "Now I kinda dread it. I won't be a kid anymore. I'll have to act like a grownup and I still feel the same as I did when I was 16." At the same time, I struggled to hang on to the guy I used to be. Part of it was that I was wising up. "I know now why parents are so wise. They've already been through it all," I wrote Mom. "I guess I'll be a daddy some day, and I will try to tell my son what's best. I hope he realizes that I too will know better. But he will probably have to try out every thing for himself. Guess that's what helps make you a wise person. All education doesn't come out of a book." But mostly, the war was turning me into someone else. "I guess I have changed over here. My temper is a lot shorter now and I would rather shove a fist than argue."

Sometime in the fall of 1967, a high-profile visitor paid us a visit. We were out on an operation with another artillery battery and four howitzer guns. As usual, we were short on men, with only three guys and one sergeant on each gun. We were firing each gun in quick succession to push the enemy away from our infantry guys. We kept raising the barrel one increment at a time to fire a bit further, driving the bad guys back. A helicopter came behind us and landed, and out came General Westmoreland. In 1967, William Childs Westmoreland commanded US military operations in Vietnam. He had been an artillery officer and had himself served in the Ninth Infantry Division during World War II.

Our major looked like he was going to have a heart attack. He told us to stop firing when Westy stepped up to our guns and to do whatever he asked. We were on live fire, so we couldn't all stop at the same time. But one gun could take a break, and the other three howitzers would take up the slack and pick up the firing pace while General Westmoreland was talking to the gun crew. The guns were set up next to one another in a straight line, and I was on the last gun, so I could hear what he was asking the other guys. Were they getting hot chow and receiving letters from home? Did we have a chaplain or rabbi? We knew the only answer we could give was that everything was wonderful. When he stepped to our gun, we quit firing, stepped back away from the howitzer, and fell in. Westy went down the line of the four of us. He stood in front of me, looked me directly in the eye, and then up and down. There was no incoming fire, so I wasn't wearing my steel pot—my helmet—or my flak jacket. The heat was overwhelming, and I had no shirt on. My pants were ragged and muddy, I had not polished my belt buckle in months, and my boots had holes in them. I didn't wear the heavy wool socks the Army issued: they held too much water. Later on, Mom sent me nylon socks that were much better suited to the Delta conditions, but I didn't have them yet, so several of my toes were sticking out of my boots. When Westy looked at my feet, I couldn't think of what to do, so I wiggled my toes. His eyes got real big.

"Son, is that the only pair of boots you have?" he asked.

"Yes, sir." I didn't explain that I could have gotten new ones, but the holes in my boots were working for me. The mud and water of the Mekong Delta gave us bad cases of foot rot, or what we called trench foot—big open running sores that would never heal and kept getting worse because they were always wet. I figured that, whenever I had a chance to get onto dry ground, the water would drain out much better from boots with holes. Most of the time we stood by our guns, and we didn't go on long hikes through the jungle like the infantry did, so I didn't bother getting new boots when the old ones got holes in them. In any case, new boots didn't last very long, as the mud ate at the leather. It all worked pretty good for me. In fact, my feet were in better shape than most of the other guys'.

General Westmoreland turned to the captain and noticed he was wearing a brand-new pair of boots.

"Captain, what size are your boots?"

"Ten wide, sir," said the captain.

Westy turned to me. "Private, what size boot do you wear?"

"Ten wide, sir," I said.

The general turned to the captain. "Captain, take those boots off and give them to that boy."

I sat down in the mud beside the captain and put on my new boots. I thought Westy was quite something. This was the beginning of a relationship that would span years.

In October, I was sent on R & R—rest and recuperation—in Vung Tau. After nearly five months in Tan Tru and eight months in Vietnam, it was as if I'd died and gone to heaven for five days. No more fire missions, no more perimeter guard, no more radio shifts. I slept in a real bed with real sheets and a real roof over my head. I ate proper hot meals three times a day. Vung Tau was a small fishing and resort town right on the South China Sea. I went to the beach every day and watched the fishermen bring in their nets. I swam in the clear and cool blue sea and, for the first time since I'd left California, I went waterskiing. If it hadn't been for the GIs swarming all over the place, I could have forgotten I was in a war zone. When the five days were over, I headed back to my battery. Leaving Vung Tau was the hardest thing. It had been wonderful, but my heart sank at the thought of getting back to the mud and the howitzers after a few days of tropical vacation. Luckily, I was sent to Kuala Lumpur on another R & R shortly after Vung Tau. I couldn't believe my luck. I wasn't certain where Kuala Lumpur was, but I sure was happy to go. I don't remember much about Malaysia, except that the beer was cold and the ladies friendly. I left for that R & R on October 31—the day before I turned twenty-one.

Just before my trip to Malaysia, I'd been out on an operation for several days. We'd been under fire, pinned down in our foxholes except when firing our guns. I'd sat in a foxhole with eighteen inches of water in it for what seemed like an eternity. My hands were white and shriveled. When I dropped my trousers, I saw that my legs were milky white and the skin was peeling off from being wet. I was pruny in places I would never have imagined. I didn't sleep for several days. When I came back, two other guns were being sent out and I was told I had to go out again immediately to stand in for a guy who'd been injured. I was so tired I could barely move. I thought things could not get any worse than that.

How wrong I was. On November 17, 1967, forty-two of us were airlifted with four of our guns to another fire mission near Cai Lay, about thirty miles west of our home base. Significant enemy movement and activity had been reported in the area, and we were part of a sweeping operation. We realized later that the Vietcong and North Vietnamese Army were preparing for the Tet Offensive that would take place two months later, and troops were gathering for what would be the largest and most daring Vietnamese offensive of the war. My gun stayed at Tan Tru, and I wasn't supposed to go. But as usual, the guns that went out were short of men, and I volunteered. I had come back from my R & R in Kuala Lumpur a few days before and figured I should be helping the guys out.

The Chinooks dropped us off in a bog by a canal. We struggled to find any solid ground to set up our guns. In a nearby rice paddy, Battery D set up three howitzers on aluminum platforms.

We were at Fire Support Base Cudgel.

★ 6 ★

CUDGEL

FIRE SUPPORT BASE CUDGEL, MEKONG DELTA, VIETNAM

NOVEMBER 18, 1967

I rolled over to lie on my back and looked straight up. Pretty blue, white, red, and green lines crisscrossed the sky.

Wow, I thought. *This is just like Christmas.*

As my head cleared a bit, I realized they were not Christmas lights, but tracers—ammunition rounds that burned so brightly they seemed to twinkle. Then the ringing in my ears eased, and I heard what was going on around me. The explosions. The *ratatatattt* of automatic weapons. Men yelling, injured or terrified. The beehive fléchettes in my legs, butt, and lower back hurt real bad. My head was heavy, and I felt as if I was underwater or in a very bad dream. Traumatic brain injury. I couldn't see Sergeant Gant, Cole, or Hart, with whom I'd been working the howitzer. They were gone. I lifted my head and looked toward the canal. Scores of Vietnamese bodies were lying on the bank, but I saw another wave of one or two hundred soldiers coming at us. I was in serious trouble.

Adrenaline took over. I moved on autopilot.

I checked my ammo. I had about 180 rounds for my M16 rifle. I fired at the enemy until I was left with three or four rounds in the last clip. For some reason, I wanted to save them. I saw the heavier M60 machine gun in another foxhole. Between two assault waves, I crawled over to get it and dragged it back to my hole, which was closer to the riverbank. I set it up on its tripod and plugged the ammo loop. I waited until new Vietnamese lines crossed the canal. The water was about waist high, but there was a trough just in front of me. As they popped up from the deep, I fired. I looked into the last box of M60 ammo: there was only one loop left.

I felt I had died and landed in soldier hell. No matter what I did and how many rounds I fired, the bad guys just kept coming at me. I shot, soldiers dropped dead, but somehow they kept advancing, like zombies rising back from the water. That same movie kept playing again and again. I was trapped in a looping nightmare with no end. Except I was fast running out of ammo.

I looked around, and my only chance was the howitzer—or what was left of it. The recoil mechanism was gone. So were the rotating wheels. The shields were hanging, and the tires were on fire. But it looked like the barrel was in one piece. So I got up, threw the M60 in the canal so the enemy wouldn't take it, and made a limping run for the howitzer. A Vietnamese soldier saw me and fired his AK-47 semiautomatic rifle. I dived. He shot me in the leg—and then stopped firing. I don't know why he did. But he gave me the seconds I needed to grab my rifle and shoot. My first shot was more accurate than his.

He was dead. I looked at my leg, and for some reason, I thought of that first rabbit I'd shot as a boy, all those years ago. It's real strange the things that go through your mind in combat. Back then I had wondered if that rabbit had felt any pain. With a bullet in my leg, I finally knew. *It's not that bad*, I thought.

The enemy was coming from another angle now. I had to rotate the howitzer. It usually took several crewmembers to move the two-ton artillery piece. I found out that in the right circumstances and with enough adrenaline, it only took one determined young man to do it. I crawled under a trail, lifted myself up to my hands and knees, and slowly stood up. I had to do this. I just had to, or die trying. I pressed against the howitzer, my ear against the trail that supported it, and pushed with all the strength I had. Adrenaline numbed the pain and made me stronger.

A loud *bang* blasted in my ear. It sounded like a Japanese gong. *Japanese gongs? Out here?* I got even more confused. Then I looked back, and a .50-caliber round whizzed past me. Then another hit the trail that extended out of the gun. I realized the Japanese gong ringing in my ear was the round hitting the howitzer. I had to take out that .50 caliber before it got me. I gave a final push, and the gun shifted in the mud. It was in the right place.

I crawled behind the howitzer to find ammunition. One of the rockets had hit our ammo supply, and everything was strewn everywhere. I searched the mess and found beehive rounds. Hallelujah! I also saw powder. It usually came in seven cotton bags strung together with cotton string. How far the weapon fired was determined by how many bags were in the brass shell, and how many were cut off. The explosion of our ammo stash had destroyed the bags though, and pellets of loose powder were all over the ground looking like hamster food. I crawled back and found a canister for the loose powder. Sergeant Gant had always told us that to get the most out of the beehive, we had to fire at maximum charge—or seven bags of powder. With the bags gone, it was hard to tell how much that was. But there was no better time to go for top impact. So I scooped up handfuls of loose powder and filled the canister to the brim. I didn't know it yet, but I'd just loaded a charge equivalent to over twenty powder bags—or three times the limit—in a badly damaged cannon.

I assembled the beehive round, set the fuse to muzzle action and rammed it into the breech. By then, the Vietnamese had figured out what I was doing, and they were bringing smoke on my butt. I lay down behind the right wheel for protection, but it was on fire. My face, neck, and arms were burning. I pulled the firing lanyard.

Nothing. Damn, this was not working.

After a few seconds, the gun started to wiggle. And *bam!* It exploded. With the overcharge and the recoil mechanism gone, it reared like a bronco, standing on its trails and spewing fire. Then the two-ton piece rolled back—and it rolled back on me. At first, I thought I was just winded. I saw my brothers Buddy and Darrell looking down on me after I'd fallen from a willow tree as a kid. *Breathe, breathe real shallow.* Then I was back in the blackberry bushes after I'd caught a wave waterskiing on the Sacramento–San Joaquin Delta. *I'm OK.* So I lay there, catching my breath. My right ribs and my back hurt like hell, but my legs were kind of numb, so the fléchettes didn't feel so bad anymore. *You don't lose 'til you quit trying, Sammy.* I picked myself up. As long as I was still breathing, I wasn't going to quit trying.

A mortar hit just a few feet away, and shrapnel flew into my leg.

I fell. Another wave of Vietnamese soldiers was about to cross the canal. So I got up and loaded a fresh round in the gun, reducing the powder charge, and I fired. Then I fired again. I used all the beehive rounds I could find. When they were all gone, I moved to regular high-explosive shells. Without the recoil mechanism, the howitzer rolled back and sank deeper into the creek behind me every time I fired. Then I was out of ammo, and the gun was almost underwater. The only thing left was a propaganda round, which spewed leaflets promising the enemy a safe passage home if they surrendered. That would do. I loaded it and pulled the lanyard one last time. As it turned out, propaganda worked real well at close range.

I couldn't see any of the guys. Was I the only one alive? Then I heard a scream across the canal.

"Help us! God please help us!" the voice yelled. "Don't shoot. I'm a GI!" At first, I thought the enemy was trying to trick us. Then an illumination round popped with a bang and brightened the sky. I looked up. Right across from me, on the other side of the canal, a brother was waving his boonie hat.

My heart broke. I had been firing beehives across the water right at him. I'd seen infantry guys cross to our side of the canal earlier as the enemy advanced, but I didn't know anyone was still stranded on the other side. For a second, the explosions, the screams, and the bad guys coming at us were gone. All I heard was my mother's voice, clear as day. "Don't you leave your little brother!"

I had to go get him.

I thought of all those days swimming in the creek as a boy, and later, ferrying my baby brother, Johnny, across the river. I was a good swimmer. But with my back and my ribs crushed, the beehive fléchettes all over my legs and lower back, an AK-47 round and shrapnel in my thigh, and burns on my face, neck, and arms, I was in no shape to swim across. I crawled and found one of the air mattresses that we'd all been issued to sleep on. They kept turning over or getting holes in them, so they were not too good as mattresses. But boy, was I happy to find one right then.

The mattress was full of bullet holes. I tied it off and blew into the part that was still intact. I got to the canal. I saw Frank Gage, our forward observer, and asked him to cover me. Then I hugged the air mattress and set to cross. Bullets were whizzing past, and I ducked underwater as much as I could, hanging on to my air mattress. I made it to the other side. I stuffed the mattress under the grass and crawled toward my brother. There were dead bodies all over the bank.

I had no weapon. I picked up a Vietnamese rifle, but the beehive rounds had made it inoperable. I checked another. Same story. I crawled forward and tried all the weapons I could find. None of them worked. All this movement was also bringing me unwanted attention. I finally got to the foxhole where I'd seen the soldier waving.

What I found was not one stranded GI. There were three. They were part of the infantry unit, and I didn't know them. They were in bad shape. The guy who had been waving his hat was shot through the back. He also had a nasty shrapnel wound on top of his head that left a gap two fingers wide. The second guy had lost the lower part of one leg. A tourniquet saved him from bleeding to death. And then there was the third man. He'd been shot in the head—which left part of his brain exposed—and his chest was open.

"He's dead," said the boonie hat guy.

Dead or not, I was not about to leave anyone behind. But I

couldn't ferry all three of them across the water in one go. Not with my injuries. I also knew I didn't have the strength for three trips. So I looked up and asked for some help from the Big Guy above.

One of the GIs still had his M16 and three clips.

After carefully pushing part of his brain into his skull, I put the unconscious soldier with the head and chest wounds across my shoulders. I linked arms with the other two and, leaning on each other, we hobbled toward the canal. The M16 was hanging from my neck. Between two enemy assault waves, off we went.

When I heard another wave of Vietnamese coming behind us, we played dead. I laid the guys down among the sea of corpses on the ground and lay faceup on top of them. For the most part, it worked. The Vietnamese ran right over us. Among their dead, we were invisible. I kept watch. They were kids, just like us. A few became aware we were there, I could see it in their eyes. I did my job as a soldier and shot them before they had a chance to shoot us.

We made it to the bank. I laid the unconscious soldier down, close to where I'd left my mattress.

"Wait for me. I'll be back!" I told the other two. Not that they were in any shape to go anywhere.

Before the next assault wave came, I grabbed the mattress, dragged the unconscious GI on it, and set off to cross as best I could. I tried to keep his wounded head out of the dirty water. I didn't know what was going on around me. All I saw was the other side of the canal. I gave it all I had.

As I got close to the other side, two men were in the water close to me. I didn't know if they were our guys or the enemy. A head popped out of the water, just inches away from mine. I saw blond hair and blue eyes. It was Bill Murray from Lenoir, North Carolina.

The other head bobbled up. Frank Gage from Buffalo, New York. They got the wounded GI onto dry land.

I crossed back to the other side. Bringing the other two was easier: they could both hold on to the mattress. As we got close, they got pulled out of the water onto the bank. They'd made it to our side of the canal.

My job was done, and suddenly I was bone tired and I hurt like hell. No more fuel in the tank. I was still in the water, and it felt so good. I just wanted to let go and rest. I sank into darkness.

Then I saw a warrior wearing a Roman helmet, a metal breastplate, and a short gladiator skirt. In my concussed dream, he lifted my head out of the water and breathed life back into me. "Son," he said, "your job is not yet done." I kicked up from the bottom. My head was out of the water again.

A few feet away, someone was reaching out to me. Frank Gage. He grabbed my arm and dragged me out of the water and into a shallow depression. I got enough strength back to thank him. Then as I lay on the canal bank, I saw a hand coming out of the water in the distance. Just a hand. Somebody was underwater, sinking. Was it another brother? I didn't know. I wanted to go back, but I couldn't find enough strength just yet to move. Then the hand disappeared, swallowed by the canal. It was gone.

There was still a war raging around us, and I managed to crawl to a foxhole. I heard someone telling me I needed a medic. The enemy was still coming at us. *I can't quit now.* I moved toward the two howitzers, further back, that were still working.

And then I saw him. There with his legs in dirty water, Sergeant Gant was lying on his back. My mean old sergeant, who made us sit out in a hundred-degree heat to polish our bullets and set time fuses blindfolded. I'd last seen him when we'd fired our howitzer, and a rocket-propelled grenade had hit our gun. One of the guys had pulled him back from where he'd fallen. A big pile of pink foam was bubbling out of his chest. Sergeant Gant had taught us that the proper response to something like that was to take a piece of our rain poncho, clean off the wound area, apply the plasticized nylon over it, and secure it with anything at hand. I'd stopped thinking straight a long while back. So instead of grabbing the first one I found, I crawled all the way back to my foxhole, found my duffel bag, and pulled out my own poncho. I looked for a piece without bullet holes. I cut it out, folded it neatly, and kept it out of the water as I crawled back to Sergeant Gant. I applied the cutout nylon and compressed it with his T-shirt. His eyes started to clear, and he coughed up a lot of blood. He held up his hand like he wanted to speak to me. I grabbed his hand, and pulled myself close.

I was a twenty-one-year-old private first class, and I'd been on my own most of the night. I was in bad shape and more tired than I'd ever been. *Please, Sergeant. Please, tell me what to do.*

Sergeant Gant said nothing. He couldn't speak. But I looked into his eyes, and all of a sudden, I understood. I understood that he was not mean or bitter. I understood that he didn't hate us. He loved us. All this time, he had been teaching us kids things he knew would keep us alive. He had done all he could to prepare us for the worst. Working blindfolded so we could operate in the dark without a flashlight. So we could do it in our sleep, or when we could no longer think. Polishing bullets so our M16 wouldn't jam. What he had failed to do was explain. He'd taught us well, our mean old sergeant. That night, his lessons saved my life, along with many of my brothers'.

I gave him a shot of morphine and pulled him out of the water. I marked his forehead with blood to signal he'd had morphine. That's all I could do for him.

I crawled to the two howitzers in our battery that were still operating. I helped in any way I could. By then, all I could do was set the time fuses. My hands were the only parts of me that still worked.

At about eight a.m., the enemy finally broke contact. The battle was over, and we'd done our job. What was left of the enemy had retreated without taking our artillery.

I looked around. Across the canal, the thick brush and tall palm trees were gone. The beehives and the bullets had mown the grass and trimmed all the trees. The change of terrain was unbelievable. And strewn on the desolate moonscape were dead Vietnamese soldiers. On the canal bank across from our howitzers—where I'd laid among dead bodies with the three GIs—the casualties piled up one on top of another. The official reports later credited us with fewer than a hundred. To this day, I cannot reconcile that official number with what we saw. I cannot reconcile it with the waves of men coming at us and the fire they took from us.

Out of the forty-two men of Battery C, only twelve of us were still standing. Barely. Cole and Hart, the two guys who worked the howitzer with Sergeant Gant and me, were hit by shrapnel but survived. Our one medic, Johnny Edwards, was very busy, and he'd been hit as well. I didn't know how the infantry was doing. Or Battery D, set up in the rice paddy.

Medevac choppers appeared, and those of us who were still able to did triage. One guy's leg looked bad: the ruptured femoral artery twirled and squirted blood like pressurized water from a garden hose. I tied it off with dental floss so he wouldn't bleed to death. I had to decide who got immediate attention and went out on the first choppers. This was a nightmare, and I don't know if I made the right decisions. To this day, it still haunts me at night.

The wounded were airlifted. Then we loaded the dead. It had been six hours, and it felt like a lifetime. A devastating sense of loneliness, despair, and exhaustion washed over me. But there was still some housekeeping to be done. We marked unexploded rounds and picked up guns. We checked the damage.

I needed to relieve myself. Our portable toilet was a three-hole bench. I found it full of bullet holes and turned it upright. I dropped my breeches. "My God, Dave, look at your leg!" Cole said.

I looked down at my bloody flesh, and I let go. I passed out cold.

This is how I remember that night. It has been more than forty-five years now, and it feels like yesterday. Every detail is so clear, the images so sharp, the screams so loud. Most nights since November 18, 1967, I've gone back to FSB Cudgel in my sleep and crossed that canal. Most nights, I am back in the water, I hear the bullets, I see that soldier waving his hat. Most nights, I fear I'm going to die.

I've told that story many times over the years. Putting it down on paper, I realize that there are a couple more things I need to say. First, what I remember is a small part of a bigger story. With bullets and mortars raining all over us, injuries crippling us, and adrenaline pumping through our veins, the world became very small for all the men who fought that night. Like everyone else, I focused on the job I had to do and was only aware of what was going on a few feet around me. And at some point or the other, I bet everyone felt very alone. I know I did.

Yet I was not alone. The Fifth Battalion, Sixtieth Infantry had been assigned to guard the fire support base perimeter. One infantry company, covering the three howitzers of the artillery battery set up in the rice paddy, was east of us, and a reconnaissance platoon was posted across the canal from our Battery C. I didn't see the guys from that recon platoon that day, but they had set up listening posts and foxholes in the tall grass. When the enemy attacked, these men—who had already been fighting for days— were in the first line, with nothing between them and the waves of Vietnamese soldiers coming out of the jungle. Vastly outnumbered, they had no choice but to retreat across the canal any way they could under heavy fire. At the same time, the enemy offensive had also targeted Battery D in the rice paddy and the infantry company defending that part of the perimeter. These guys resisted the Vietnamese assault as well, and the enemy retreated. When dawn broke, the infantry had lost six men, and seventy-six others were wounded. This is the bigger story of FSB Cudgel, but I became aware of it much later.

That night, I didn't know any of that. All I knew was this: I had to push back the Vietnamese that kept coming at us and make sure they didn't get our guns. And I had to help those three soldiers stranded on the wrong side of the canal. I just had to—or die trying. That was all there was, and I put everything I had into it. In that moment, nothing else mattered. I clearly remember feeling that these guys depended on me. I can't even say *thinking*, because I couldn't think: I moved on autopilot. Knowing they depended on me gave me strength. It also filled me with overwhelming loneliness. I couldn't think or see anything else. The bigger story, I got from history books, or memories that are not mine, so whenever I tell people about that night, I tell them only what I remember.

But now I also realize that, no matter how sharp the images and how loud the screams still are, memory is not perfect. We only believe it is. Over the past year, I read eyewitness statements collected ten days after that night. I talked to several men who were there and read accounts from the infantry unit. We all have slightly different versions. All of us were in it together, but we all fought different battles. It is hard to describe the confusion and chaos we were in that night. It was dark, it was mayhem, and we were all fighting for our lives. It's not like anyone stopped to observe and take notes. As the infantry recon platoon retreated across the canal, many were helping these guys reach the other side. I wasn't the only one.

Even reading my Medal of Honor citation—for the first time in years—I don't remember it exactly that way. I have no final answer or explanation to offer, and I have to accept that maybe I never will. All I can do is tell the story to the best of my recollection and listen with an open mind and an open heart as others do the same. Memories of traumatic events feel very real, and every little detail seems carved in our minds forever. I know mine are, and I know they will never leave me. Haunted by these images that replay night after night, it is tempting to believe we own the Truth. But listening to the many accounts of that night, I know now that there is no such thing. We each carry our own truth. They overlap, but sometimes they do not perfectly match.

I don't doubt for a second that everyone is sincere. This makes me wonder about how, and why, we remember what we remember.

★7★

DUDE, I THOUGHT YOU WERE DEAD!

Ting.

Sound came first. My eyes were still closed, but the fog in my head started to clear. I was slowly coming back to the world as if being pulled through a long dark tunnel.

Ting.

I was lying on my belly. Then I heard voices behind me.

"How did he get hit with these? I thought they were ours!"

Nurses were pulling beehive rounds from my legs, buttocks, and lower back and dropping the fléchettes into a metal pan. *Ting.* One from my kidney. *Ting.* One from my fourth lumbar vertebra.

I was in a military hospital. After passing out in mud and blood at Fire Support Base Cudgel, I woke up in a top-notch air-conditioned tent with inflated walls and a canvas top. I had been loaded with the wounded on one of the medevac helicopter ambulances—known as Dustoffs, after their radio call sign—and evacuated to Dong

Tam, less than twenty miles from Cai Lay. Bill Few and Jimmy Picket, two of the guys from my howitzer battery, were there with me.

"We didn't think you were hurt too bad," said Jimmy.

"Well," I replied, "I wasn't."

That night, I hadn't had a chance to take stock of the damage. When I woke up in the hospital, I could sense that a lot was wrong, but I was heavily medicated. I only found out a bit later the extent of the injuries that would keep plaguing me for years. Some of the beehive fléchettes had perforated my left kidney and lodged into a lumbar vertebra. A doctor explained that, ironically, the injury to the vertebra was probably what had kept me going that night at Cudgel. The dart and the howitzer rolling back on me had caused swelling that had compressed the spinal cord. I'd still been able to move my legs, but everything below my waist had been kind of numb. I understood then why getting shot in the leg and having beehives buried in my flesh hadn't felt all that bad. I was also told that the AK-47 round probably hadn't hit me directly—which would have broken my leg—but had bounced off something else. When the beehive fléchette was pulled out of my vertebra, the bone started healing, and the swelling gradually went down until I was able to fully feel my feet and legs again—and, unfortunately, the pain.

My chest, on the other hand, was a different story. There was nothing numb there, and every breath or movement was excruciating. The ribs on my right side were no longer attached to my sternum. The howitzer that had rolled onto me had ripped the connecting cartilage. I also had small shrapnel wounds all over and burns on my face, hands, and neck. To top it all off, the hit from the enemy recoilless rifle to our howitzer had given me a big old bang to the head, and I had traumatic brain injury. Other than that, I was in pretty good shape. I was banged up, but compared to what I had just seen, it really wasn't that bad. I was lucky to be alive and more or less in one piece.

I didn't stay in Dong Tam for very long. After a few days, I started running a temperature of 106 or 107 degrees, and passed out again. With a perforated kidney, the bacteria from the mud and dirty water at Cudgel—and, I later realized, exposure to Agent Orange—sent me into toxic shock. The weeks that followed are fuzzy. Between the bouts of fever, the blackouts, and the heavy medication, I can't be sure of the exact sequence of events.

What I know for sure is I was at the Third Field Hospital in Saigon for Thanksgiving less than a week after Cudgel. Major General Forsythe, who was then number two in the US program to win hearts and minds in rural Vietnam, invited eight or ten of us in the hospital for the traditional turkey dinner. I didn't know him, and I have no idea why or how I was picked. We were rolled out in wheelchairs, and ambulances drove us out to the general's colonial mansion. It was one of these fancy dinners with six different sets of spoons, forks, and knives, multiple plates, and crystal glasses in all shapes and sizes. After several months of C rations and tin cups, I thought I was hallucinating. All that silver and china would have been real confusing even if I'd had all my wits about me. But somehow, I made it through dinner all right. I sure was happy to be fed such fine food.

I also remember waking up in Camp Zama in Japan, but I can't be sure whether that was before or after Thanksgiving. During the Vietnam War, the US Army hospitals in Japan were real busy and cared for six to eight thousand patients a month on average. Zama, with its seven hundred beds, was the only general Army hospital in

Japan and had every kind of doctor. Thousands of lives were saved over there. Casualties of all ranks and from all kinds of units across Vietnam ended up at Zama. The Lurps and the pilots, the grunts and the cooks. The privates and the generals. The evacuation chain worked pretty good. The medics' job was to keep the wounded alive until the Dustoff choppers came in. I've read that medevac flights averaged thirty-five minutes in Vietnam, and the more seriously wounded usually reached a hospital within one or two hours of being hit—provided they could get picked up. Every casualty was first dusted off to a hospital in Vietnam to be stabilized and patched up. The wounded who could survive a six-hour flight and needed a longer stay in the hospital were sent to Japan to free up beds in Vietnam. Those who made it to Camp Zama had a very good chance of survival—and, depending on their injuries, headed home to the United States or back to Vietnam to finish their tour once they were back on their feet.

Not too long after I woke up, a doctor came in to see me. I was heavily medicated and feeling kind of weak. "We're sending you home," he said. "You'll probably be retired from the Army."

This should have been like Christmas coming early. From the moment I'd arrived in Vietnam, I'd been counting the days until I could go back home. That was the ticket that could shave three months off my little Vietnam adventure. But instead of celebrating, my heart sank. At the time, I could not have explained why I wanted so bad to go back to Vietnam. Now I know it is called closure. That morning at Cudgel, after loading the dead and the injured onto the helicopters, I'd passed out before I had the opportunity to talk to the other guys. The guys who'd been there and, like me, were lucky enough to see another day. They were the only ones I could talk to about what had happened to us. Who else could have understood what it was like to have gone to hell and back? But lying in that hospital bed in Japan, I didn't yet understand it all that clearly. All I knew was I needed to be with my brothers real bad. I wasn't about to let any doctor stand in my way.

"I don't want to go home," I heard myself slur.

The doctor probably thought I was off my rocker. "We're sending you home!" he repeated louder and slower, as if talking to someone who was slow or whose English wasn't too good. Doctor or no doctor, he was the slow one. He evidently wasn't getting it.

"And I'm telling you I want to go back to my unit!" I yelled. In my condition, raising my voice almost finished me. Then I figured that arguing with the guy who controlled my medication wasn't too smart. I changed course.

"Please call General Westmoreland," I said. If anyone could understand, surely Westy would. I thought he'd let me stay and go back to be with my brothers. After all, he'd given me a pair of boots a few weeks before. I figured that meant something, and that maybe, with a bit of luck, he'd remember me. "The general and me, we're just like that," I told the doctor, crossing my index and middle fingers.

I still don't know how I managed to convince anyone to call the highest-ranking US general in Vietnam. But a while later, I was carried on a canvas stretcher down to a colonel's office in the hospital. My stretcher was balanced on four chairs, and the colonel handed me the phone.

"General Westmoreland is on the line," he said.

And, amazingly, he was. "Just what is it that I can do for you, son?" General Westmoreland said.

"They want to retire me from the Army and send me home, sir,"

I blurted out, "but I want to go back to Vietnam. I need to go back to my unit."

Westy was silent for a few seconds. "Well, son, let me speak to the colonel," he finally said.

The colonel was put back on the line. He just sat there, nodding. All he said was "Yes, sir. Yes, sir. Yes, sir."

It was agreed that, as soon as my health stabilized, I would be sent back to Saigon. And as soon as I could walk, I would be allowed to go back to my unit. If I'd been able to, I would have jumped up and down. But I was hurting too much to move anything. I just gave the colonel a real big smile. "Thank you, sir."

Years later, during one event we both attended, General Westmoreland asked me if I remembered that conversation at the hospital. "Yes, sir," I said. How could I ever forget? Then he told me that just before I'd called, he'd been at his desk, reviewing the testimonies and paperwork that would eventually become my Medal of Honor citation. Just when he'd finished reading it, he'd received the call from Camp Zama. "I would have given you the world," he said. "And all you wanted was to go back to your unit in Vietnam."

The colonel at Camp Zama kept his word. I was flown back to Vietnam and admitted to the Third Field Hospital in Saigon. I still ran a high fever, which pushed me in and out of reality much of the time. But I remember this civilian lady who came and talked to me. The first time she came, I was dozing off. She touched my arm, and I opened my eyes, my brain still gripped by fever.

"Wes said I should come and visit you," she said.

I had no idea who she was, who Wes was, and what on earth she was talking about. But I was too tired and weak to figure it out or ask. Her hand felt soft and cool on my arm, and that was fine by me. Who was I to argue?

She came back several times. When I was feeling better and my brain was starting to work again, I heard the nurses on the floor whisper to each other.

"Here she is," they said. "Here comes Mrs. Westmoreland."

I realized the mysterious visitor was the general's wife, Kitsy. She was a regular in the hospital to visit wounded servicemen.

I also got a visit from some top brass from the Ninth Infantry Division when I was in a hospital. I can't say whether this was in Saigon or in Dong Tam. It must have been a few short days after Cudgel, because I was still in bed and unable to move much. A general presented me with the Purple Heart, a medal awarded to servicemen wounded or killed in action. I'd never been awarded anything before, and even though I was weak and heavily medicated, I was very grateful. In light of my sorry condition, the general pinned the medal to my pillow. A few days later, I was told that my name had been put forward for a Medal of Honor. I couldn't believe it. I was really moved that anyone in my unit thought I deserved the highest military award for bravery. "I know that sometimes I didn't do so good," I told Mom in a letter. "So I do hope you can afford to be proud of me now." That made my heart feel good, but I was also mystified. This was the medal awarded to guys like Audie Murphy and Pappy Boyington, the World War II heroes. I knew I was no Audie Murphy or Pappy Boyington. Surely, someone along the chain of command would soon realize that I'd only been doing my job. So I quickly put it out of my mind and went on with the business of getting back on my feet.

Another surprise visitor also appeared at my bedside in Saigon. One night I felt a big pressure on my chest. There was something in my mouth, and I couldn't breathe. I thought I was having a heart attack. The idea that, after all I'd been through, I was going to die in a hospital bed was enough to jolt me out of my sleep. I opened my eyes and there, standing by the side of my bed, was Gwyndell Holloway, the infantryman who'd called out and waved his hat across the canal at Cudgel. He'd put a Lucky Strike in my mouth, and was pushing down my chest so I would smoke it.

At first, I thought I was dreaming. But I wasn't. As luck would have it, he was being treated in the same hospital. He later told me he'd found out I was there when doctors had all but given up on me. I'd been rolled out of the ward and parked in a corridor to free up a bed when he saw me. He raised hell until someone told him what was going on: my fever was out of control, I was severely dehydrated, and I needed blood the hospital didn't have. We had the same blood type, and he had a doctor run a tube from his arm straight into mine. He saved my life. I often think of the many ways Gwyndell has changed my fate, and how lucky I was to be in a position to help him when he needed a hand. Because he sure returned the favor many times over, and I wouldn't be here today, doing what I do, if it weren't for him. After that blood transfusion, I got better and was moved back into a bed. He took the bed next to mine. When I was out of the woods, I guess he figured I could use a smoke.

Next, I had to get back on my feet. I was supposed to go back to my unit as soon as I was able to walk. That was the deal. I had a note from General Westmoreland that said as much. My doctor in Saigon decided to be much more specific: I would not be discharged before I could walk down three flights of stairs, go to the armory in a separate building, clean a weapon, and then walk back to the colonel's office. If I could do that for three days in a row, I'd be sent back to Tan Tru. That was easier said than done. I was still pretty feeble, and my leg was not fixed yet. I would manage to complete the prescribed routine once or sometimes two days in a row. Then the fever would spike again, and I was out.

That was real frustrating to me, and I told Gwyndell as much. The three-day rule was nonsense. I couldn't wait to get out of that hospital and be where I belonged, with the guys of Battery C. Gwyndell had a great idea.

"My legs still work okay," he said. "So why don't you hop on my back, and I'll carry you down the steps."

I thought that was a brilliant idea. I weighed about 210 pounds. Gwyndell was about 175 pounds, and he had severe back and head wounds. I was still hooked to a glass IV bottle, and so was he. What could possibly go wrong? I climbed on his back, holding both our bottles, and off we went down the outside fire-escape stairs, so no one would see us. Of course, Gwyndell slipped. We fell down the metal steps, the glass bottles shattered, and we crashed to the ground. Not the result we were hoping for. Gwyndell helped me back up the stairs and we limped to our beds, our tails between our legs, and with glass cuts all over us. We found a nurse and had to explain how we'd lost our IV bottles and why we probably needed to be checked. She wasn't pleased.

My legs may not have been working too good, but other parts of me still were. Because of my injuries, I needed a catheter to urinate. Being a twenty-one-year-old boy took precedence over being banged up. Each time some beautiful young nurse came to insert the catheter, I would get an erection, and catheters cannot be placed in an erect penis. One of the nurses thought of an effective solution. She'd evidently seen it all before. She took out a pencil from her pocket and whacked my man part into submission. It worked wonderfully—for her and for the catheter. From then on, she took to carrying a pencil behind her ear every time she came to see me. Just seeing it made me sweat, and she never had a problem with the catheter again. To this day, I am wary of pencils.

Part of our treatment was to walk to a therapy room in another wing of the hospital. Many of us had spinal injuries, so, leaning on each other, we helped each other as best we could. These hundred yards felt like such a long distance. We might as well have been walking to the end of the earth. The therapy room was empty except for a pool table. No chairs, no sofa, nothing. We all hurt from the long walk, but we couldn't sit. We had to stand and play pool. Boy, I'd never thought playing pool could be such a pain. We couldn't understand why we had to do it, and we all hated it. No one had thought of telling us that it helped strengthen our backs and improved our hand-eye coordination. The pool therapy must have worked, because today my coordination is still better than most.

All that standing and playing pool also helped my legs. Gwyndell and I went back to our plan, but we were a little more careful. For three days, he helped me down the stairs, and helped me walk to the arms room, where I cleaned a weapon. Then we walked toward the colonel's office. Just before we got to his window—where he would be able to see me—I stood by myself as tall and straight as I could and walked into his office. On the third and final day, I took General Westmoreland's note out of my pajamas pocket. The colonel already knew what was in it, but he held it up and read it slowly.

Being presented with the Medal of Honor by President Johnson, November 19, 1968.

Lyndon Baines Johnson Presidential Library

Grandpa John Helle in his WWI uniform.
Author's private collection

Mom and Dad—Bonnie and Bob Davis—in Savannah, Georgia, March 1945.
Author's private collection

Above: Mom, Dad, my baby sisters, Delilah and Charlene, and me.
Author's private collection

Left: My baby brother, Johnny Davis.
Author's private collection

My big brother Buddy Davis.
Author's private collection

Early morning at Tan Tru, after a hard night's work.   *Author's private collection*

My friend "Lurp," Sergeant
Johnston Dunlop.
Vietnam Veterans Memorial Fund

Playing the harmonica at Tan Tru.

Author's private collection

At the White House with (L to R) James Taylor, Gary Wetzel, Dwight Johnson, and Angelo Liteky, November 19, 1968.

U.S. Army photograph

After the Medal of Honor presentation ceremony. Grandpa Helle is shaking President Lyndon B. Johnson's hand, behind Mom, Dad, my sisters, and Peggy. *Lyndon Baines Johnson Presidential Library*

Left: Reuniting with Gwyndell Holloway in Manteca, California.
Author's private collection

Below: With Peggy Jo Martin at the White House, November 19, 1968.
Author's private collection

With my wife, Dixie Davis. *By Katie Kunzelman; author's private collection*

Still standing, still speaking, 2015. *By Karen Haworth; author's private collection*

"Private, you're making a poor decision," he said. "But I'll arrange transportation back to your unit."

I was finally clear to go. I mailed home the fléchettes and pieces of shrapnel that the doctors had extracted from my flesh. In the last few days of December 1967—six weeks or so after Cudgel—I boarded a helicopter and flew back to Tan Tru. The chopper dropped me off on the landing pad, about three hundred yards from the base camp. I was taped up real tight to keep my ribs and lower back in place, and I walked with crutches with IV bottles taped inside each one. Looking down, I took a few steps. By then the dry season had settled in, thank God, and the mud was gone. The tips of my crutches hit the dirt, sending up little clouds of dust with each step. *Puff. Puff. Puff.* I looked up. I'd barely made any progress. These three hundred yards kept stretching ahead of me. I took a few more steps. *Puff. Puff. Puff.* I looked up again: still a long way to go. I kept my head down and kept going. *Puff. Puff. Puff.* I was finally getting close, and I kept walking down the path leading to the gun area.

"Oh my God look!" someone yelled. "It's Dave!"

Several guys came running out. I was home.

"Man, we thought you were dead!" one of them said.

They carried me into the orderly tent. Of the guys who had been at Cudgel, only seven or so were left. Some had been wounded and were still recovering, and the rest had rotated home. New guys had arrived as replacements.

"Davis, what the hell am I going to do with you?" First Sergeant Verle Johnson said. My condition did not make me fit for much. "I guess I'll make you a cook."

So I was back in the kitchen again. The first few days, I didn't really cook though. For all the pool therapy I'd gone through in the hospital in Saigon, I still could not stand up for very long. I had to go to the infantry aid station every day so the medics could change my dressings and tape up my chest and back again. I started off slicing bread. That wasn't much, but it made me happy. I was doing something useful. At mealtime, the guys were starving. Those of us in the kitchen joked that they looked like a bunch of pigs running to the trough. So instead of ringing the triangle for meals, I squealed like a pig and watched everyone come running.

The new year started off with some good news. On January 1, 1968, I made corporal. There was a little ceremony to mark the occasion. I was real proud and also happy that this meant a bit more money every month. I was also presented with the Silver Star, a medal awarded for gallantry in action against an enemy of the United States. It was such an honor, but I still wasn't sure what exactly I'd done to deserve it. Then the first sergeant told me I was going on R & R to Sydney, Australia. I couldn't believe how lucky I was. Australia was the favorite R & R destination. In July 1967, the Australian government had added Sydney to the list of cities that US servicemen could visit for their leave, and the first contingent had been there in October. I remembered how fondly the Aussies I'd met in Bien Hoa had talked about Sydney and how I'd wished to see it someday. And there I was, about to head down under for a whole week.

There were a few snags: I did not have any money or civilian clothes. Since I was supposed to be retired from the Army, everything had been sent home. Without any money, I wasn't allowed to go. I'll never forget what the guys did for me then. They passed a hat around and collected three hundred dollars for me to go to Australia. It was a fortune back then. Over four decades later, their generosity still warms my heart. I also wasn't well enough yet to travel alone. Although the IV bottles were finally gone by the time I was due to travel, I was still on antibiotics, my back and ribs were still bandaged tightly, and my dressings needed to be changed. A medic was assigned to me out of our battery's headquarters in Tan An.

In January 1968, just a few days into the new year, we flew to Sydney. We stopped over in northern Australia to refuel. We all got out of the plane and headed to the airport bar, where rows of cold beers were already lined up on the counter, waiting for a planeload of thirsty GIs. I was still taking heavy meds and wasn't allowed to drink alcohol, so I had to settle for a Coke. I was probably the only one. The second leg of the trip was quiet: after all that good, strong beer, most of the guys dozed off—or lined up in front of the aircraft's only toilet.

Once in Sydney, we headed to the R & R center in Kings Cross. We were given neat little folders with brochures, maps, and information about the city and sat in a large hall for a pep talk about do's and don'ts that would keep us on the right side of local authorities. Public drunkenness and indecent language—as well as spitting—could set us back over eighty dollars in fines. Since I had to stay sober in my condition, there was no risk I would run into any trouble there. But the main message was to get rid of all narcotics and weapons we might have brought with us. Narcotics? Really? It sure was easy to procure anything in Vietnam, but I hadn't realized that anyone actually used, let alone traveled with drugs. Yet it was common enough that some guy in Sydney had to advise us to flush them down the toilet. I certainly didn't play with any of that stuff, and as far as I knew, neither did any of the guys at Tan Tru. With fire missions coming at all hours of day and night, we were always on call and far too busy and too frightened to be high. We couldn't afford to be wasted: we would have risked our own lives and the lives of others.

After the welcome briefing, the medic and I were sent to the Koala Alamain Motel on Ward Avenue. The Cross—as people in Sydney called it—was wild. It was all bright flashing neon lights, bars, and nightclubs with girls in bikinis dancing in cages. There were also a lot of working girls, their wares on display in shop windows. I was still a country boy through and through, and I'd never seen anything like it before. Kings Cross blew my mind. The medic would not let me go to bars, so we walked around the area in the evening to enjoy the scene, feel the vibe, and look at the girls. But we did go to the Whiskey-a-Go-Go, a famous nightclub that was cleaner than most and offered GIs free food on special nights. I was in too much pain to dance, but just talking to the beautiful young ladies there made me feel a whole lot better.

During the day, we walked around the city. We went to the zoo and rode the ferry. We went to the beach and watched surfers riding unbelievable waves. I had surfed a little when the family lived in California, and I was aching to go into the water. But my wounds were still bandaged, and I had to watch from a distance. The city's now famous opera house was still under construction, but its roof, shaped like white sails, already overlooked the harbor. It was all so beautiful. We did a lot of walking during our eight days in Sydney, which strengthened my legs a great deal.

People in Sydney were very friendly to us. Local associations organized get-togethers for GIs and arranged visits with Australian families in their homes. It was good to be around nice people who didn't want to kill me and spoke English. Some kind of English. I had a ball listening to their accent and turns of phrase. "They call bars 'pubs' and men 'blokes,'" I wrote in a letter home. "And if they call you a bloody bloke, you're in bad shape." I thought Australian girls were really something else. Most of them wore miniskirts and were very good looking. I met very nice young ladies. There was one in particular I grew real fond of. I first met Christine at the Whiskey-a-Go-Go. She'd come with her roommates to dance, and we ended up talking. They all lived on Bondi Beach, and they invited us to a party they were having the following day. Christine and I spent much of the next few days together, talking, holding hands, and dreaming big. I met her mom and dad. It was good to fall in love again. We wrote each other real often after I left, and her letters helped me a great deal through my last few weeks in Vietnam.

I can honestly say that these few days in Australia helped heal my body and my soul. After the nightmare of Cudgel and weeks fighting pain and fever in a hospital bed, I remembered how good it felt to be alive. Sydney looked something like San Francisco, and it was almost like being home. Feeling the sand under my feet, soaking up the sun, and strolling in the streets with normal people having a normal day, I had the time of my life—even though all I was allowed to drink was Coke.

After a week, I had to go back to Vietnam. It was real hard to leave Australia—and the nice girl I'd met there. I promised myself I'd visit again someday.

In Tan Tru, I went back to work in the kitchen. By then, I was well enough to cook. I was also well enough to drive to Tan An for the ration runs and to help with the guns whenever I could. The battery was still short of men, and many bunks were empty. There was a bunch of cherries—new guys fresh off the plane—and I tried to show them the ropes the way my gun sergeants had done with me when I was a rookie. I also spent a lot of those weeks talking to some of them late into the night. I thought it was very nice of them to stay up with me and listen to my stories. It was only years later that I discovered that First Sergeant Verle Johnson had told them that if I wanted to stay up all night and talk, it was their job to stay up with me and listen. They did their job well.

There were FNGs in the air as well. Not long after I came back to Tan Tru, a chopper brought us pads of ammunition. A few months earlier, during the rainy season, the pads were often dropped off into knee-high mud, and I was glad that now the ground was dry. But that day, the guys in the helicopter managed to drop one ammo pad bang onto one of the flares. I thought the whole pad was going to blow up—and all of us with it. I ran to the pallet, trying to dig underneath to knock the flare out and move the rounds away as quickly as I could. Luckily, nobody got hurt.

Besides my work in the kitchen, I was flying into and out of Tan Tru regularly. When I got out of the hospital in Saigon, I had once again met with General Westmoreland before heading back to Tan Tru. He'd introduced me to Colonel James Newman, one of the top officers involved in the Phoenix Program in Vietnam. The program, which would later come under a great deal of controversy, was administered by the Central Intelligence Agency and sought to destroy the political infrastructure of the Vietcong. I didn't know much about it. All I knew was that Westy asked Colonel Newman to take care of me. I believe he wanted to keep me busy but out of harm's way during the rest of my tour in Vietnam. I became a courier, delivering briefcases of documents to various parts of the country a couple times a week. I sometimes traveled with Colonel Newman, who was a keen harmonica player. We hit if off from the get-go.

Sometime after my trip to Australia, I broke into a high fever again and everything ached. I couldn't see straight, and I had fever sores all over my mouth. The medic thought that maybe I had malaria, and I was sent back to the Third Field Hospital in Saigon. The doctors then told me my kidneys and urinary tract were all infected again. After a few days on antibiotics, I was back on my feet and back in Tan Tru. "Well, I'm back among the living now," I wrote home. "Course, I knew I would be all along. It isn't like a Davis to give in just because the whole world fell on him." I didn't know yet that this was only the beginning of a long battle. These episodes of high fever were to plague me for years to come.

I also didn't realize I was just about to make another trip back to Saigon. On January 30—the day of the Vietnamese New Year known as Tet—and the days following, the enemy launched a massive offensive against US and South Vietnamese military installations and dozens of towns and cities across Vietnam. In Saigon, enemy sappers briefly broke into the grounds of the US Embassy. This was to be the largest and most daring offensive of the Vietnam War. We were all taken by surprise. The US military command had been aware of troop movements throughout the summer and fall of 1967—the operation we'd been part of at Fire Support Base Cudgel was in response to those movements. But they didn't believe the Vietcong and the North Vietnamese had the capability to launch such a big offensive. On top of that, the North Vietnamese had declared a cease-fire for the lunar New Year, and a lot of Arvin troops were on leave.

We were trucked to Saigon with several of our howitzers. I was not in great shape, but we were short of men, so I went along. We set up in the Phu Tho Racetrack in Cholon after it had been taken from the insurgents. The Cholon section of Saigon was mainly Chinese. Little bitty alleyways and narrow streets ran between a few major roads. There were lots of shops, bars, restaurants, and opium dens in that area. The racetrack, right in the center of Cholon, was in a strategic location between several major boulevards. It had been built by the French in the 1930s and was popular with the Chinese and Vietnamese—even though the races were said to be rigged. The Cholon district was fiercely contested. We fought from the racetrack for several days before being moved outside of Saigon. Then we went back to Tan Tru. "Suppose the TV has been telling you how it's been over here," I told Mom in a letter in early February. "Well, they know about the half of it." By the second week of February, the enemy had been pushed back in most places. This felt like a victory. But the Tet Offensive sent shockwaves that traveled thousands of miles to the United States and had lasting consequences that were not yet visible to us back in Vietnam.

By then, my time in Vietnam was running short. I was supposed to fly out in early March, one year after I'd landed. On my last evening in Tan Tru, the major in charge of Battery C invited those of us who were leaving the next day for a drink. He told us how proud he was of what we'd accomplished during our time with the battery, and we downed some whiskey in his office. It was hard to believe it was all over. I wasn't on guard that night, and there was no fire mission, but I couldn't sleep. I tossed and turned on my cot inside the gun bunker. The heat was stifling in there, and I couldn't stop thinking. I had survived for a year, I had made it, and I was so relieved. I was excited to go back home and be with Mom and Dad and my brothers and sisters again. At the same time, Tan Tru had become a kind of home. After the year I'd just had, how would it be like to be back home? I had a feeling something in me had changed.

After a while, I climbed up on top of the roof. Our gun bunkers were quite low, but at least there was some air and it was cooler up there. I lay on top of the sandbags looking at all the stars. There still wasn't much light in our camp, so they shone brightly, and the night sky was beautiful. I was still restless, so I got up and walked around the roof. Next thing I knew, I heard the rattle of machine-gun fire, and a few rounds came flying my way. What the hell was going on? I grabbed my M16 and jumped down real quick. I reckoned the enemy was coming at us and firing. Everybody got excited, and the phones started buzzing. It turned out that one of the guys on perimeter guard had seen me in the dark and took me for a bad guy. We sorted him out on the radio, and everything was okay in the end. I wasn't hit, but that gave me a good old scare. I almost got myself killed on my very last night—and by friendly fire.

The next day, I said my good-byes and drove to Tan An for the very last time. So much had happened on that road, but fortunately, everything was quiet that morning. No land mines, and no ambush. From Tan An, I flew to Long Binh and headed back to the Ninetieth Replacement again, this time to be processed out. Then, on March 5, I boarded my aircraft. I took one last look through the window. I would never see Vietnam again.

I was alive.

Over the years, I have often had to remind people that I am still alive. In most cases, it is not too surprising. Back in the days of no Internet or Facebook, those of us lucky enough to survive Vietnam lost track of one another. In any given unit, guys came in and out all the time. Cherries filled in for those who'd gotten killed or injured or had rotated out. Guys who'd served together and shared so much went back home and often didn't see one another again for years—if at all. There was no easy way to track people down. In any case, a lot of guys who were at Cudgel didn't think I'd made it, and I've lost count of the number of times I've found a brother at some veteran reunion who thought he'd just seen a ghost. I can't blame them: there are times I find it hard to believe that I'm still here. But my Vietnam comrades are not the only folks surprised to find me still breathing. Whenever I can, I go visit my old high school in Mooresville, Indiana. My portrait hangs on the wall, so each generation of students knows my face. Every time I go and walk down the corridors, there's always some kid walking past me who stops, looks at me, and, without fail, blurts out: "Dude, I thought you were dead!" *I get that a lot,* I'm always tempted to say, but I just smile. For most veterans, the Vietnam War feels like yesterday. But I guess for these youngsters, it is ancient history, and they can't imagine that anyone is still alive.

More surprising was when the good people at the White House thought I was roaming the afterlife. In 1996, I received a letter from the Clinton administration stating that a federal building in St. Louis, Missouri, was to be named after me. The year before, I'd received a phone call from my friend Don Kelby. Don and I had first met in

1984 at the dedication of the Three Servicemen statue honoring Vietnam veterans in Washington, DC. We'd become good friends, and we stayed in touch over the years. Don, who's also a Vietnam veteran, worked for the US Army Publications Distribution Center in St. Louis, Missouri, and he'd invited me to speak to the men and women who worked there, which I gladly did. A few years later, when the colonel in charge of the center wanted to name the building after someone who'd been in the Army, he asked Don for suggestions. Don asked me. I thanked him and said I'd be very honored.

Don got the ball rolling, approached local politicians, and worked through the mountain of paperwork. It is no small achievement to get a thing like that done. The publications center is a federal building, and naming or renaming federal buildings requires an act of Congress. I was very moved when I heard that people working at the publication center all supported the initiative and had petitioned the district representative to sponsor the bill. It was introduced in Congress in March 1996. It went through a maze of committees and votes, and was approved unanimously in the House and the Senate before being sent to the White House for signature in October.

There was only one snag: I wasn't aware that federal buildings are supposed to be named after dead people. There are very few exceptions, none of which apply to me. I guess nobody wants to have a federal building named after someone alive enough to misbehave later in life. I'm not exactly sure what happened, but the folks in Washington, DC, evidently believed I was dead. By the time they realized there'd been some snafu and I was very much alive, the situation got really confused. Eventually, somebody in Washington must have determined that it was too late to backpedal, and

★8★

WELCOME HOME, SOLDIER

On March 3, 1968, I landed at Travis Air Force Base near San Francisco. For the first time in a year, I walked on American soil. It felt good to be home, where everything was familiar and no one wanted to kill me. I was relieved I'd made it back alive and in one piece. I looked forward to putting Vietnam behind me and moving on. I looked forward to a life of no crouching in mud, no radio shifts or perimeter guard, and no fire missions or mortars coming my way. I still had eighteen months left in the military until the end of my three-year service, but right then, I couldn't think past the thirty-day leave I'd been granted before reporting to Fort Hood in Texas. Thirty days to be with Mom, Dad, and the family. Thirty days to be with my buddies and chase girls. Thirty days of freedom. Thirty days of sleeping. Boy, was I ready for that.

I wasn't prepared for what was coming.

For three days, I stood in line at Travis Air Force Base to get my shots and navigate the unbelievable amount of paperwork I had to sign to be allowed back into the United States. We were processed in groups of one hundred, and we walked or were bussed from one building to the next, wondering when we'd see the end of the red tape. On the third day, we lined up on a parking lot. We were given a choice: those of us who wanted to fly home on a military aircraft were instructed to go to one side, and those who preferred commercial airlines had to join the other line. Flying military cost nothing, but it meant going the long way round, being routed through Anchorage or Guam or wherever, before eventually heading to your home destination. That could take four or five days. Not one of us on that parking lot was willing to wait that long. We all fell in the commercial airline group prepared to pay for our transport back home. Then we were informed that, to fly commercial, we had to pack up our military uniforms. I was confused. I wanted to go home like my dad, my uncle, and my brothers had done before me, wearing my uniform. I had earned it. I had served my country, and I was proud of that. Why did I have to take off my uniform? That really upset me, but I could hardly question an order. I figured I could put it back on once I was at Mom and Dad's house.

Fresh out of Vietnam, none of us had much civilian clothing. We were instructed to get on a bus that took us to the base's commissary store to gear up. With the influx of troops coming home, the store didn't have much left to offer. They had suits, but none of us wanted to wear a suit. So we settled for the only other outfit available: Levi's 501 jeans, a Hanes white V-neck T-shirt with a breast pocket, and Red Ball Jets tennis shoes. I still remember paying $1.25 for those high-top canvas sneakers, which I thought was a good deal. And it was: I wore them for years, until they eventually fell apart.

We changed quickly, right there at the clothing rack of the commissary store. We folded our military clothes, carefully packed them in our duffel bags and fell in once again in the parking lot. The sergeant looked us over. We were in civilian clothing, as instructed. But every single one of us had on the same white T-shirt, blue jeans, and Red Ball Jets tennis shoes. We all sported military haircuts, and carried Army-issued duffel bags. The hundred of us looked exactly the same, and there was no mistaking where we were all coming from.

We finally got on the bus. On the way to San Francisco International Airport, we asked the sergeant who rode with us what was going on. Why couldn't we fly with our uniforms on? He explained that soldiers returning from Vietnam had run into a lot of problems at the San Francisco airport for several months. No matter what happened, he said, we were not to respond to provocations. He warned us that some of the people protesting the Vietnam War would go to great lengths to get us to respond in a negative manner, which would tarnish the image of the US military and then get all over the news. The bus fell into heavy silence.

I couldn't believe anyone would do anything like that. I knew from letters that I'd received from home that a lot of life had gone on without me while I was away, but I was expecting to find the same old America I'd left a year earlier. My only news source in Vietnam was the Army radio, which didn't give us an accurate picture of what was really happening stateside. I thought I knew what was going on, but in truth, I had no idea how bad it was. I'd read or heard about antiwar protests here and there, when some of the guys at Tan Tru received letters with newspaper clippings. I attributed those rumblings to a small fringe. The America I knew didn't shrink from its responsibilities, and helped people fighting for freedom around the world. The America I knew welcomed with open arms those who had fought in its name.

But America was changing. The Tet Offensive in January 1968 had stunned the American public. For months, people had been told that the war was being won. The enemy was suffering heavy casualties and other indicators being measured suggested progress. The official line had been that with more time and more men, victory was a sure thing. The scale and audacity of the Tet Offensive dispelled the notion of an exhausted enemy on the brink of defeat. Watching American soldiers in street battles and fighting back the enemy on the very grounds of the US Embassy in Saigon was a shock. Although the offensive ended up being a military setback for the North Vietnamese and the Vietcong, it planted the seeds of defeat in the American psyche. The national mood turned, and an increasing number of folks lost confidence: maybe victory wasn't imminent after all, and maybe the military and the government had been lying to the public. These folks were losing patience and were no longer sure what US troops were trying to accomplish in Southeast Asia.

At the same time, the draft was sending an ever-increasing number of young men to Vietnam, and more and more American families were losing their sons. In 1968, over half a million American troops were fighting in Vietnam—a big swell over the twenty-three thousand or so who were there four years before. Casualties peaked in 1968 as well: close to seventeen thousand American soldiers died in Vietnam that year. Protests against the war were gathering steam in the United States, particularly on university campuses. San Francisco, a breeding ground for the hippie movement, was a nexus of antiwar protests.

Sitting on the bus driving to the airport, I didn't know much about any of that yet. Three of us were flying to Indianapolis that day.

Once at the San Francisco airport, we went to the Eastern Air Lines counter and bought our tickets. As we walked toward our gate carrying our green duffel bags, a group of about twenty long-haired, flower-robed hippies saw us. One of them stepped in front of me, blocking my way. "Hey, dude," he slurred, "if you want to get to your aircraft, you have to run our gauntlet." I hadn't heard of a gauntlet since high school, when I played football in Manteca High in California. Our coach had incorporated the old military punishment into his teaching very effectively. Back then, after field practice, he used to line us up in two rows, each facing the other. "Assume the position and run the gauntlet!" he'd yell. Those who had made mistakes during practice had to walk off the field on their hands and feet between the two rows, butts up in the air, while their teammates whacked their rear ends. It became a big joke among us that whoever had the biggest, reddest handprints on their butts in the shower had learned the lesson the best. I ran that gauntlet and got my butt smacked many times. We were all good friends on the team, and it felt pretty harmless. Our coach used to say that those who didn't make mistakes now and then were not working hard enough. It worked real well too: we all listened to him with ears wide open, trying to do everything right so we wouldn't get our butts whacked.

So I knew what a gauntlet was, and so did the other two guys flying to Indianapolis with me. We backed up, looked at one another, and talked among ourselves. What should we do? That was such nonsense, and we didn't feel like doing what they said. But we remembered what the sergeant told us on the bus to the airport. We opted to go with the flow and do the best we could. I'd done it before. The greasy-haired kids standing in front of us were not my friends, so I suspected this wouldn't feel nearly as good-natured as football practice. But how bad could it be? At least I'd be on my two feet, and I assumed no one would be whacking my butt. Surely these guys were not going to severely hurt us. Weren't they supposed to stand for peace and love? They were just trying to humiliate us, but we'd just survived a year in Vietnam. This was small beer. We took a deep breath and turned to the hippie-in-chief who had stopped us.

"We won't run your gauntlet," I said. "We'll walk it." We didn't want to make waves, but we didn't want to give them the satisfaction to make us run either.

The band of hippies lined up in two rows, and the three of us fell in. We hadn't noticed that they had little brown lunch bags tucked under the cordons they wore as belts over their flowing robes and tunics. They pulled the paper bags out, put rubber gloves on, and reached into the bags. We started marching down the middle. As we walked past them, they rubbed some foul-smelling brown stuff all over our hair and faces. It smelled like dog poop. It probably was, or worse even. They tried to push it in our mouths and inside our ears. We kept our cool and kept walking.

I was in front, and right behind me was Wabash. I'd met him a few days before at Travis Air Force Base, and I didn't know his real name. He was from Wabash, Indiana, and that's what everybody called him. Before we reached the middle of the gauntlet, I heard him grunt. I looked over my shoulder: blood was running down his face. The peace-loving hippies with flowers in their hair and round rimless spectacles had just hit him. Just as I realized that a few of them had clubs in their hands, I got whacked on the head as well. I hadn't noticed those clubs earlier, and I don't know where they came from. They were heavy wooden canes, beautifully carved up. I was stunned. *Keep walking*, I thought. *Keep walking. One step at a time.* We kept going, and they kept clubbing us and rubbing dog poop all over us. I guess when they'd realized we were not going to respond to their provocation, they'd decided to try harder. There were dozens of people in that part of the airport, but nobody lifted a finger. Everybody just stood there and watched.

When we finally cleared the gauntlet, we kept walking to put some distance between us and our crap-shoveling friends. We stood as tall and proud as we possibly could, trying hard to hang on to our dignity. Then we dropped our duffel bags, looked at one another, and assessed the damage. Our faces and hair were smeared with blood and dog poop, and our brand-new white T-shirts were filthy. Blood was still running down Wabash's face and dripping from his chin. We realized later that it wasn't too serious: he had a cut by his hairline, and skull cuts always bleed a lot. But for a moment, I feared that he'd been injured real bad. Forget the sergeant's orders. How were we supposed to ignore that kind of assault? When he'd talked about "incidents," I'd never imagined that meant being buried in poop and whacked on the head.

Just as we turned to run back and beat these twenty or so hippies into a pulp, we saw a big TV news camera and two technicians. The red light was flashing, which meant the camera was rolling. They'd taped the whole gauntlet, and the camera was on us. We could either give them footage of crazed soldiers out of Vietnam beating up civilians, or we could swallow our rage and walk away. So we gave them a military salute, picked up our duffel bags, and walked away. As far as I know, the footage of what we'd just gone through never made the news.

When we got to our gate, we walked to the desk to hand in our tickets. The airline lady behind the desk told us the plane wasn't ready to leave for another hour. My heart sank. I didn't want to spend another minute in that godforsaken airport terminal. We looked real bad though, and she'd evidently seen it all before and knew exactly what had just happened. "But you gentlemen may board right away," she added. "Follow me."

This was long before the time of retractable jet bridges, and she walked us downstairs and across the tarmac to the steps going up to the aircraft. As soon as we boarded, everything changed. We'd bought the cheapest possible tickets, but the airline ladies on the plane sat us right up front in first class. They apologized profusely and were real nice to us. They took our filthy T-shirts, gave us water and towels, and helped us clean up. They put Band-Aids on our cuts, and gave us clean white shirts. I'm not sure where these shirts came from. They were probably the pilots' shirts, and we were sure glad to have them. Mine and Wabash's fit pretty well, but the third guy's shirt was big on him, and he had to roll up his sleeves. Funny, the things we remember. I don't recall his name, but for some reason, I haven't forgotten his shirtsleeves. Go figure.

Once we'd cleaned up and settled in our first class seats, they served us champagne. We had the aircraft to ourselves, with a crew of nice ladies taking real good care of us, treating us like kings. I wasn't sure what to make of all this. I'd never had champagne before or sat in first class. The bubbly and plush leather seats sure felt good, but they left a bittersweet taste in my mouth. I was still trying to wrap my head around what had happened in the terminal. I could not believe that people back home would punish us for having served. We'd done nothing wrong. The way I saw it, we'd gone to Vietnam to help the Vietnamese people be free. We'd done our job, and done it the very best we could. We had just made it out of hell, and we were treated like the devil himself. It made no sense. I'd spent a year in Vietnam counting the days until I could come back home, where I figured life would get a lot easier. Now I was finally back—only to find out there was another kind of war to be fought.

Wabash, who was sitting across the aisle from me, summed it all up real neatly. He raised his glass and said, "Yeah, life's a bitch, ain't it?" I laughed, picked up my champagne, and tried to put San Francisco out of my mind as I drank up.

The reception we got in Indianapolis was much different. Mom, Dad, and a good portion of the family were waiting with big signs. "Welcome home, son!" It was like I had landed in a different country. There were hugs, tears, and congratulations. Mom and Dad told me how much they loved me and how proud they were. This was all I needed. What had happened at San Francisco Airport had shaken me up pretty bad, but the welcome party in Indianapolis helped me push it to the back of my mind way better than all the champagne and first class in the world.

It wasn't until we were in the car driving home from the airport that Mom asked me about the two Band-Aids covering the cuts and bruises on my forehead. I told her about the gauntlet, without getting into too much depth. She shook her head in disbelief. Once we got home, I opened my duffel bag, undressed, and put on my uniform.

Robinson, Illinois, was a world apart from what I'd just experienced in San Francisco. There, in small-town America and among my family and friends, I experienced nothing but support, gratitude, and pride. The only protests and confrontations I saw were on television when we watched the news after supper. I had a thirty-day leave before having to report to Fort Hood, Texas, where I was to finish my enlistment. Although my health was a whole lot better than it had been a few months earlier, I still had episodes of high fever that no one could explain, and every part of my body ached. But for a whole year, I'd been dreaming about what I'd do when I got home, and I was not about to let pain get in my way.

It was March, so none of the hunting seasons were open, but fishing was just starting to get good. I didn't have many acquaintances in Robinson—Mom and Dad had moved there when I was in Vietnam—so I drove back to Waverly, Indiana, to visit my old friends. We went to bars, but I quickly found out that drinking too much made me feel a lot worse, so I was careful. Some friends and I visited a big local dance hall a couple times. I played a lot of guitar. I also encouraged my sisters, Delilah and Charlene, to introduce me to some of their friends. Shortly after I'd gotten back to Mom and Dad's home, I'd called Christine, the nice girl I'd met during my R & R in Sydney. We talked for a bit, and we decided to move on with our lives separately. By then, I couldn't foresee having the money to fly to Australia or to fly Christine to the United States. It was a sad decision, but it was the fair thing to do.

Delilah and Charlene were still in school, and when they got off the bus one evening, I saw a young lady waving at the window. She had the flip hairstyle so popular in the 1960s, short with the tips curling up. She was real pretty.

"Who's the girl sitting in the third seat by the window?" I asked Charlene.

"That's Peggy Jo Martin," Charlene said. "She's a real nice girl. You need to meet her."

Delilah and Charlene arranged for me to meet Peggy. I took all three girls to a "sock hop." A sock hop was a dance in the school gym, and everybody had to take their shoes off so the basketball court wouldn't get all scratched up. Everybody's shoes were lined up against the wall, and we danced on the polished gym floor in our socks. Peggy and I danced together a lot that evening. She was a sweet and innocent seventeen-year-old, with her white blouse and plaid skirt and tall white socks. After my year in Vietnam, sweet and innocent was exactly what I needed. She was also real smart, and I quickly knew she was a very special girl.

We started dating, and we fell in love. I would pick her up after school and drive her home. Her mama was always waiting by the door, making sure we'd arrive within the twenty minutes it took to drive straight from Robinson, with no unscheduled stops or detours. I can still hear Peggy's dad, a Korean War veteran: "I remember coming back from the war, son," he told me. "I know what you're after." But I got to know her mom and dad better, and then I met her grandmas and grandpas. Everyone was real nice to me.

Before I knew it, the thirty days were over. With a heavy heart, I said good-bye to Peggy. Once I was stationed at Fort Hood, Texas, we wrote. Every time I was able to spend a day or two at home, I would pick her up, and we'd go out on a date. On July 4, I went to her parents' house for a family gathering and asked her to marry me.

"I guess," she first said.

That wasn't the kind of reaction I'd expected. "What do you mean, you guess?"

"I mean I will! Of course I will!"

We went to the jewelry store and got a ring, and I slipped it on her finger. We had to wait for a few months though. Her daddy would not let her marry before she turned eighteen. Her birthday was on December 27, 1968. We got married that very same day at the Methodist church in Robinson, Illinois, with both our families celebrating with us. I had a week's leave, and we went to Texas for our honeymoon. She moved to Fort Hood with me.

I'd rented a house outside the military base, and we tried to make it our home. I usually came home from the base at around five p.m., and Peggy did her best to have something ready for me. Peggy grew up as one of four girls, but the family house had a one-butt kitchen, and her mama never taught any of them how to cook. Peggy had many talents—she was a wonderful singer and painter—but cooking wasn't one of them. Her mama sent her recipes, but Peggy didn't know the first thing about cooking. I am not a fussy eater; I can eat almost anything. But in those early days of our marriage, I admit there were many home-cooked dinners that I couldn't stomach. But I would have starved before I'd hurt her feelings. "Thank you so much, honey," I'd say after a few bites. "I'm just not that hungry tonight." I sure didn't put on any extra pounds in those first few months.

In Fort Hood, I made sergeant and became a section chief. I was in charge of a howitzer and was teaching new recruits to operate the artillery gun. Early on, Lieutenant-General Beverly Powell—the commanding officer of Fort Hood—asked me if I would go talk to his kid's high school. He knew I'd been put in for a Medal of Honor, and I can't think of any other reason he asked me. I'd never spoken in front of any audience before, and I wasn't sure I could do it right. But he was the commander in charge. "Of course, sir," I said. I went to the neighboring high school and talked to the kids there. I guess it went well, because next thing I knew, General Powell asked me to go to his daughter's grammar school. So he set that up, and off I went. Then other officers and sergeants asked me to do the same. Before too long, I was speaking in schools all around Fort Hood. I really enjoyed it. I've always liked hanging out with kids and speaking to them, and they were asking excellent questions. "Why is my daddy in Vietnam?" "What are we doing there?" Those were tough questions, but they were real questions. Most of these kids were too young to have any political agenda. They were looking for answers, and they had a genuine interest in what I had to say.

While I was in Fort Hood, I met General Westmoreland again. I had seen him several times in Vietnam before I finished my tour, both in the hospital and out. After he'd arranged for me to return to my unit and introduced me to General Newman, he had checked up on me several times. I looked up to him, and I felt he'd taken me under his wing. In June 1968, General Creighton Abrams had been put in charge of US military operations in Vietnam, and Westy came back to the United States to serve as the Army's chief of staff. In that capacity, he started touring university campuses, keen to improve perceptions of the military and of the Vietnam War. He came to Fort Hood, and he knew I'd been speaking at local schools. Maybe he thought that college kids would be more receptive to someone their own age. Maybe he thought it would be a good education and experience for me. In any case, as 1968 was coming to a close, he asked me to come along with him on some of his visits. His office would call my commander, and I was sent to speak wherever he was. I got to know Westy a great deal more, and I came to consider him something of a father figure. Soldiering through fever spikes and unexplained pains, I ended up traveling a great deal all across the United States and no longer spent much time at Fort Hood.

My job was to deliver a written speech on the greatness of the US military and its involvement in Vietnam prepared by the Pentagon. No more, no less. It was one page long, basically promoting the values of the Army and the US government. In 1968 and 1969, many university campuses were hotbeds of antiwar sentiment, and this was a message many college students were not prepared to hear. The first time I realized what I was in for was at Texas A&M University in College Station, Texas. General Westmoreland and I were scheduled to speak as part of a bigger event that also involved local politicians. A group of protesters marched into the hall where we were speaking and interrupted the function, screaming and waving big placards. It was mayhem. After my visits to high schools around the base, which had gone really well, that was a big shock.

Wherever we went, General Westmoreland was typically first received with great pomp, but whenever protesters managed to slip in, they treated him like a war criminal. It bothered him greatly. He'd shake his head, but he brushed it off and kept going. He'd learned to not let it get to him. To me, on the other hand, this was new, and none of my training, military or otherwise, had prepared me for that. Westy instructed me to stick to my speech and to not respond to provocations. It felt like San Francisco all over again. Sometimes, I managed to do my job without incident. But most of the time, these campus visits felt like walking the gauntlet all over again.

When I was onstage, I managed to keep it together. But back in my hotel room, I often wanted to scream and punch the walls. I usually had a few days between speaking duties, and I went home as often as I could when en route to my next engagement. I would talk to local grammar schools or high schools around Mom and Dad's home as well, and I was treated real well. But I couldn't crack the big campuses in big cities. The country was at war with itself, and all the booing and yelling and name-calling was taking a real big toll on me. My poor health was not making it any easier, and at times while I was on the road, I could barely stand or see straight through the fever.

In some ways, the battle I found myself fighting back home was more challenging than the year I'd just spent in Vietnam: I'd been trained to be a soldier, but I had no idea how to be a politician or a spokesman—or whatever it was I was now supposed to be.

On one of my short visits home, Mom and I were driving home from Indianapolis International Airport. I was feeling particularly discouraged, and I told her that I didn't know if I could go on doing this. It was my job, and I wanted to do it the best I could, but I didn't know what to tell all those hostile young men and women. I didn't even know how to talk to them. It was as if we came from different universes and didn't speak the same language. She listened to me and was silent for a moment. "Well, son," she finally said, "all you have to do is just open up your heart and let them look in." I've carried her words with me for over forty-five years and done my very best to follow her advice.

This is not to say it was easy. In June 1969, I traveled to the University of California, Berkeley. By then, I often traveled by myself, and Westy wasn't there. I usually spoke to small crowds, but there was a big rally there that day, with hundreds of people. The university was very radical, and in May, there had been violent confrontations between protesters and the authorities over a vacant lot near the campus. Student activists and local residents had decided to turn the derelict lot, which was university property, into a park. On May 15, the governor of California, Ronald Reagan, sent in the police to clear everybody from the park and fence it off. A rally that started on campus moved toward the park, and thousands of protesters clashed with the police. Governor Reagan declared a state of emergency and sent in the National Guard.

In June, the violent confrontation was still fresh in people's minds. When General Westmoreland told me I was to go speak at Berkeley, I was skeptical. They'd never let me speak there in a million years, I told him. He explained that they had to, because they received government funding. I read and reread the speech that had been prepared for me. It was promoting the values of the US Army and justifying our military involvement in Vietnam and the government's position. *Oh boy*, I thought. *This is not going to go down well.* But General Westmoreland had asked me to go. If he'd asked me to jump off the Empire State Building, I would have. So I boarded a military plane and flew to San Francisco.

The rally I was supposed to address was held in a big common with trees, some kind of park. A stage had been set up. Bands were playing, and speakers took the stage between music numbers. I was the only one speaking on behalf of the military. The organizers made it very clear to me that they were not at all happy to have me there, and I was not officially part of the program. I was behind the stage, waiting for my turn to speak, when I heard Country Joe and the Fish—a big protest rock band back then—sing their "I-Feel-Like-I'm-Fixin'-to-Die Rag":

> *And it's one, two, three, what are we fighting for?*
> *Don't ask me I don't give a damn*
> *Next stop is Vietnam.*
> *And it's five, six, seven, open up the pearly gates,*
> *Well there ain't no time to wonder why,*
> *Whoopie! We're all gonna die!**

---

*Words and music by Joe McDonald, Copyright © Alkatraz Corner Music Co, 1965, renewed 1993.

Perfect, I thought. How was I to take the stage in my dress uniform and read my speech after *that*? I took a deep breath and got ready to do my job. I went onstage, stepped out front by the microphone, and took out my one-page speech. The crowd started booing before I even opened my mouth. When I started reading, slowly and clearly, a deluge of projectiles rained down on me. Garbage, beer bottles, cans, you name it. As I stood there, reading and trying to avoid all the debris coming my way, I could hear the crowd screaming and yelling. "Drug-smoking baby killer! Mother rapist!" There were hundreds and hundreds of people in front of me, and my very presence seemed to enrage them. They didn't know anything about me, but they hated me. It only took a few minutes for me to read my piece, but I barely managed to finish. By the time I walked out, there was trash all over the stage.

I was seriously shaken. I'd had it rough on many campuses, but it had never been that bad. It wasn't the cans and bottles bouncing off me that hurt the most. Those bruises healed quickly. But the names they called me, and the memory of all those faces contorted by anger and hate are still with me. I remember it as if it were yesterday. I never smoked drugs. I never raped anyone. I never killed any babies. The reason I went to Vietnam was to help the Vietnamese people be free, and freedom is always worth fighting for.

As I went down the few steps taking me backstage, I saw a group of girls wearing long, loose robes and flowers in their hair running around the stage toward me. "Sergeant Davis! Sergeant Davis!" they called. My blood went from icy cold to a full boil. I thought they were going to throw more stuff at me or scream at me or club me. I was already seriously aggravated, and I'd already had more than enough for one day. All I wanted to do was jump on all those kids in the crowd that had thrown stuff at me and called me names, choke them, and tell them to wake up. But I managed to calm down and tried to think of a proper response. I would listen calmly to what the ladies had to say, keep my cool, and move on.

They stopped by the small stairwell, panting. "Sergeant Davis," one of them said.

I braced myself. "Yes, ma'am?"

"We just want you to know that we're here to protest the war," she continued, "but not the warrior."

It was so astounding that at first I thought I hadn't heard right. "Pardon me, ma'am?"

"We," she said, pointing to the other eight or nine girls who were with her, "want you to know that we're protesting the war, but not the warrior."

I was speechless. This was the best thing I'd heard in all my university tours, and it helped salve my wounds that day. I have never forgotten it. It's okay to protest the war. That's what democracy and free speech are all about. War is about politics, and politics should be debated. But it's never okay to take it out on the warriors who fight it. Soldiers only do their job, willingly putting their lives on the line for their country, their countrymen, and the comrades who fight beside them.

I learned plenty other lessons during those months touring universities. Up to that point, my first instinct was to grab people by the throat and beat the daylight out of them. I learned to control my anger. I learned to listen to other people's opinions, even though I didn't share them. I learned to be understanding.

Difficult as it was, speaking to young men and women who fiercely opposed the war was not the most trying experience. Some wounds cut much deeper still. Sometime during my eighteen months at Fort Hood, I attended an event at a veterans organization in neighboring Copperas Cove. I was standing there, minding my own business, when a World War II veteran approached me. We started talking. When he found out I had recently returned from Vietnam, he poked a finger into my chest. "Vietnam?" he sneered. "Let me tell you about *real* war, son." Blood drained from my face. I just stood there, my heart silently breaking. The *real* war? The war in Vietnam felt very real to me. I had real injuries to prove it. I had seen men die for real. I didn't know what to say. I'd been taught as a kid that all veterans deserved to be honored, and I believed that I had earned the same respect. It was one thing to have a bunch of hippies spit on me and everything that I stood for. But another veteran, someone I looked up to, belittling my service? That shattered me. It also knocked my respect for him down a few notches.

Over the fifteen years that followed, I lost count of how many times I was poked in the chest by a World War II or World War I or Korean War veteran keen to educate me about the *real* war. I can't fully make sense of it. I can only guess that, in their eyes, they'd brought victories home, and we didn't. Many of them had served for several years, and I suppose the twelve months most Vietnam veterans spent risking their lives on the other side of the world didn't tally up in their ledger. Not all veterans from earlier wars felt that way. But it only takes one or two "real war" chest pokers in any given gathering to sink a spirit.

Most Vietnam veterans I know had the same experience back then. During the 1970s and part of the 1980s, many of my Vietnam brothers didn't feel welcome, even among other veterans. The isolation and shame were crushing. We'd fought for our country, and our country had turned its back on us.

On November 9, 1982, I traveled to Washington, DC. I was on sick leave from work, recovering from another surgery for my legs, but nothing could have kept me from heading to the nation's capital that day. I arrived late at night, and after I checked into my hotel in Arlington, I put on my military uniform and drove to the Lincoln Memorial. It was maybe two in the morning by then, and it was dark and eerily silent. I walked past the memorial toward the Washington Monument and turned left. There, in a wooded area, I walked along a brand-new shiny black wall. Rows and rows of names were carved into the stone. Some fifty-eight thousand names. I first searched for the names of those who had died the night of November 18, 1967. I found them on panel 30E. Their names all stood next to one another in the black granite, just like these men had stood together at Fire Base Cudgel. Then I walked a bit farther and stopped in front of panel 50E near the end of the V-shaped structure, searching for a name. On the thirteenth line from the top, I found it.

Johnston Dunlop.

I reached for the harmonica tucked in my breast pocket. I had brought my old harp, the one Mom had sent me in Vietnam. Seeing Johnston's name etched on that black wall right in front of me, I went back to all those times I'd played for Johnston sitting in foxholes all those years before. With my eyes closed and a lump in my throat, I played "Shenandoah" for my Vietnam brother again, so he could rest one more time. There were a few people around, but I figured they wouldn't mind. By the time I was done and I'd opened my eyes, dozens of men stood around me in the dark, silent. At first, I thought they were the ghosts of the dead and missing soldiers whose names were etched on the wall, and for a few seconds, I was concerned that I'd completely gone off my rocker. But all these men were alive and breathing. They were Vietnam veterans who'd come to visit their fallen brothers for the first time. They'd been a bit farther out, and came down when they'd heard the harp. Like me, they'd come to touch the names of their brothers at night, so they could cry in the privacy of darkness. They'd come in the tens of thousands from all over the United States. They'd come by car, by bus, or by plane. Some even came on foot, walking hundreds of miles to be there. Some had spent their last dollars to attend the event. Like me, they had traveled to Washington, DC, to inaugurate the Vietnam Veterans Memorial a few days later.

It had been a long time coming. Like most of my Vietnam brothers, I had too often been shunned and screamed at and chest-poked for fifteen years. I felt that the way we'd been treated had actually grown worse over the 1970s. Every time I attended some event, there would be protesters. I learned to stay calm and give them a big old military salute. Only a year or two before my trip to Washington, DC, I'd sat with Jan Scruggs on a park bench in Los Angeles, and things were looking bleak. Jan, a wounded and decorated Vietnam veteran, had come up with the idea of building a memorial to honor all those who had served in Vietnam, and to heal the wounds that the war had inflicted upon America. He'd put in his own money and was working real hard to make it happen. His efforts were being met with a lot of resistance, there were many complications, and raising the money to build the memorial was tough. That day in Los

Angeles, Jan was disheartened. I had just attended one of his big fund-raisers, which had not produced the results he was hoping for. We sat on that bench in a little park just outside the hotel, sharing a bottle of wine. But Jan didn't quit trying. He didn't quit when some people objected to the memorial design or its architect—a twenty-one-year-old Chinese-American lady from Ohio—and tried real hard to sink the project. When the secretary of the Interior blocked it, Jan kept going. He eventually gathered over $8 million in private contributions and got it built.

Over the days before the dedication, Washington, DC, was swarming with Vietnam veterans. There were receptions and emotional reunions. The wall was open to the public all week ahead of the big day. For three days, a round-the-clock vigil was held at the Washington National Cathedral, where volunteers working in shifts of thirty minutes read the names carved on the memorial. When someone asked me if I wanted to read, I gladly accepted. In the chapel adorned with only two large candles and red roses, I stood in front of rows of people—mothers and fathers, brothers and sisters, and comrades who'd fought side by side. They'd all come to hear a name. With a list on a sheet of paper in my hand, I started reading slowly. Each name a young man fallen for his country, each name a life ended much too soon, each name now spoken out loud for all to hear and honor. Each name saying, "I once lived. I was here. I gave my life for you." These names would now be known and remembered, not just by loved ones, but by the whole nation. A nation that, in its struggle to come to grips with a war that had scorched its soul, had tried to forget them and all they had sacrificed. As I kept reading, a tidal wave of grief washed over me. I broke down and fell to one knee. I managed to keep reading, but I couldn't get up. Someone helped me back to my feet, and it took all I had to keep going until I'd spoken the very last name.

On November 13, 1982, one hundred fifty thousand people converged on the Mall. Thousands of Vietnam veterans finally marched down Constitution Avenue toward their memorial. Some of us had our uniforms on, some wore civilian clothing. Some of us walked—alone or with our arms locked with one another—and some could only move in wheelchairs. There were flags and music and speeches about healing. On that cold, cloudy Saturday, thousands of us touched the names of our brothers on the Wall. We laughed, we cried, and we hugged, hanging on to one another like rafts. "Welcome home," we kept telling each other. "Welcome home."

It took another four years before we got our proper Welcome Home parade. Since no one had thrown one for us—and it looked like no one was going to—a group of Vietnam veterans organized it themselves. On June 13, 1986—eleven years after the Vietnam War ended—two hundred thousand Vietnam veterans marched on the streets of Chicago. General Westmoreland was our grand marshal. We marched under a rain of confetti and ticker tape, as more than half a million men, women, and children cheered and waved flags on the sidewalks. Veterans came from all over America—and beyond. I realized that day how many Vietnam brothers I'd gotten to know since the war. I could hardly take a step without shaking somebody's hand or giving a hug. During the parade, I saw several Australian veterans, wearing their uniform and their slouchy hats. I went to talk to them, and we became friendly. It felt real good to hear that accent again. I told them about the Aussies who'd shared many beers with me in Bien Hoa and the others I'd met when I was with the Second/Fourth Artillery. I told them about my R & R in Sydney. The following year, they would invite me to help beat the drum for their own Welcome Home march in Sydney.

In Chicago, we started in Milton Lee Olive Park and ended in Grant Park—once the site of many antiwar protests. The route was less than three miles, but the parade lasted for nearly five hours. A lot of wounds started healing on that day. I was overwhelmed by conflicting emotions. It had been eighteen years since I'd come home from Vietnam. I thought about the gauntlet I'd walked in San Francisco's airport all those years before. I remembered all those times I was booed and scorned on college campuses. I felt all those fingers poking my chest, and heard all those men telling me again and again about the "real" war. But now, the huge crowds that welcomed us in Chicago brought me to tears. All these people had come to celebrate us and our service. After eighteen years, the tide had turned. I thought about the young girls who spoke to me at Berkeley. Finally, the warriors were no longer being blamed for the war.

I outlasted them, the protesters and naysayers, and held on to my beliefs. My homecoming from Vietnam contributed greatly to who I am today. It made me more determined to tell my truth. I never quit traveling to colleges and universities to speak about honor, duty, and country. But now, students want to hear what I have to say. And once in a while, I get a chance to marvel at the long road we have all traveled. In 2009, I addressed middle-school students in Illinois and answered questions about my return from Vietnam. After we finished, one of the teachers walked up to me and took off his necklace. It was a silver peace symbol hanging on a chain. He put it in my palm, closed my hand around it, and said, "I've been wearing this for forty years.

I don't need it anymore. I am so sorry: I was one of those protesters." Sometimes it takes forty years for old wounds to heal.

In retrospect, it was a poor political decision to go to war in Vietnam. Just as it has been in Iraq or Afghanistan today. Don't send kids to die in wars you can't win. But hindsight is a luxury we don't have when tough choices have to be made. Somewhere along the way, America's purpose in Vietnam got muddled and lost. But my reasons for going to war were pure, and I am proud to have served in Vietnam. In spite of everything, all the insults and the gauntlets, I have always been proud of my service, and I always will be. I had a job to do and I did it the best way I knew how. Freedom is always worth fighting for. The rest is politics and is of little concern to me.

Every time I meet a Vietnam brother—or sister—today, I give them a big old hug, and I still say it: welcome home. Until we started saying it to each other as we marched toward the Vietnam Veterans Memorial, we didn't even know what it meant to us. We'd never been welcomed home, so we didn't comprehend what it would do to our hearts and to our souls. But when we finally did welcome each other home, it felt so good. A weight was lifted from our hearts. There was no need to hide. We could stand tall and be proud again, and find comfort knowing that our service and the price we paid was being acknowledged. So I still say it to the brothers I know, and I say it every time I meet one of those men with a thousand-yard stare. They don't have to tell me that they have served in Vietnam. I can feel it. I cannot describe it, but within a few minutes, there is just something that rings in my soul, a silent recognition. Part of it is a look in their eyes that I've come to rec-ognize. So many Vietnam veterans, burdened by some memory they can't shake off, have that thousand-yard stare, looking far off in the distance. Part of them is still someplace else.

Welcome home. We still need to hear it. Only ten years ago or so, Steve Rogers, one of my Tan Tru brothers, was out of work and looking for a job. He sent his resumé to a headhunter. Among his accomplishments, he listed that he'd been a section chief in Vietnam. It meant that when Steve was only twenty years old, he'd made gun sergeant and was in charge of a howitzer crew of several men, making life-and-death decisions every day. The recruiter called him up. "Please remove that," he said. "That says *drugs* to anyone reading your resumé." In spite of all the memorials and parades, our work is not done.

I also say it to a new generation of veterans. I now see that same thousand-yard stare in the eyes of so many of these kids who are coming back from Iraq or Afghanistan. Those of us who served in Vietnam have sworn that we'll never let other veterans be treated like we were when we came back. No one deserves it. Once again, a new generation of kids has gone to fight wars far away from home. Once again, America has been divided about our military involvement. Once again, there are questions about our purpose and our mission, and about what victory or defeat looks like. But this time, we as a nation have to honor the young men and women who serve and put their lives on the line. Every chance I have, I go speak to our new veterans. I speak to them in hospitals, at military bases, or at veterans events. I welcome these kids back home, tell them they make us proud, and thank them for their service.

It is part of my job as a veteran and as a human being. But it is also part of my responsibility as the guardian of a shiny medal hanging on a light blue ribbon.

★ 9 ★

THE MEDAL

In early November 1968—a day or two after my twenty-second birthday—I was at Fort Hood, working on my howitzer, when one of the sergeants came by and said the captain wanted to see me. I got into a jeep and drove over to the squad building. Once there, all the captain said was that the battalion colonel wanted to talk to me. I walked up to Lieutenant Colonel James O. Day's office and knocked.

"Come in, Sergeant Davis."

I walked in and saluted.

"Sergeant, I have some news," he said. "I want to inform you that your Congressional Medal of Honor citation was signed by the President of the United States today."

The enormity of the news just about knocked me over. I knew that the proposed citation had been traveling through the various military echelons and had been sent to Congress. But I'd always maintained a great deal of disbelief that it would go through and that I would ever be awarded the medal. Somewhere along the way, someone would wake up and realize I had done nothing special.

I couldn't have imagined a better birthday gift. "Thank you, Colonel," I managed to blurt out.

"Congratulations, Sergeant Davis. You are expected at the White House on November 19."

A couple of weeks later, I traveled to Washington, DC. Mom, Dad, Delilah, Charlene, Johnny, and Grandpa Helle also made the trip, and so did Peggy Jo. I don't specifically remember why my big brother Darrell was not there. I imagine he couldn't get off work. I'd also invited Sergeant Quinones, who'd pushed me so much during basic training. After a year in Vietnam, I'd come to appreciate how his tough instruction had prepared me well for what was to come and had saved my butt over there.

On November 19—one year and one day after the battle at Cudgel—I put on my uniform and headed for the White House. My stomach was in knots and my throat was dry. Never in my life had I ever imagined that I, a country boy from the Midwest, would one day meet the president of the United States, let alone receive a Medal of Honor. President Lyndon Johnson was in the last months of his presidency. Earlier that month, America had elected its next president. President Johnson had declined to run for a second term, and Vice President Hubert Humphrey had carried the Democratic ticket but lost. Richard Nixon was to be inaugurated in January.

Before the ceremony, I briefly met the other four guys who were also receiving the Medal of Honor that day. I was in awesome company. Gary Wetzel was a door gunner from Wisconsin who did two tours in Vietnam. When his helicopter was shot down in a rice paddy a few days before he was supposed to go home, Gary kept operating his machine gun until he neutralized the enemy's automatic fire. He then helped his fellow crewmen to safety while he himself was bleeding profusely, and he had sustained terrible injuries to his chest, legs, and both arms—one of which couldn't be saved. Angelo Liteky, from Fort Hamilton in New York, was a chaplain in an infantry company that came under fire from a much larger enemy force during a search-and-destroy operation. Ignoring his own injuries, he moved toward enemy fire to administer last rites to the dying and to evacuate the wounded. He carried over twenty men to safety and kept encouraging his men until the bad guys withdrew. Dwight Johnson was a tank driver from Detroit, Michigan, who never gave up fighting to push back enemy forces that had ambushed his platoon. When his tank was immobilized, he came out and faced heavy fire armed with only a pistol. He inflicted severe damage firing whatever machine gun he found—and, when he ran out of ammunition, engaging in close combat—all while saving an injured crewman. James Taylor, a California native, was a captain in the cavalry who under heavy fire pulled several of his wounded men from burning vehicles, carried them to safety, and faced mortar rounds to direct Dustoff helicopters to pick up the wounded. Each one of us was the first living Medal of Honor recipient in our specific military field.

We were all nervous walking on the plush carpets past portraits of former presidents hanging on the walls. We'd been well trained to be soldiers, but we had not received any instruction on how to behave at the White House and visit with the president. Before the ceremony, we were directed to a little room next to the big East Room, where the medals would be presented. An aide went over protocol with us. How we should address the president, how we should look straight into his eyes, the do's and don'ts, all these things we didn't know. Then President Lyndon Johnson came in and sat down with us. Being the man that he was, he talked to each of us, trying to put us at ease, and found something personal to say to all five of us. It didn't take him long to figure out I was a country boy, because within two minutes, he and I were talking about catching catfish and eating crawdads. He knew everything about it and made me feel like I fit right in. By the end of our sit-down with President Johnson, the five of us were feeling a whole lot better.

Then we moved to the big East Room for the ceremony. Before our families and other guests, President Johnson, with General Westmoreland standing to his left, spoke. To be honest, I was too nervous to hear a single word he said. Mom later told me that my legs were shaking so badly that she could see my knees knocking. Then each of us stood before him as our citations were being read. I was third in line. I stood as tall as I could, and looked him straight in the eye as I'd been instructed, barely daring to blink. I remembered watching Roger Donlon on TV at the Big M bowling alley: it had only been three years, but it felt like a lifetime. As my citation was being read, memories of Fire Support Base Cudgel came rushing back. The fire, the explosions, the mortars. The waves of enemy soldiers and the drowning fear. Gwyndell waving his hat across the canal. But most of all, the screams. My mind went to all the men who'd fought so hard that night, and to those who didn't come back. Without them, I wouldn't be here. They had paid the ultimate price. They deserved that medal, not me. It was an intense moment, and I swallowed hard to push back tears. Then President Johnson placed the blue ribbon of the Medal of Honor around my neck and shook my hand.

The president said another few words to close the ceremony. "I want to remind you of what another president said upon another occasion. That I'd rather be able to have that blue band around my neck with a Congressional Medal of Honor than to be the President of the United States. . . . It goes to a very select and special group of men, and you are a part of that group. So to you and your families and on behalf of all the people of this country and the free world, whom you have sought to protect, and whose freedom you have tried to ensure, I say we thank you and we are grateful to you. . . . I hope and I believe that your efforts will not have been in vain, and as long as Americans love their liberties and revere their freedom, they'll owe a very special debt to you men who wear that blue ribbon." President Johnson's words felt like a cool, healing balm on a festering sore. I was a long way from gauntlets and booing crowds. I realized there and then how much I had longed to hear a simple thank-you. I experienced firsthand the power of gratitude, and it has never left me. I've been striving to pass it on to others ever since.

Years later, I watched footage that looked curiously similar to the moment when I had been presented with the Medal of Honor. The year was 1994, and I was at the movies with Peggy. I watched as President Johnson hooked a Medal of Honor around my neck. Except it wasn't me on the big screen, but Tom Hanks. The movie was *Forrest Gump*, and, as I sat watching, I realized for the very first time that a few other details had been borrowed from my own life. I was astonished.

Shortly after the ceremony at the White House in November 1969, Mom, Dad, and the rest of the family went home. Dad had not been feeling well in Washington, DC. He'd had chest pains and couldn't breathe well. An Army doctor checked him out but released him. After he got home, his heartbeat was all over the place, and he went to see his doctor. His doctor said he'd probably had a mild heart attack. His job at the asbestos mine back in California had also damaged his lungs. He'd been very lucky to make it back to Illinois. The news must have given Dad a scare. Maybe he realized he was not going to live forever and that there were a few things that needed fixing. He hadn't talked to my older brother Buddy in years after they'd fallen out. He told me he wanted to see him. The trouble was, we had no idea where Buddy was. None of us had seen him since we'd left California in the summer of 1965. He'd called Mom a couple times just to say he was okay, but he always refused to give an address or a phone number. I'd been real worried about Buddy, wondering where he was, and if he even had a roof over his head. I told Dad I would try to find him.

There wasn't much I could do right away. Right after the ceremony at the White House, I headed to New York with three of my fellow recipients. We'd been invited to appear on *The Ed Sullivan Show*. This was almost as intimidating as the White House. The CBS TV show—which back then hosted all the big names in music and film—had been a popular entertainment number since the 1950s, and Ed Sullivan was a real big star. So was singer Nancy Wilson. She sang "Face It Girl, It's Over" on the show that night. Dwight Johnson had been a fan for a long time, and he was so taken with her that he could hardly stand. Ed Sullivan was supposed to introduce us to the public onstage, but after speaking to Nancy Wilson, Dwight was feeling real weak in the knees and they had us sit in the front row of the audience instead. Dusty Springfield, who had just released "Son of a Preacher Man," was also on the show that night. It was the very first time I heard what would become her trademark song. She kissed me on the cheek and told us how proud she was of us. That was quite an evening, and it left us starstruck for some time.

Besides being a star, Ed Sullivan was also a real gentleman. He told us we could order anything we wanted at the hotel and he would cover it. Of all the things on offer, the guys and I settled for a good old burger and fries. Boy, did it feel good, having a juicy burger in some fancy hotel in New York City. Ed Sullivan also had a bottle of very good whiskey sent up to each of our rooms. I brought mine home and gave it to Dad. "With Mr. Ed Sullivan's compliments!" I said. Everyone who visited Mom and Dad's house after that was treated to a short little shot of Ed Sullivan's whiskey— and to the much longer story of how it came to St. Francisville, Illinois. The bottle lasted almost a year.

After New York, I had a few days before going back to Fort Hood. I flew to Indianapolis. My uncle Boo picked me up at the airport to drive me home to Illinois. For as long as I could remember, he'd been living in Indianapolis, running a machine that polished chrome for car bumpers. Bruce, or Uncle Boo to us, was Dad's older brother, and I'd always had a soft spot for him. He was the funny one in the family. When we were kids, he was always playing with us, doing silly things. He would stand on his head and spit marbles just to make us laugh. And of course, that always did crack us up.

Uncle Boo, wearing his Sunday suit and hat, was waiting for me in the baggage claim area. He evidently had been there for a while talking to anyone who would listen, because when he saw me, he gave me a big hug and then introduced me to everyone there as if they were old friends. "This is my nephew, Sergeant Sammy Davis. He's just received the Medal of Honor from President Johnson," he said over and over. I was embarrassed and touched at the same time. When we finally stepped out of the terminal, I expected to walk to the airport parking facility, but he'd parked his 1965 Chevy Impala right in front of the door. Four poles carrying stars-and-stripes flags were bolted on the four corners of the car, and the sides had big signs with my name on it. We drove all the way home with those flags flapping in the wind. We stopped for gas twice during the two-hour drive—not that we needed any gas—so he could introduce me to whoever was there. He was a special guy, my Uncle Boo. Special in an over-the-top, marble-spitting kind of way.

After a few weeks back at Fort Hood, I picked up the phone and called President Johnson's home. During the reception after the medal ceremony, we'd exchanged a few more words. When he realized I was stationed in Texas, he'd said his family ranch happened to be just south of Fort Hood and kindly invited me to visit. Lady Bird Johnson, the first lady, picked up the phone. "We've been expecting your call," she said. I told her I was free over the weekend, and asked if I could still come to visit. She said that President Johnson had business to attend to in Washington, DC, but she would be delighted to have me come over. So the following Saturday, I drove to the president's family home. The ranch was a large cattle estate by the Pedernales River with a beautiful Southern mansion—known as the Texas White House—sitting by a big old oak tree. There was even an airplane hangar. President Johnson was born and lived there, and even while in office, he still spent a good portion of his time at his ranch. It was also where he would later die and be buried.

Lady Bird was a very gracious hostess and made me feel very much at home. She put me up in the pool house, which had very nice accommodations, and we got to talk over the weekend. She asked questions about my family and made easy conversation in her distinguished Southern drawl. My country-boy charm did not work on everyone, though. The first morning, as I looked out the window of the pool house, I saw Lynda, the president's elder daughter, in her bathing suit sipping ice tea in a lawn chair by the pool. She was about the same age I was, and I figured I should go introduce myself. I put on my bathing suit, threw a towel over my shoulder, and stepped out. I pulled a chair toward her and sat at a respectable distance. "Hello, ma'am," I said, looking in her direction. She looked back at me over her sunglasses, and then pushed them back up. Without saying a word, she got up, grabbed her chair, and walked to the other side of the pool. I was crestfallen, and not too sure what to do with myself. Luckily, Lady Bird came out and sat with me awhile, and then told me that I was expected later in the main house for aperitifs. At the end of the weekend, I was invited to visit again.

After that first weekend, my speaking engagements kept me real busy, and I couldn't go back to the ranch for a while. When General Westmoreland and I went to Stockton, California, I looked for Buddy. I talked to his friends, but none of them knew where he was. I went through every listing I could think of. There was even an article in a local paper, which I hoped he would read, saying I was looking for him. I wasn't even sure he was still there, but I had to start somewhere. Unfortunately, the trail was cold.

Back in Fort Hood, I managed to go down to President Johnson's family ranch a couple more times before I left Texas for good at the end of my enlistment. Besides sitting by the pool—making sure after my first visit that the coast was clear—I spent my time there talking to Lady Bird and everyone working at the ranch. Mrs. Johnson was quite something. Besides being the first lady, she was also a very successful businesswoman, but her manners remained down-to-earth, warm, and generous. We took long walks around the ranch. We talked about the cows and the horses and the flowers she loved so much. She asked about Vietnam and how I'd earned the Medal of Honor. I told her what I could at the time. And I told her about all those kids we'd tried to help, how we'd washed babies in villages with washcloths and bars of soap our moms had sent us.

President Johnson was never there when I visited the ranch. But during one of my visits, Lady Bird informed him over the phone that I was over for the weekend, and she handed me the receiver. I didn't quite know what to say—except that I found his ranch to be a real nice place and my visit very enjoyable.

Not too long after my very first visit to President Johnson's ranch, I was to meet another president. On January 20, 1969, Richard Nixon was sworn in. Now a Medal of Honor recipient, I was invited to the inauguration. By then, Peggy Jo and I were newlywed, and we flew to Washington, DC, together. On a cold and cloudy day, I sat by the Capitol with other guests of honor as the new president swore he would protect and defend the Constitution. A couple days earlier, Gary Wetzel and I had watched James Brown work his magic from front-row seats at the All-American Gala at the National Guard Armory. I'd been propelled into a whole different life.

Then there was the inaugural ball at the Shoreham Hotel. It was my very first function as a Medal of Honor recipient. Peggy Jo got all dressed up, and I put on my uniform. When we got to the hotel that evening, we took the elevator down, and there was the ballroom behind big, open arched doors. Just on the other side were all these Medal of Honor recipients sitting at tables decked with crisp white linen. Back then, there were still close to 350 living recipients, and I didn't know any of them except for the four men who had received the medal the same day I did.

At the very first table, closest to the door, were three legends: Pappy Boyington, Eddie Rickenbacker, and Jimmy Doolittle. I'd never met them, but I knew exactly who they were. Pappy Boyington was a Marine Corps fighter ace pilot in World War II, commander of the Black Sheep squadron, and a former prisoner of war. Eddie Rickenbacker had been a formidable ace pilot during World War I. And Jimmy Doolittle, also an outstanding pilot, was famous for planning and executing the first air raid on Japan's major cities during World War II. Jimmy Doolittle and Eddie Rickenbacker were in their seventies by then, and Pappy Boyington in his fifties. I was barely twenty-two years old. The first thought that crossed my mind when I saw them was that I didn't belong in the company of these men. To me, they were giants. And there was a big ballroom full of them. How could I possibly breathe the same air they breathed and sit at the same tables? I froze. There was an ashtray by the elevator, so I lit up a Lucky Strike. And then another. And another. I just stood there, my feet glued to the carpet. Thousands of things were running through my mind, but none of them involved walking through that door. Other guests kept coming down the elevator and walking in, and Peggy Jo was wondering why we kept standing by the ashtray. When I was on my fourth Lucky Strike, I saw Pappy Boyington nudge Eddie Rickenbacker and point at me. I would have given anything right then to melt into the wall. All three of them stood up and walked over to the elevators.

Pappy Boyington jolted me out of my daze. "You must be one of the fucking new kids," he said, giving me a big old handshake.

I could tell the cursing made Peggy Jo real uneasy, and I felt bad. As I got to know him, I later came to appreciate his vernacular.

"Yes, sir," I said. "I'm Sergeant Sammy Davis. I received the medal for Vietnam."

Then I shook Eddie Rickenbacker's hand and Jimmy Doolittle's hand as they introduced themselves—not that they needed any introduction. Pappy Boyington got my arm and led me into the ballroom, and Eddie Rickenbacker and Jimmy Doolittle each took one of Peggy Jo's arms and escorted her. They sat us down right at their table. For the rest of the evening, they made sure we met every recipient who came in.

That was my introduction to the Congressional Medal of Honor Society, and what an introduction it was. It feels like yesterday. Many of the men who were there that evening are no longer with us, and it has been an immense privilege to get to know them. Eddie Rickenbacker, ever the gentleman; Jimmy Doolittle and his twinkling blue eyes; Audie Murphy; and so many others.

Shortly after I returned to Fort Hood from Washington, DC, I received a letter.

Dear Sergeant Davis,

I want you to know how honored I was that you attended my Inauguration as President of the United States.

Your magnificent service to the cause of peace and freedom as so eloquently demonstrated by the honor you have received will be a constant source of inspiration and strength to me in the years ahead.

Sincerely,
Richard Nixon

I had to read the letter several times to make sure I wasn't dreaming. I'd received a personal note from the new president of the United States. And *I* was a source of inspiration? Oh boy. If only he knew I'd almost smoked myself to death at his inauguration ball, maybe he'd have been less impressed.

And if he'd known then what was to come at his second inaugural ball, four years later, he sure would have chosen his words more carefully. Four years had evidently cured me of any trace of shyness. If I remember correctly, Wisconsin was one of the sponsors of the inauguration ball in 1973. On each table of ten people was this big wheel of cheese, and the cheeses were all different. Gary Wetzel was sitting at the next table over.

"What kind of cheese you got, Sam?" Gary asked.

I read the little sign. It was some kind of Swiss cheese.

Gary read me the name of his cheese. "Is your cheese any good?" he asked.

"Yeah. It's pretty good."

"Why don't you throw me a slice?"

So I cut off a slice of cheese and tossed it lightly over to him. Gary—who lost his left arm in Vietnam—caught it with his hook. Then he threw me some of his cheese, but I missed it. Instead, it hit a guy at the next table, who grabbed the piece of cheese and threw it back at Gary. Then Gary threw another piece of cheese and hit somebody else, and I threw one piece and then another. More people joined in. Pretty soon, we were having a big cheese fight at the inaugural ball. It was awesome. Until the Secret Service stepped in and killed all the fun.

If President Nixon ever came to know about the big cheese fight, he never said. Neither did he bear any grudges. He sent me all the books he wrote with a personal handwritten dedication and called me up a few times. It still amazes me that I have had the rare privilege to attend every single inauguration since 1969 and meet every president of the United States since Lyndon Johnson.

I have received far more honors than I deserve, and I owe every single one of them to the medal on the blue ribbon. All were special, but some were particularly memorable. New Zealand's Maori, a people of great warriors, welcomed me as one of their own in a ceremony among the mud baths and geysers of Rotorua. I was also initiated into the Oglala Lakota Nation of Native Americans. In 1987, I went to Minot, North Dakota, to speak at an event organized around the Moving Wall, a replica of the Vietnam Veterans

Memorial in Washington, DC, that travels around the country. I met several Native American Vietnam veterans from the Pine Ridge Indian Reservation who'd come over for the occasion, and we stayed in touch. The Moving Wall was scheduled to come someplace closer to Pine Ridge in South Dakota, and I was invited to speak. The Oglala Sioux Tribe said they wanted to honor me. I was humbled. It was nothing like the White House, but it was just as moving. I learned how to dance for the ceremony. They presented me with a feather fan: a warrior never dances with an empty hand. There was a lot of chanting, and private rituals were held in a sweat lodge. It was a beautiful initiation. Every time I have a chance, I go visit my Oglala Sioux brothers at Pine Ridge.

In April of that same year, the Medal of Honor also took me to Australia. It had been almost twenty years since my R & R in Sydney. The year before, I'd met several Australian vets at the big Welcome Home parade in Chicago. I'd become friends with one of them in particular, Bob Gibson, and we'd stayed in touch. Bob told me that the Australian veterans were trying to organize their own Welcome Home parade in Sydney that year. I kept a special place in my heart for Australia and its veterans: I remembered all those guys who'd shared beers with me in Bien Hoa and my trip to Sydney in January 1968, which had helped me a great deal. So I was keen to assist in any way I could, and when Bob asked me if I could come beat up the drum for the Sydney parade, I gladly accepted.

I had a few extra hours in Indianapolis before my flight. There was a gun show near the airport, and I went to kill some time. Displayed on one of the tables at the show was a Medal of Honor. The guy behind the stand was trying to sell it. I took a good look at it to make sure it was a genuine one. It was genuine all right. It was a display medal, which looks exactly like the medals presented to recipients, except there is no name engraved at the back. Quite a few of these medals had been circulating, and they were very popular among collectors. But they were not supposed to be: Medals of Honor may not be sold.

It became enough of a problem that the FBI later got involved. Special Agent Thomas Cottone, the son of a World War II veteran, became the first federal agent to track down medals circulating on the black market and people pretending to be recipients. Over the years, he exposed countless impostors—including a judge—and recovered probably over thirty Medals of Honor. Some of these medals had been stolen, but he also realized that medals that had not been assigned to any recipient were being sold. Yet these medals were genuine, not knockoffs. In 1996, he investigated the company contracted by the US government to manufacture the Medals of Honor and found out that HLI Lordship Industries had stamped an extra three hundred medals on the side and sold them for seventy-five dollars apiece. After pleading guilty to illegal manufacture and sale, the company was fined and ordered to return the proceeds of its illegal sales. It also lost its government contract.

Back in 1987, as I stood at the Indianapolis gun show looking at that Medal of Honor for sale, there was no one to call yet. I also had a plane to catch. So I took matters in my own hands.

"Sir," I said to the man displaying them, "selling a Medal of Honor is against the law. Where did you get this?"

The man didn't take me seriously, and I was in no mood to argue with him. So I confiscated the medal, and put it in my pocket. He became agitated and threatened to call the police.

"Please do, sir," I replied. "Then you can explain why you're breaking the law trying to sell a Medal of Honor."

I walked away. By then it was time to catch my flight, so I took the display medal to Australia with me. I had a wonderful time in Australia. It was awesome to meet all these Australian brothers, and Sydney was just as beautiful as I remembered. I went back to Bondi Beach and visited Kings Cross again, reminiscing over the good time I'd had. I talked to newspapers and on TV to advocate for the Welcome Home parade in Sydney—which eventually happened in October that year and was a big success.

During my visit to Australia, I was privileged to attend the Anzac Day celebrations at the Australian War Memorial in Canberra. Anzac Day, which is on April 25, celebrates the anniversary of Australian and New Zealand soldiers landing on the Gallipoli peninsula in Turkey—their first major military action in World War I. It is a day of remembrance to honor the country's servicemen and -women, and it is a very big deal in Australia. I'd been asked if I would consider leaving my Medal of Honor on display at the War Memorial museum. I wasn't comfortable parting with my own medal, but I said I happened to have a specimen Medal of Honor in my hotel room and would be proud to donate it. And that's how a Medal of Honor with no name on the back is still there today, hanging in the Australian War Memorial museum among Victoria Crosses—Australia's highest award for bravery—and other honors and awards. I have sent maybe two or three new ribbons over the years to keep it looking nice. It is probably about time to send another one.

It is ironic that, after retrieving that wandering medal in

Indianapolis and giving it an appropriate home in Australia, another trip to Indianapolis almost cost me my own. In July 2005, I was invited to address the United Automobile Workers union. My wife and I drove the night before and checked into a hotel near the airport. I didn't want to leave the medal in my hotel room while we were out getting something to eat. I had been advised this wasn't safe. Several recipients had had their medals stolen. Fellow recipient Charles Coolidge, for instance, had been approached at an official Medal of Honor event by an individual who'd told him his original medal needed to be exchanged so he could wear the newer design. He was given an illegally manufactured replacement. Luckily, Special Agent Tom Cottone recovered his medal some years later. Art Jackson, who'd been awarded a Medal of Honor for his action in the Pacific during World War II, was not that lucky. He had his medal stolen from his bedroom at the Waldorf Astoria in New York only a few weeks after he received it from President Harry Truman in October 1945. To my knowledge, it was never recovered. So I locked up my medal and its case in my heavy-duty Pelican briefcase, which contained a lot of personal papers and photographs, and left the briefcase in the trunk of my car. It was parked in the hotel parking lot, and I figured it was safe. The next morning, when we came down at around seven a.m. or so, I went to the car to put on my medal for the next event. I unlocked the trunk, and my heart sank. The briefcase was gone. In fact, everything that had been in the trunk was gone. My tools, a bag of harmonicas, family photos, personal papers, some speeches. All gone.

I couldn't believe it. For almost forty years, the medal had been my companion, traveling with me across America and around the world. It was more precious to me than anything in the world. That shiny piece of metal held the memories of that terrible night at Fire Support Base Cudgel. It belonged to all the men who had fought so hard that night. It stood for those who had died. With the medal gone, I felt I had let down all those men, and tears rolled down my cheeks. I immediately called Tom Cottone at the FBI. I also called my friend Alan Jones, a detective supervisor for the Indianapolis Police Department and a Vietnam veteran. The police moved real quick. The days that followed were among the longest in my life. I was worried sick that we would never find that medal and that it was gone forever.

Four days later, I got a call from Alan and then from Ron Gray, the police detective who led the investigation. The medal had been found at the bottom of the White River. I was so relieved that I almost jumped up and down. Once my nerves settled down, the news sank in. "The bottom of the White River?" I asked. "How on earth did it get down there?"

A man who'd already run into trouble with the law had been burglarizing cars around the hotel where I was staying, looking for cash and valuables. He popped up my trunk and took everything in it. He happened to be staying at the hotel where I was, where he'd partied with two friends. One of them was a troubled kid named Bradley. A few years before, when Bradley was in sixth grade, I'd spoken at his school. He made poor decisions as he grew older, and he was in a bad way—doing drugs. When the guy who'd popped my trunk went back to the hotel room with his loot, he opened my briefcase and took everything out, including my medal in its case. Bradley immediately knew what it was: like all the kids in his class, he had held my Medal of Honor in his hands when I visited his school. And since there were photographs and documents with my name on it in that briefcase, he also knew who the medal belonged to. He figured this could get them into real trouble, and that his buddy had to get rid of it. Although he'd fallen into drugs, stealing in general didn't sit well with him. But stealing my medal made him real queasy.

My waterproof Pelican briefcase was thrown into the White River with all its contents. They put rocks and drilled holes in it so it would sink to the bottom. But the police caught up with the car burglar, and then with Bradley. Troubled as he was, Bradley had his heart in the right place. When the police paid a visit to his parents' house, he told them exactly where the medal was. He pointed to the exact location on the bridge where he said he'd seen the other guy throw my briefcase in the water. He helped out as much as he could. The fire department sent divers, and a young fireman went in. It was his first official dive, and with the currents and bad weather, it was a long shot. Yet when he resurfaced, in his hand was the briefcase. All the papers and photographs were ruined, but the medal was in it. It had been gone three nights and four days. When I received the call, a real big burden was lifted off my soul. I swore to myself I would never let the medal out of my sight again.

A few days later, I stood on the steps of the Indiana War Memorial in front of a big crowd. All the policemen and firemen who'd worked so hard to find and recover the medal were there. A lot of them had come forward and volunteered to help when they'd heard it was missing. I was humbled that so many people cared so much. The medal went from hand to hand until Detective Ron Gray, who had led the efforts to retrieve it, hooked it back around my neck. The Congressional Medal of Honor Society had sent a brand-new blue ribbon, and a local jeweler had volunteered his time to buff and polish it. I wiped away tears. I was so relieved and so grateful. I could have gotten a replica of my original medal, but a real big part of its history and soul would have been missing. So many people—including several United States presidents and Pope John Paul II, as well as tens of thousands of veterans and school kids—had held that medal in their hands over the years. I've always felt that touching the Medal of Honor helps people connect with what it stands for.

The medal touched Bradley's life. He straightened himself out and turned his life around. He quit all the drugs and went back to school. We became friends. He wanted to become a Navy Seal, so I made some introductions. But sadly, Bradley's past caught up with him. About a year later, his mama went to wake him up one morning and found him dead in his bed. He was only twenty years old or so. Some of the hard stuff he'd taken in the past had consumed his body and killed his kidneys, and he hadn't told anybody how bad he felt and how bad he hurt. He was a good kid who had made real bad decisions. Without him, my Medal of Honor would still be at the bottom of the White River.

Over the years, I've come across many other kids who are inspired by the Medal of Honor to be the best version of themselves. This is why I enjoy speaking to them so much. I believe something of the values that the Medal of Honor represents stays with them. Seeds are planted. I see it on their faces when they hold the medal in their hands. I hear it in the letters they send me. So any chance I get, I pass my medal around so they can touch it, only asking that they don't get it dirty.

Besides Bradley, another kid stays in my mind. In March 2005, the Medal of Honor Memorial in Indianapolis was vandalized. The memorial, dedicated in 1999, is a collection of twenty-seven curved-glass panels along the downtown canal walk that list the names of all Medal of Honor recipients. Several panels were smashed, and spray-painted graffiti defaced some of the walls. During a fund-raiser and presentation about the restoration of the glass panels, I met a seven-year-old boy. Standing among the veterans who'd come to contribute to the repair, Spencer was holding a container full of quarters, nickels, and dimes. When he'd found out what had happened to the memorial, he'd gone straight to his piggy bank. He'd collected seventy-five dollars in coins that his grandpa taped to his letters. He asked his mom and dad to drive him to the event so he could donate all his money. I thanked him and put my Medal of Honor around his neck for a photo. Today, Spencer says that experience sparked an ambition to serve. About twelve thousand dollars in contributions were eventually collected to fix the damage, but none was more moving to me than the seventy-five from a small boy with a very big heart.

Over the years, I have witnessed over and over again what a special place the Medal of Honor holds in the hearts of people, young and old. I've learned how it can inspire them. But back when I completed my three-year enlistment in the Army in September 1969, I knew none of that yet. All I knew was that my health was poor, and I wondered when I would get better. I was still running high fevers on and off, and my whole body ached. After waiting for the end of my time in the Army for so long, part of me was glad it was over. Talking on behalf of the military in 1969 was very tough, and I needed a break. I thought I'd done my job, and I was ready to leave it all behind. At the same time, I was very sad to leave. I was proud to be a soldier, and I felt in my heart that I wanted to keep serving. I needed it. So when the time came to leave, I realized that I would have gladly reenlisted for another few years. But unfortunately, I wasn't in any shape to do so.

Once again, General Westmoreland looked after me. He and the then governor of Illinois, Richard Buell Ogilvie, thought it would be a good idea to have a Medal of Honor recipient join the National Guard and promote it, and they made a deal. As soon as my health improved, I was to join the Guard's summer-camp program.

Peggy and I moved from Texas back to Illinois, and I tried to get on with the rest of my life.

★ 10 ★

SURVIVING PEACE

On a hot summer afternoon a few years after I'd left the Army, one of my good buddies Paul Stallings, another Vietnam vet, came over to my house with a cooler full of beer. This was back when I enjoyed drinking a cold beer on occasion. That spring, Peggy Jo and I had moved with our baby daughter from downtown West Salem, Illinois, to an old farmstead about three miles out in the country. Part of the deal with the landlord was that we would help take care of the barn and the animals, and the rent would be only thirty-five dollars a month for the house. We'd use an old Ford tractor to scoop the barn out, and there was a big pile of straw and cow poop sitting in the barnyard. Paul and I sat under an old maple tree resting our bones in the shade. We'd been fishing and hunting a lot, and we were talking about where we caught this or that fish, and how good the season was. After several beers, Paul got silent for a moment.

"You know one thing I really miss about Vietnam?" he said.

"The explosions. Like throwing a hand grenade in the water, feeling that *bang*, and then go gather the fish."

I knew exactly what he was talking about. That feeling that our chests were going to burst. "Yeah, man," I went. "I do too!"

By then, I was a section chief in a combat engineer company at the National Guard in Lawrenceville, Illinois. In the back of my pickup truck, I carried the combat engineer's big watertight footlocker with a mile of detonating cord, forty pounds of C-4 explosives, and all the accoutrements to make it work, like blasting caps and such. In those days, explosives were not closely guarded the way they are now, and it was perfectly acceptable to take all that stuff home with you. When I think of it now, I realize how crazy that was, but I didn't think much of it back then.

So I was sitting in the shade on a slow day with a cool beer in my hand, reflecting upon Paul wanting to feel an explosion. I thought about the chest in my pickup truck and looked at the big pile of cow poop staring at me. *Let's have some fun*, I thought.

I went to the pickup truck and got some C-4. I climbed on top of the poop pile and buried a quarter-pound charge about two feet in, ran the wires out, and went back to sit underneath the tree again.

"Just tell me when you're ready," I told Paul.

"I'm ready!" he immediately said.

I flipped the switch, and there was a *bang!* Poop flew everywhere. We laughed and rolled on the ground, thinking that was a really big hoot. We drank another beer or two.

"You know, that was pretty good," Paul said. "But that wasn't the kind of explosion I'm talking about. Remember those big bangs that you can kind of feel in your chest?"

"Yeah, I remember that."

"Well, that's what I'd like to feel!" he said.

I thought for a second. "I think we can do that."

I went back to the pickup truck for more C-4, and came back with half a pound. The wires were still there. I just had to restring them. I buried the charge, climbed down the dung pile, and sat underneath the tree and asked Paul to tell me when he was ready.

"I'm ready!" he said.

That was a much bigger bang. Boy, half a pound of C-4 flung dung like you can't believe. Big hunks of it flew up in the sky and rained down all over the barnyard. By then, we were laughing so hard our ribs hurt.

Things had no more settled that Paul spoke again.

"That was pretty good, Sam. But that still wasn't that feeling like we got when we were in Vietnam," he said, thumping his chest.

I took another sip of my beer. "I can fix it."

I figured that the reason that we weren't feeling the concussion the way we wanted was because the charge was buried too deep in cow poop. So I took a whole pound of C-4 and stuck it right on the end of a ten-foot section of electric conduit pipe. I planted the pipe on top of what was left of the poop pile, which still was pretty tall, so it was sticking several feet in the air all by itself. I restrung the wires again. I was pretty sure this was going to be the explosion we were after. I walked back to that big old maple tree. I'd run out a hundred yards of wire, and we were just about a football field away. Before I sat down or had a chance to ask, Paul said he was ready. So I picked up the detonator and flicked the switch.

That third time, we felt it all right. The explosion was so unbelievably loud that our ears rang for a few minutes. It broke three big full-pane windows in the house and knocked some of the wedding china out of the cabinet. When Peggy Jo later came home and found out, she was not amused. Not one bit. But right then, Paul and I thought it was awesome.

We stood up and went, "All right! That's what we're talking about!"

That's when I heard sirens. We lived south of town, but the house was on top of a hill, so in the distance, Paul and I could see fire trucks and their red flashing lights rushing out of West Salem. They were driving at full speed toward a little propane station that was three or four miles straight west of town. When the fire department heard the explosion, they'd evidently thought the station had blown up. I quickly gathered my stuff and put it back in the pickup truck. The fire department never figured out what had happened. Neither did the National Guard. I wrote off the missing C-4, and no one ever asked me about it. But after that day, I decided to leave the combat engineer demo pack at the armory. I figured drinking beer and playing with explosives didn't mix too well.

I also realized something else: I was reckless and a bit crazy. I had left Vietnam, but Vietnam hadn't left me.

In September 1969, I had decisions to make. I was just out of the military, and I'd never really thought about what I'd do with my life. When I graduated high school, I wanted to get my military obligations squared away first and figure it all out later. That *later* was now staring me in the face, and I didn't know what I wanted to do. I had always figured I'd get a job somewhere. I didn't have any big plans. Dad was working in West Salem at Champion Laboratories, a company that manufactured oil filters for vehicles.

He talked to the people over there, and they said they could use an extra pair of hands. So back in Illinois, with no more howitzer to operate, I went to work for a buck and a half an hour at Champion Laboratories. I first worked a punch press that made oil filters, and then became a machinist in the tool-and-die section. The folks at Champion treated me real nice. In 1970, STP Corporation and Andy Granatelli, a car-racing enthusiast, bought the company. Andy Granatelli found out I was a Medal of Honor recipient and looked me up whenever he came to West Salem. He also invited me to the big car races up in Indianapolis a couple of times. Besides working a good job in a good company, I also got to see Dad every day, which was a big bonus. We got to go fishing a lot.

In 1974, I went to work for Central Illinois Public Service Company, a local power utility, and we moved to West York, Illinois. I was working with the high-pressure pumps that moved water from the Wabash River in and out of their power-generating station in Hutsonville. Suddenly, I went from making $2.30 an hour to $12 an hour. I was making the big bucks.

I was also part of a combat engineering unit in the Illinois National Guard. I first operated bulldozers and drove trucks, but my back was killing me. So when a position in explosives opened up, I took the test. I hadn't received formal demolition training in the Army, but I'd worked as a powder monkey in California and used C-4 explosives in Vietnam to blow holes for howitzer trails when the ground was too hard. I'd always liked to blow up stuff ever since my experiments with cherry bombs as a kid. I passed the tests. From then on, I worked demolition jobs one weekend a month, and every summer, I taught EOD—explosive ordnance disposal—at the National Guard summer camp for two weeks.

I had everything I'd always wanted: I had a good job. I had a wonderful wife, and in January 1972, our first child, a baby girl, was born. She was the most beautiful thing I'd ever seen. Two boys followed in November 1975 and July 1978. As soon as my babies could walk, I took them fishing and trapping, and showed them all the good stuff I'd learned as a kid. We walked the woods around our house and sat by the river. Peggy Jo had the voice of an angel, and in the evening, I'd play the guitar or the banjo or any old wooden box with strings I could lay my hands on, and she'd sing. Life was good.

Except it wasn't.

My body wasn't working properly, and I felt increasingly weak. The injuries I'd suffered at Cudgel explained some of it: there was so much scar tissue from the beehive injury around my left kidney that it didn't work too good, and I would get kidney infections two or three times a year. Although my lumbar vertebra had closed up and healed, there was also a lot of scar tissue and excessive calcification around it, which created problems. Some of my ribs had detached from my sternum when the howitzer crushed my chest, and I pulled them loose again many times over the years when lifting something heavy. Every time that happened, the pain was real intense for a few weeks and then eased again.

Overall, my injuries had healed pretty good and couldn't be held responsible for the debilitating episodes of high fever I still suffered. They didn't explain the oozing sores that kept appearing on my skin either. They didn't explain the painful muscle spasms in my back and legs or the tingling in my feet and hands. They didn't explain the constant diarrhea, the dizzy spells, or the sharp pain around my heart. They didn't explain why I always felt I was about to throw up, and why my joints were so stiff. I became so weak I could hardly grip anything, and so dizzy I fell at work. I walked miles of hospital corridors seeking answers. Doctors from Veterans Affairs could not tell me why I was feeling so bad. They ran all kinds of tests and speculated and wrote prescriptions, none of which offered any answer or solution. They kept telling me the reason I was hurting was because I was running a fever all the time. But when I kept asking why I was still running a fever, they'd just shake their heads and shrug. Unable to come up with answers, they'd tell me there was nothing wrong and that I couldn't be hurting like I said.

Telling me it was all in my head made me want to pinch *their* heads off. It was already bad enough that I felt like a shadow of my old self. All these things I used to do, I couldn't anymore. I felt sick to death and had to watch all these people walking around in perfect health. I remembered how once I could run faster, jump farther, and lift more than practically anyone going. But I'd become this man who could hardly walk at times, let alone run. Every time I tried to pick up something heavy, my back and legs were killing me. I was in and out of hospitals, and there were times Peggy Jo wasn't too sure she'd be able to bring me home. Some days I was so weak I could barely do my job. I had to run up and down all day at the power plant to check and operate the high-pressure water pump. I often struggled to drag myself up and down those stairs. I kept pushing past the pain, but I was getting worse and felt I was dying slowly. My health turned so bad I was on sick leave for nearly four of the nine years I worked at the Central Illinois Public Service Company in Hutsonville.

Talking to other Vietnam vets, I found out I wasn't alone. A lot of guys were in bad shape as well, or even dying, and no one could tell them why. So whatever was going on, I was pretty sure it wasn't in my head. In the early 1980s, a veteran friend advised me to consult a well-known expert in environmental health at the University of Illinois in Chicago. In March 1983, I went to see Dr. Bertram Carnow. He put me through a series of tests and concluded what VA doctors had failed to identify for over fifteen years: I was suffering from dioxin poisoning due to Agent Orange exposure.

Until I met Dr. Carnow, I didn't know much about dioxin. I remembered Agent Orange though. From 1962 to 1971, the US military sprayed close to 20 million gallons of various tactical herbicides and defoliants over Vietnam, an operation known as Ranch Hand. The herbicide mixtures were named according to the colors of identification bands painted on their storage drums. Agent Orange was the most common. The objective was to remove the thick tropical vegetation that provided cover to the enemy and also to destroy crops that fed them. Herbicides cleared tall grasses around US base camps and fire support bases. It allowed us to see the bad guys coming. At the time, it sure helped us and saved lives. But we didn't know there would be a very high price to pay. Agent Orange contained a highly toxic dioxin compound, an unintended contaminant generated during its production.

In Vietnam, we had been told that Agent Orange wouldn't hurt us. I still remember sitting through a presentation at Bearcat meant to impress upon us that there was nothing to worry about. I watched some guy from one of the chemical companies that sold Agent Orange to the military drink water with Agent Orange in it. Or so he said. So I wasn't worried when I treated the ammo piles at Long Binh. I got real scared when I was sprayed so bad at Bearcat that I couldn't see for three days, but then my eyes recovered, and I didn't think too much about it. When Dr. Carnow told me about Agent

Orange and dioxin, I was filled with dread, thinking of all the times we established firebases right after the vegetation had been cleared. Over and over, we slept on the ground that had been sprayed with Agent Orange and drank or bathed in the foul-tasting, rainbow-colored water that contained it. I thought of all those pineapples from the old French plantation I'd eaten. I'd never tasted or even seen real pineapples before I went to Vietnam, and I so wished I hadn't touched them. I remembered the white blisters that had appeared on my skin at Bearcat. I hadn't paid much attention back then. I had plenty other things to worry about.

In September 1985, I met Paul Sutton at the Vietnam veterans reunion in Kokomo, Indiana. Following pressure from Vietnam vets, the state of New Jersey had created its Agent Orange Commission to study the effect of dioxin on the human body. Paul explained that the commission's Pointman Project tested Vietnam veterans and compared results with people who hadn't been exposed to "rainbow" herbicides, and he was looking for research candidates. Peggy Jo convinced me to participate, and a year later, I spent a few days at the Barnert Memorial Hospital Center in Paterson, New Jersey. Researchers from Rutgers University ran every test imaginable, including fat biopsies from different parts of my body. The results confirmed Dr. Carnow's diagnosis. Again, I was told that I had dioxin poisoning from Agent Orange. But the folks at the Pointman Project explained in much greater and clearer detail what dioxin does to a human body and what it all meant for me.

As Peggy Jo and I sat in a doctor's office in New Jersey at the end of my tests, a veil lifted. Suddenly, a lot of things made sense. For the first time, I was given an explanation for the fever that had been running for years for no apparent reason: my immune system had been trying to fight off the dioxin, and my body had worked real hard to excrete it. It had done a pretty good job: by the time I was tested, I had far less dioxin left in my body than most other Vietnam veterans.

Yet the damage was evident—and extensive. When Dr. Carnow had first looked at my liver, he'd asked me point blank if I was an alcoholic. I drank some, but no more than a few beers now and then. Yet I had advanced cirrhosis, and my liver was very close to clunking out on me. My kidneys were also packing up, a fact that VA doctors had failed to either notice or admit. My heart, my brain, my nervous system, and my lungs were all affected as well, and I was told I would need bypass surgery. My platelets were damaged, which caused my blood to be real thick and to clot too easily.

Finally understanding why my body wasn't working right was a relief. I wasn't crazy after all. It was also terrifying. I was not even forty years old, but my organs looked and worked like those of a seventy-year-old man. I had the explanation I'd been looking for all those years, only to find out there was no cure. I was told that I might not live for very long. Even more frightening was finding out that dioxin damages not only the people who have been exposed directly—it may also affect their children. My son, Beau, suffers from the same blood condition and had to have surgery to remove multiple blood clots in his lungs. We're both on blood thinners.

As years rolled by, I developed new ailments. I was driving one summer in the early 1990s when I noticed that the road was undulating. I first thought I was seeing heat waves rising from the tarmac, until everything became blurry. I consulted my doctor, who ran some tests. He told me I had diabetes and probably had had it for a while. This was another gift from dioxin, which damages the cells' mitochondria and their ability to process insulin. Over the years, research has linked dioxin to a growing list of serious health problems, from multiple types of cancer and diabetes to Parkinson's disease and severe birth defects. Fifty years after the end of the Vietnam War, the damage continues to be devastating not only for veterans, but also for Vietnamese men, women, and children.

At the time I was first diagnosed in 1983, I wouldn't have bet too much on my prospects. My future looked mighty bleak and mighty short. After I consulted Dr. Carnow, I sent his report to the VA, and I was put on permanent disability. I had been on sick leave and in and out of hospitals for the best part of the previous two years anyway. I had also left the Illinois National Guard. Sad as I was to go, I'd been in no shape to do my job properly over there either.

Then started a lifelong battle I've been trying to win ever since. I was lucky. Thanks to my body's ability to excrete dioxin and the care I have received, I have recovered a great deal. Dr. Carnow put me on a diet and vitamin regimen that helped me feel better. I was instructed to quit drinking, quit smoking, and quit anything else that was hard on my system. I had to be kind to my body, rest when I was tired, and avoid excessive stress. I was never a big drinker, so staying off the sauce was no problem. Smoking was another story. I'd been hooked since basic training in 1966, and for years I couldn't kick the habit completely. But I tried to smoke less.

My heart kept going for years, and I was able to postpone the quadruple bypass surgery until a few years ago. When the surgeons split my chest open, they also fixed up my ribs by wiring them to my sternum so I'd no longer pull them out of place. Every few months I develop skin tumors, and every few months I have them removed.

I owe a great deal to Clamato. Yup, Clamato: the tomato juice with clams. When Dr. Carnow told me that drinking it every day would help my liver regenerate and clean itself out, I was skeptical. But what did I have to lose? It turns out the Japanese have been using these same clams for a long time to repair liver damage. So for twenty years, I drank a quart of Clamato every single day, and even today, I still down the occasional glass. It worked. My liver is now working perfectly well. The rest of me, less so. I've lost count of how many surgeries I've had over the years to patch me up. But I am still here and I am still standing, and at nearly seventy years old, I am in much better shape now than in my thirties.

Besides Agent Orange, I brought another insidious enemy back from Vietnam. I had spent a year trying not to get blown up or shot. I'd looked into the eyes of the enemies I'd killed and seen the lives of too many young Americans cut short way too soon. I was back home, but part of me hadn't come back from Vietnam, and I felt no one could really understand. All my senses were still on high alert. The sound of a fork dropped on the floor made me jump. Any sudden noise sent my heart racing and left me panicked. I was hypervigilant all the time, expecting an enemy behind every tree. I avoided crowded supermarkets and school events. I had a short fuse, and sometimes lost my temper for no reason at all. In Vietnam, I'd spent twelve months thinking that being back home would sort me out, and now I felt I'd left my real family in Vietnam. I felt out of place and disoriented, caught between two worlds. I kept waiting to feel like me again, but I had changed. My mama would ask me if I was okay. "Yeah, Mom, I'm doing pretty good," I always told her. I didn't know what else to say. Then she'd shake her head. "You just aren't the same since you came home from that damned war."

Days were no picnic, but nights were much worse. Whenever I could sleep, I was back in Vietnam. Night after night, I kept seeing waves of Vietnamese soldiers coming my way at Fire Support Base Cudgel. I kept seeing the life snuffed out of their eyes as I fired the howitzer. Every night they kept coming, and every night I kept firing, but there were always more. Every night I heard the screams and witnessed the bloodshed. Every night I floated in the canal, and every night I saw that hand coming out of the water, asking for help. I kept wanting to go and pull it out, but I was tired, so tired. Too tired to move. And the hand kept going under, and then it was gone. If only I'd been stronger. If only I hadn't been hurt so bad. If only I'd made one more trip across the canal. I never knew whose hand it was, but it kept haunting me. Some nights, I was carrying Smitty's mangled body back to the ration truck, his head and arm blown off and his chest hollowed by the blast of the recoilless rifle. The same Vietnamese lady, carrying off the dead in her cone-shaped hat, black trousers, and bright red shirt, often visited my dreams. I wanted so bad to forget that young soldier who'd called for his mama on the road to Tan An, but I couldn't get his voice out of my head. I kept hearing him gurgle, struggling to breathe with a bullet in his chest. I couldn't escape, and I dreaded the sleep I so badly needed. Nightmares bled into the day, and I had flashbacks even when I was awake.

When I met Peggy Jo, she became my anchor to reality. I wanted to fit in her world. The world of war I had just left, I wanted to forget. I did my best to leave Vietnam behind, to push it out of my mind, lock it away in some dark basement and throw away the key. I believe I adjusted to civilian life reasonably well, considering.

There was no one to talk to. Post-traumatic stress is well known now, but in those days, it didn't even have a name. Men came back from wars, their bodies and their souls all broken up, but the manly thing to do was to shut up and get on with life. Those of us who'd fought in Vietnam faced such hostility stateside that we were even less inclined to talk. We suffered in silence. We were prisoners in solitary confinement, trapped behind invisible walls of our own making. Some veterans retreated. They just went to work—if they were able to work at all—and locked themselves up at home. They didn't want to be identified as Vietnam veterans, ashamed or worried about how they'd be treated and judged. They kept denying a whole part of themselves and their histories.

For at least a decade, we didn't really talk about Vietnam, even to one another. We were all trying to forget what we had been through. We were trying to forget what we had done and what had been done to us. Most of us were failing miserably, but we thought we were alone in our failure and somehow defective. We were trying to feel alive when parts of ourselves felt dead. We thought we were crazy. And because we thought we were crazy, we did crazy things. When I wasn't busy blowing up poop piles in my backyard, I jumped out of airplanes and raced motorcycles way past reasonable speed. I needed that adrenaline rush. I needed to wrestle with death again and again and get the upper hand. I couldn't sit still.

During one visit to Mom and Dad in 1976, I took the kids on the back of a six-wheeled buggy up and down the long lane that joined the road to the house up on the hill. It was one of these all-terrain vehicles that went in the water like a boat or on land like a tank.

There'd been a lot of rain, and the front yard was underwater. With the kids in the back, I was real careful. The buggy sprayed water everywhere, and the kids were clapping and loving it. My little brother, Johnny, and his wife, Paula, were there as well, and when the kids were all wet and muddy, happy as clams, Johnny, with a smile on his face, yelled out what he'd said so many times as a kid. "What about me?"

I took him on a ride. With each pass through the water, John would ask me to hit it harder and make the splash bigger. I was happy to oblige. I stepped on the gas and spun the six-wheeler around full speed in 360-degree turns, spraying giant arcs of water and mud. I felt the adrenaline rush, and it was awesome. I pushed harder and went faster. Then the buggy slid on some dry ground, and when it hit, it flipped over. Luckily, Johnny was okay. I flew out, but my left leg got caught in the buggy. I was lucky it didn't get ripped off completely, but my knee was destroyed. That joyride cost me five surgeries on my knees over the years, and it's a miracle that I can still walk the way I do. Agent Orange had weakened my immune system, and I got a nasty infection from the first surgery. I had to go back on the table to have it scraped off, and I had tubes sticking out of my leg for a couple of months. That put an end to my academic ambitions. I'd been going to night school at the community college in Robinson, Illinois, learning about metal work and tool and die, but I couldn't keep it up. I dropped out before I could complete my associate's degree.

I wasn't the only one to think I was crazy. Sometime in the mid 1970s—I can't remember exactly what year it was—one of my monthly visits to the VA hospital in Danville, Illinois, nearly drove me over the edge. I was supposed to get my meds, talk to the psych unit, and spend the night for observation. That day, I was sitting on a couch in a doctor's office, trying to answer questions from two psychiatrists without losing my cool. "How do you feel about killing people?" Really, dumbass? That's what you want to ask me? Behind me was a two-door closet. Without any warning, some guy jumped out of the closet, screaming. The two clever doctors figured this little surprise was an appropriate method to check my startle response. I was startled all right. I grabbed the poor guy's throat and tried to break his neck. Before I knew it, I was in a straitjacket and locked up in a padded room.

I ended up spending part of the night there. After several hours, I managed to wriggle out of the straitjacket, picked the door lock with the metal buckle, and walked out. I borrowed a quarter from another patient in the hallway and called Peggy Jo from a payphone. She came to pick me up, and we drove off. Furious, I contacted the governor's office. It turns out the two doctors were conducting unauthorized psych experiments. They never did it again.

Crazy doctors apart, there was little help for veterans like us. The VA was at best ineffective. We didn't know yet how to help ourselves, let alone help each other. The first few years, I didn't even talk to my wife. When we still lived in Texas, I slept in two-hour increments. Every couple hours I would get up, check the doors, look out the windows. At first, she didn't understand what I was doing. Then she did, long before I was able to tell her anything. She saw how it affected me and other Vietnam vets and accepted it. She guided me and gave me strength. She calmed my anxieties. Playing with my three kids also helped me a great deal, and I spent as much time as I could with my family. Then came a day when I was able to sit down and talk to Peggy Jo. I would not have survived this long without her. I was so lucky to have her and my babies by my side.

You would think that with so many vets in my own family, we could have talked to one another. But we didn't. I don't remember ever talking to my dad about Vietnam. Maybe a few words here and there, but I don't think we ever had a proper conversation about it. He was old school, my dad, and we just didn't talk about that sort of things back then. And then, he was gone. After his heart scare when I was presented with the Medal of Honor, he'd been diagnosed with lung cancer. Working for the asbestos mine in California had caught up with him. On September 4, 1978, his heart gave in. My sister rushed him to the hospital, but he died in the car. I was devastated.

A few short weeks later, Buddy called. Dad hadn't had a chance to patch things up with him. After he'd told me a few years before that he wanted to talk to Buddy, I'd looked for my big brother but hadn't been able to find him. Buddy had called home maybe once or twice from a payphone to let Mom know he was still okay. He lived largely off the grid, and I never had an address or a phone number. Each time he called, I kept asking him when we could see each other again, but it never happened. I hadn't seen Buddy since we'd left California thirteen years before. When my phone rang that day in 1978, he told me one of his kids was sick. He needed money. I had no idea he was married and had children. He said he lived in Phoenix, Arizona.

"I'm real sorry, Bud," I said, "but I can't right now." I had a wife and three kids to care for, and with my health so poor, money was tight.

He was silent for a few seconds. "Okay," he said, and hung up.

That was the last time I heard from him. At first, I didn't worry, because he called so infrequently. But within a year of his call, things started getting better money wise and I had a few hundred dollars I could send him. So I asked Mom to tell him to call me when she spoke to him next. He never called her or me or anyone in the family again. He just vanished.

The worst was still to come. On May 28, 1979, the phone rang. I was at home with one of my legs in a cast. I barely recognized Mom's voice, strangled and hoarse.

"It's about Johnny," she said. "There's been a terrible accident."

Johnny and a bunch of his buddies had been riding motorcycles and dune buggies down on the riverbank, playing on the great big sand dunes. He really liked riding bikes and was real good at it. When Peggy Jo and I moved back from Texas to Illinois, Johnny was twelve. I took him fishing and hunting with me as much as possible on weekends, but I never had a chance to spend as much time with him as I had spent with Delilah and Charlene at that age. When Johnny got older, riding motorbikes was one of the things we did together. We both did some pretty serious racing for several years. Johnny was really good at it, but that day in 1979, his dune buggy rolled over. The roll cage broke, and a pipe from the frame went right through the back of his head.

Peggy and I immediately drove to the hospital. That one hour in the car was one of the longest in my life. When we finally got there, we rushed to the waiting room, where Mom, Delilah, and Charlene were waiting. Johnny's wife, Paula, was talking to the doctors. When she came back, her eyes were red, and all the color had gone from her cheeks. "The doctors asked for our permission to pull the plug," she said, her voice flat. "His body is young and healthy and may continue on for a time, but his brain is dead. They can't fix it." Tears ran down her cheeks. "Please help me. I can't make that decision on my own."

We all went into Johnny's room and stood by his bed. He was hooked to tubes and machines, but he looked perfect. Not a scratch, not a bruise, nothing. He just had a two-inch hole at the back of his head where the pipe from the dune buggy cage had gone in and severed his spinal column. It was hard to believe that my baby brother, who only a few hours earlier had his whole life ahead of him, would never wake up. He had just turned twenty-three, and he had two little boys.

We gave the doctors the go-ahead. I got to hold his hand and tell him that I loved him before the line on the heart monitor went flat. He was gone.

Looking at him lying on that hospital bed, I remembered Johnny when he was nine years old, just before I left for Vietnam. He used to ride his horse, Crickett, in the field across from our house. From the living room, we could see John, waving his hat at us like a cowboy. "Boy, what a ham!" we used to say. Even as he grew older, Johnny had remained the life of the party everywhere he went.

My heart broke, and everything went cold. I wanted to scream. After I came back from Vietnam, I had hoped I would no longer have to watch young men die. Now my little brother was gone, his life switched off in front of my eyes, and there was nothing I could do to repair it. How was it that Johnny was taken and I was alive? It should have been me. I had almost died at Fire Support Base Cudgel, seventeen days after my twenty-first birthday, when I was killing Vietnamese soldiers who were no older than me. I should have died that night, so why hadn't I? Why did it have to be Johnny? It all weighed on my heart real heavy.

I would have given my life for his. He'd always been such a special, funny kid. At his funeral, I was standing on the steps outside of the funeral home, smoking a cigarette with Johnny's classmates and the friends he used to run with. We talked about John and remembered how funny he was. One kid turned to me.

"Sam," he said, "I still got a piece of shrapnel that I got off John."

I had no idea what he was going on about.

"Oh yeah!" another guy piped up. "I've got one of your fléchettes too!"

When the doctors in the Dong Tam hospital gave me the shrapnel and fléchettes they'd extracted from my body, I'd sent them home to Mom and never asked for them when I got back. John, ever the enterprising one, had evidently taken the fléchettes and shrapnel pieces out of the envelope that Mom had saved in a jewelry box. He'd taken them to school and sold them. I laughed. That was my little brother through and through. Two of Johnny's friends handed over one piece of shrapnel and one fléchette. By then, I was able to take a look at the pieces of metal that had caused me so much pain without going into a tailspin. Later, Peggy Jo had a necklace made for me out of the fléchette.

Johnny's death pushed me to the limit. I wasn't sure I could take any more grief. I was carrying so much in my heart already, so much that I didn't know how to handle. I wanted to scream and break things and cry, cry for all the wrongs in the world that I knew I couldn't correct. Yet I somehow retained enough sanity to withhold. I screamed deep inside, hoping it would release the spring that had been wound so tight. I thought that if I could somehow keep my mind straight—or what I thought was straight—perhaps I could make it. The sadness that filled my heart was overflowing, drowning me. It was harder and harder to see the bright edges of life, for the black spots were enlarging. How do you tell someone that you feel like killing people without them thinking you are stone-crazy? I didn't want to kill people, but somehow I felt it would release the tremendous pressure that had built up inside me. It seemed like if I could find the right spot high on a hill and sit very still, maybe I could get my head straight. During one of my visits to the hospital, some doctors asked me if I'd ever thought of committing suicide. "Who hasn't, at one time or another?" I told them.

I saw John-John in my dreams. He was little again, running and running, looking for me. He was so tired and dirty-faced, his clothes all muddy, and he was calling to me for help. There were hordes of people, all shot up and blown away, chasing him. I recognized some of them: they were the men I'd killed in Vietnam. They were trying to get back at my little brother for what I'd done to them. Johnny was so tired, but he kept running, forever trying to escape, calling and waiting for me to help, because I'd always helped. But I couldn't save him. I used to wake up crying, half crazy, trying to sort this out in my mind. It nearly destroyed me. But I had to continue the very best I could, one day at a time, one night at a time. So that's what I did.

Besides Peggy Jo and the kids, I got help from an unexpected corner. Uncle Jess, my father's younger brother, was a commercial fisherman. Once in a while, he would take me with him to run the nets early in the morning. "Sam, it has just rained four inches upriver," he'd say. "With that kind of current, we're gonna lose all our nets if we don't move them. Why don't you come up and help us? Bring some of your Vietnam buddies along."

So I'd call up a few guys, and we usually headed to Uncle Jess's at four o'clock in the morning. Aunt Arlene had a great big breakfast fixed for us. As soon as daylight broke, we'd get in the truck and go down to the river, which was only a quarter mile down the road. We'd get on Uncle Jess's small boat, run all the way upriver, and work the nets back to where we'd started. Uncle Jess had built a little cabin on the boat. It wasn't really tall enough to stand in, but it would keep us from the wind. In the wintertime, when it was real cold, we huddled in there between nets. "Tell me, son," Uncle Jess would say as we moved downriver, "what did you do in Vietnam?" So we would tell our stories. After a while, Uncle Jess would always ask, "And how did that make you feel?"

To understand how weird that was, you have to know that Uncle Jess was not the touchy-feely type. He was a mean, rough, tough veteran from Korea, a poster boy for the Marine Corps. His own children would tell you that at home, feelings were not for sharing. The very first time he asked us how we felt, there were three or four of us on the boat, and we were stunned. We looked at each other, but because it was Uncle Jess asking, we told him the truth. I told him about Cudgel, and I told him about Smitty. We'd run a net, then get back in the little cabin and ride to the next one. And again, Uncle Jess would ask us about Vietnam. We didn't understand back then. But he knew that talking about it would make it better for us. The irony is he never talked about Korea. Not that I know of, at least.

I can still feel the fresh air on my face and hear the tranquil hum of the motor from riding the boat down the Wabash River, running between Indiana and Illinois. Pulling the nets, offloading the fish. And here I was, with my friends, and this was the only place we talked about Vietnam. Really talked about it. During those five or ten minutes between nets, we would offload to Uncle Jess. And he would ask questions encouraging us to open up some more. It worked, the fishing therapy. Uncle Jess, the most unlikely shrink in the world, helped a lot of us.

So did John Finn, a World War II veteran and Medal of Honor recipient. In 1981, I attended a Medal of Honor reunion in Hawaii. We went to the big white memorial structure that sits on the water above the wreck of the USS *Arizona*, sunk during the attack on Pearl Harbor on December 7, 1941. The Congressional Medal of Honor Society had provided a big wreath of long-stem roses. When everybody was seated, I carried the wreath with another recipient and brought it to John, who was standing by the rail looking out over the ocean. John, who had earned his Medal of Honor at Pearl Harbor, pulled one rose out of the wreath, and as he laid it on the water, said a man's name, and then the name of that man's wife. Then he pulled another rose and said another name. I don't know how many roses were on that wreath, but John pulled every single rose off, and with each one of them said the name of someone he'd served with and who didn't get to go home. He remembered their wives' or girlfriends' names—in some cases even their dogs' or horses'.

It astounded those of us who'd served in Vietnam. Up to that point, we'd been told to forget about what had happened during the war, that it wasn't important. When we got back to the island, some of us walked over to John and asked him how, after forty years, he could remember all those names and so many minute details about these men's lives. John looked at us, tears blurring his sparkling blue eyes. "How could I forget?" he said. "You're not supposed to forget. You're supposed to remember, so you can put it in its proper place and go on with life." We all looked at each other, and that's when it finally hit me: All these years I had been trying so hard to put what had happened in Vietnam out of my mind, and couldn't. But I was supposed to remember. And by remembering and talking, I could finally move on.

That's what I've been trying to do ever since. I have been lucky. My family has helped heal my soul and my heart a great deal. John Finn's wisdom has stayed with me and carried me all these years. My job as a Medal of Honor recipient has kept me out in the world, talking. Sequestering myself was never an option. Just like my body excreted dioxin, my heart let go of the pain over the years, and gradually, the wounds didn't hurt so much. I got better. Of course, some wounds never heal completely. I still carry all these memories with me. Memories of my dead brothers and memories of Vietnam. I have a big old truckload of them. But they no longer stand in my way or cloud my outlook. They're part of me, but they do not define me.

A lot of guys haven't been so lucky.

Fellow Medal of Honor recipient Kenny Kays was from Fairfield, Illinois, not too far from my home. As often as I could, I'd drive down there and spend some time with him. Kenny had been a conscientious objector, but he was drafted all the same. In 1969, he accepted going to Vietnam when he was promised he could serve as a medic, but he refused to carry a weapon. His company came under heavy attack while guarding an artillery position, but Kenny ignored the heavy fire and moved to help his brothers. When he became a target and an explosive charge blew up the lower part of his leg, he made a tourniquet for himself and kept going, treating a wounded comrade and pulling him to safety. Although he was losing a lot of blood and was in excruciating pain, he then dragged himself back to treat another soldier and moved him to safety as well, shielding him from bullets and fragments with his own body. He then went straight into enemy territory to assist another soldier lying there. Only when all the wounded were taken care of did he allow his own injuries to be looked after.

When he came back from Vietnam, Kenny had a very hard time adjusting. He lived on the margins of society, went into and out of mental institutions, and turned to drugs to ease the unbearable pain in his soul. He often lived in a little trailer. When I came to visit and check on him, he often would not open the door. He would just slide open the little window in the trailer door and talk through that. I'd talk to him for fifteen or twenty minutes or however long he was able and willing to talk to me. Pretty soon, he'd say that he'd talked enough and he would close the little slide. In November 1991, Kenny took his own life. He was forty-two years old.

For many veterans, whether they served in Vietnam or elsewhere, that long, hard personal battle continues. This is a silent war that claims many casualties long after soldiers have left the battlefield. Every day in the United States, twenty-two veterans take their own lives—nearly one every hour. Many of us who served in Vietnam are now reaching out to the new generation of veterans, these kids coming back from Iraq and Afghanistan. Although the terrain is totally different from where we served, it's basically the same experience. The same things that frightened me to the bone, as well as my dad and grandpa before me, are frightening our kids today, right down to the core of their being.

Like John Finn before me, I tell them they're not supposed to forget. I tell them they're not alone, and there is help for them if they need it. I tell them the memories and the pain that haunt them are best brought out of the darkness and exposed to broad daylight, or they risk festering and poisoning their souls. I tell them to talk about it. Talk to their spouses, talk to a counselor, talk to a fellow veteran. Doing so doesn't make it go away. It will never go away. It's not supposed to go away. But bringing it up to the surface and into the light takes the rot off it. If you work it right, you can transcend all those things that trouble you, those things you've seen or done, or those things that have been done to you, those things that impede you from moving forward. You can move them from in front of you and put them in the toolbox that we all drag along, that toolbox that carries all the lessons that we have learned. We can use those tools to repair what's broken in our lives and fix what's needed for tomorrow. It makes it easier to deal with, so you can move past it and move on.

Talking serves us, but it also serves the brothers who weren't as lucky. I believe that if we remember those who have left us and carry them in our hearts, we honor them. For as long as someone remembers who they were, part of them lives on.

I hope so. I pray so.

★11★

"SHENANDOAH"

"Freedom now!" I hollered into the microphone.

The crowd cheered. It was November 11, 1984—Veterans Day—and I was addressing thousands of veterans in front of the Lincoln Memorial. I'd come to Washington, DC, to attend the dedication of The Three Servicemen statue commemorating the Vietnam War, which stands right by the Vietnam Veterans Memorial.

"For the mother of a prisoner of war who cries every time she sees his picture—*freedom now!*"

More cheers. Only two years before, I'd played "Shenandoah" for the first time in years in front of the brand-new Wall. Only two years before, I'd reunited with so many brothers and marched proudly toward our memorial.

"For the sons and daughters of the missing in action who do not remember what it feels like to be hugged by their father—*freedom now!*"

I'd traveled a long road over those two short years. And there I stood, where so many who were far more deserving had stood before me and spoken out to right some wrong. There I was, looking at the path ahead of me with a renewed sense of purpose. Many were dead, but I was still alive. I didn't know how much longer I had, but until my time was up, I knew in my heart what needed to be done.

As a Medal of Honor recipient, I had been invited to speak throughout the 1970s. Working full-time, and with three kids and failing health, I couldn't do much in those years. In any case, even though I was proud of my service, I was trying real hard to put Vietnam behind me and go on with my life. But I spoke locally and attended Memorial Day or Veterans Day celebrations whenever I could.

In the early 1980s, several events made it real clear to me that I had a job to do. First, John Finn opened my eyes and changed my perspective on the memories I was trying so hard to forget. I was ready to talk—and to tell others that they were not alone. At the dedication of the Vietnam Veterans Memorial the following year, so much of the grief and pain that had been festering inside so many of us started healing. I also realized how good it felt to be among Vietnam veterans, and how important it was to remember and honor those who, like Johnston Dunlop, had given their lives. Then, when Dr. Carnow told me that I owed much of my poor health to Agent Orange, I wanted to share the news and raise awareness, so those who were still in the dark could finally get answers, and together we could push for solutions.

Since Vietnam vets were not getting much help, I felt we could at least help each other. In my heart, I felt an obligation to promote the values that were dear to me and talk about duty, honor, and country. I wanted to be with my veteran brothers as much as possible, tell them that their service mattered, and help out in any way I could with all the challenges we were all facing. I also wanted those who had lost their lives to be remembered and their sacrifice honored. Since that night in 1982 at the Wall, I've carried a harmonica everywhere I go, and have played "Shenandoah" more times than I can remember. Every time, my heart aches for Sergeant Johnston Dunlop, who loved that tune so much. I hope it brings some peace to others as well.

This is why I started speaking then, and this is why I still speak today. I realized that the Medal of Honor gave me a platform and a voice to speak to veterans and to speak on their behalf. Then, in 1984, my medical retirement gave me time. Time to travel, time to spend with my Vietnam brothers, and time to speak. I had a job to do, and now I could do it. I started accepting a lot more invitations, and I hit the road.

When school was in, I traveled on my own. But any chance we got, Peggy Jo and I sat our three kids in the backseat of our Dodge Omni hatchback and drove across the country. Every summer, the five of us drove the roads of America, singing and talking for hours in the car. Most of the money we had was spent on traveling to speaking invitations or veterans reunions and events. When my health was still poor, it sometimes took me days to recover from the travel and the strain of public speaking. But it was all worth it.

I became a regular at the annual Vietnam veterans reunion in Kokomo, Indiana, and Freedom Fest in Skidmore, Missouri. In 1984, several Vietnam veterans built a half-size replica of the Wall in Washington, DC, that started traveling around the country. I was often invited to speak at this Moving Wall, and it was always special to witness the power of that memorial on so many people and in so many towns across America. While speaking around the country, I regularly found myself at the same events as General Westmoreland. After he retired from the military in 1972, he kept speaking on behalf of the warriors who had served their country in Vietnam but had been shunned. In the early 1980s, we both addressed several gatherings around the Last Patrol, a movement that encouraged veterans to march across America to raise the profile of veterans issues. One of the marches went from Springfield, Illinois, to Daley Plaza in Chicago. Tim "Doc" Holiday Taylor and Michael Martin, who'd founded the Last Patrol, performed at the concert at the end of the march, and I'd been invited to speak. Tim and Michael were very involved in the veterans movement, through music and otherwise. In 1985, they first marched from Dallas to the Alamo, and in 1987, they trekked the sixteen hundred miles from the Alamo to the Wall in Washington, DC. Over the years, the Last Patrol organized over forty marches around the country. That day in Chicago, I briefly met Dixie, who would later become Tim's wife. Over the years, Peggy Jo and I became good friends with Tim. He lived in Texas, but we often met at veterans events and reunions. I also visited military bases and talked to our troops. Then came business invitations and charity events. And I kept talking to schools as often as possible, as I'd done when I was still in the military.

There was much to talk about. Many Vietnam vets like me suffered from exposure to Agent Orange. I raised the alarm bell whenever I could. In June 1983, I traveled to Washington, DC, to testify in front of the House of Representatives Committee on Veterans Affairs. The committee was considering legislation proposed by then Representative Tom Daschle of South Dakota to offer compensation to veterans suffering from three disorders thought to be caused by the dioxin contained in Agent Orange. The VA—the very agency that was supposed to take care of us—didn't want to hear about it, arguing there was no conclusive evidence linking Agent Orange to major health problems. Before my testimony, I'd received several phone calls from members of Congress and chemical companies trying to convince me that I shouldn't go. It all happened so long ago, they'd all argued, and what good would it do to dredge this all up? I heard over and over that my testimony wouldn't make any difference. I listened politely but ignored them. I fully supported the legislation, not only for the financial help it would bring to suffering veterans, but also because it would signal that a problem did indeed exist with Agent Orange. It would call for more research toward the damage it had caused—and hopefully help find a way to cure it.

Dressed in my full uniform and with the Medal of Honor around my neck, I sat in front of the committee and spoke about my service and my deteriorating health. I also spoke of my visit to Dr. Carnow a few months earlier and of the diagnosis that had finally shed light on years of suffering. And I explained that I might not live for much longer.

"I am thirty-six years old, gentlemen," I said, "and that terrifies me. . . . I did not travel the miles from West York, Illinois, to the Capitol to accuse anyone or any organization of any wrongdoing, indifference, or malpractice of medicine. Nonetheless, certain questions exist in my mind and the minds of thousands of other Vietnam veterans. What can one doctor in Chicago

do that the largest health care delivery system in the world cannot? What can one man examine, understand, and diagnose that the largest health care delivery system in the world cannot? Can men who may not have years to wait for the completion of research be asked to stand by while there is a doctor who can answer their questions today? I submit, gentlemen, that we have a right to know, just as we did in Vietnam, why we may have to die. . . .

"I am an American, gentlemen, and therefore too proud and too bullheaded to beg you. But I humbly request that you do not break faith with those of us who answered the call that came from this very building. Think of the legacy you will leave for the next Army you may have to raise to stand under our flag, should you turn your backs on us. I can only ask you to do what is right."

The bill was approved in the House but died in the Senate. The VA kept refusing to compensate veterans suffering from debilitating diseases by claiming they were not related to their service. We didn't give up. Veterans associations kept pushing. Over the years, I gave dozens of interviews on Agent Orange, often with Paul Sutton of the New Jersey Agent Orange Commission, who'd brought me into the Pointman Project. I kept talking about Agent Orange and dioxin every chance I had. I encouraged vets to participate in research and to speak up. People needed to know, and something had to be done.

I met with Admiral Elmo Zumwalt several times. Admiral Zumwalt had served in Vietnam before becoming chief of Naval Operations. During the war, he had ordered the use of Agent Orange in the Mekong Delta to clear vegetation along waterways and protect the boats under his command. His oldest son, who had also served during the Vietnam War, had been exposed to dioxin. The admiral's son was diagnosed with cancer in 1983—he died a few years later at age forty-two—and his grandson was born with severe disabilities, most likely due to his father's dioxin exposure. Admiral Zumwalt fiercely supported the legislation.

A few years later, after the bill was first defeated in Congress, a US district court unsealed documents from an Agent Orange lawsuit settled out of court. The papers suggested that chemical companies, and possibly some of the military, knew of Agent Orange's health risk in the early to mid-1960s. Then, in 1990, Admiral Zumwalt wrote a report on Agent Orange for the VA concluding that scientific evidence linked dioxin exposure to several cancers and other serious health problems. The report also found that various government-sponsored studies concluding such links didn't exist had been scientifically unreliable and characterized by "deception, fraud and political interference." The VA, it said, had acted improperly in denying compensation to veterans. The report was classified, but it was leaked, and its conclusions became public. In 1991, following years of efforts, pressure, and studies, Congress finally approved the Agent Orange Act, which entitles veterans having served in Vietnam and who suffer from specific illnesses to compensation on the presumption that they have been exposed to dioxin. The list of illnesses was subsequently expanded. Yet it took several more years before the VA started paying out compensation, and the red tape that veterans have to go through to claim what they are entitled to is mind-boggling.

The fight continues. Younger generations of veterans have been facing similar challenges, whether suffering from Gulf War syndrome or from exposure to old stocks of chemical weapons in Iraq. In October 2014, the Pentagon admitted that it had failed to react appropriately to the American service members who had told the military they thought they'd been exposed to chemical warfare agents in Iraq. A few months earlier, a VA facility in Phoenix was found to have cooked the books to hide the long delays that veterans had to wait to receive medical care. This exposed to the broader public the inefficiencies and serious problems plaguing the VA— from floors of unopened files and unattended disability applications to delayed or poor medical care—that veterans had long been battling. Those who have put their lives on the line to serve their country deserve better. Much better. Yet I have also met extraordinary people at VA facilities around the country, people truly dedicated to this country's veterans. This gives me hope that the machine can be reformed, as long as we keep pushing.

In the early and mid-1980s, another serious problem was high on my list. For many families whose husbands, fathers, sons, and brothers had fought in Vietnam, the war continued long after the 1973 Paris Peace Accords officially put an end to American involvement. That agreement included provisions for all American prisoners of war to be released and allowed to return home, and for the remains of the dead to be located and repatriated. By then, over twenty-six hundred Americans were missing, many of them pilots shot down over North Vietnam or Laos. Some of them had been captured; some of them had died. Between February and April 1973, Operation Homecoming organized the return of 591 POWs. That still left a staggering number of men whose fates remained a mystery.

Following the Paris Peace Accords, families and organizations

working on locating POWs and soldiers declared missing in action—
or MIA—worked tirelessly to find out what had happened to these
men. Evidence and satellite pictures suggested some were still alive
and being held against their will in camps in Southeast Asia. One
specific case I became aware of was Charles Shelton's, after I met
his wife, Marian. Captain Shelton had been shot down in April
1965 while on a photoreconnaissance mission over Laos. Evidence
suggested he was held captive with another POW thought to be
Colonel David Hrdlicka. Many others were being held in prison
camps in the same area. Some had been moved to Laos. Yet Charles
Shelton did not come back home in 1973. For years, Marian kept
looking for answers.

Like many other veterans, I wanted to help. The idea that men
had been left behind and were still alive was unbearable. Even worse,
our government didn't seem to care much. It wasn't until 1979 that
our government proclaimed the first National POW/MIA Recognition Day. Little was being done, and families looking for their husbands, fathers, and brothers were getting no traction in Congress.
For years, families and veterans had been hitting a brick wall. We
actively campaigned in Washington, DC, to convince politicians to
do more to return prisoners still being held in Vietnam to their
families. I publicly spoke about the fate of POW/MIA soldiers every
chance I had. At the dedication of the Three Servicemen statue in
November 1984, a concert was held on the Mall, and between
musical numbers, the mothers and relatives of missing men came
to the microphone and appealed to anyone present to come forward
with information. After my friend singer-songwriter Britt Small and
his band Festival sang their songs "Missing" and "Still in Saigon,"

I stood onstage and, in front of a crowd of tens of thousands, demanded clarity on the fate of those prisoners of war and those missing in action still unaccounted for:

In 1963, two-hundred fifty thousand people were drawn to our nation's Capitol by a promise that was spoken in two words. Two words that went on to shape the soul of this nation. Two words which expressed a concept so simple, so basic, yet so far away from life, as it was at that time, that the words changed history.

Those words must be spoken again. We have dedicated a statue honoring our living that has been placed in the shadow of a monument honoring our dead. I suggest to you that the two words of 1963 speak directly to those of us today who have yet to find a place on this Mall.

Freedom now!

Freedom now for the prisoners of war and the missing in action yet to be accounted for from the Vietnam War. Accounted for is a contemptible term to begin with—money and property are accounted for, not men—and not accounted for is simply unacceptable.

It is unacceptable to even think that men are still imprisoned in a war no longer being fought. It is unacceptable that families sent sons, brothers, and husbands to their country and got question marks in return. It is unacceptable that the business of nations cannot allow the pain of the unknown to haunt them to the point of action.

The Reverend Martin Luther King brought pain and suffering into the face of a nation and he demanded it be healed.

He insisted that a country born of justice and equality extend that justice to all citizens. He refused to accept that America left anyone behind in chains and simply went about its business.

And he said two words—freedom now—which became a cry; a cry for justice, a cry for decency, a cry for fairness.

For the mother of a prisoner of war who cries every time she sees his picture—freedom now!

For the sons and daughters of the missing in action who do not remember what it feels like to be hugged by their father—freedom now!

There have been promises enough that there will be action and there have been all too many guarantees of results that have not been followed through on. If campaign promises of a renewed, stronger America are to be believed, it is up to us to ensure that our past be settled.

An organizer of Dr. King's march of 1963 was asked, somewhat rhetorically, why the march ended at the reflecting pool and did not continue to the steps of the Capitol building. "It is simple, man," the organizer replied. "The man in the White House can hear us from here."

The man in the White House—who already claims to support our goals—can hear you from here as well.

Freedom now!

Firsthand testimonies from Vietnamese and Laotian witnesses who had seen POWs still in camps and whose accounts were supported by satellite photographs, were collected. It was clear from the photographs that the subjects were white males, even though they could not be identified. Armed with the evidence we had, I approached General Al Gray, then the commandant of the Marine Corps, and convinced him to speak up on behalf of the POWs. We lost an advocate when he retired in 1991. In 1992, I personally handed a file containing such evidence to Tom Foley, who was then speaker of the House of Representatives. Nothing came of it.

American teams started being dispatched to Vietnam to search for the missing only in 1988—fifteen years after the Paris Peace Accords. The remains of nine hundred servicemen have now been returned, but more than forty years after the war ended, over sixteen hundred men who fought during the Vietnam War are still missing. This is unacceptable, and for their families and friends, it is a pain that will never heal.

This is a pain I feel in my heart. I know firsthand what it is like to wonder what has happened to a loved one. I know the hoping against all hope that someday the phone or the doorbell will ring, and the despair gnawing at your soul that maybe it never will. Although I haven't lost my brother Buddy to war, to this day I don't know what happened to him. After his last phone call in 1978, I kept looking for him. I went to Phoenix several times over the years and talked to the police there. I gave them descriptions and the little information I had, but I didn't know where he lived, I didn't know where he worked, and I didn't know his wife's name. I don't even know his kids' names. I don't know anything. I have his social security number, but he evidently didn't use it, because there is no record. I can't be sure he truly lived in Phoenix, yet that's where he said he was. I can't find death records or obituaries. For all I know, he may have been going by another name.

Not knowing what happened to my brother has been a particularly cruel form of torture that I don't wish on anyone. For years, I carried a little spark of hope in my heart. Hope that I would one day see him again, and then hope that I would find out what happened to him. As time went by, the spark grew smaller and smaller, until one day, it went out altogether. I know he's dead, because he stopped calling, and for all his wandering and his demons, I believe in my heart that he would never have completely cut the cord that still tied him to us. I know he's dead, because he was drinking too much too often. But I don't know where, when, or how he died. I have now accepted that I probably will never know. I will never know his children either, and get to see Buddy living on in their eyes or in the shapes of their faces. Sometimes, that pain still keeps me awake at night.

Unfortunately, the fight to find out what has happened to those who went missing in Southeast Asia has lost some of its fire, as most—like Charles Shelton—are now presumed dead. Charles Shelton remains "unaccounted for," and the Vietnam War claimed another casualty long after the war ended: his wife, Marian, committed suicide in 1990.

Over the years, invitations to speak have kept on coming, and I've crisscrossed the United States and traveled abroad to speak about duty, honor, and country. Along the way, I've met incredible people—some famous, and some not. The warmth and generosity of ordinary people has kept me going. And the country boy that I am still has to pinch himself whenever I am in the company of talented musicians, entertainers, or athletes. I got to play the harmonica with awesome musicians like Carlos Santana, Willie Nelson, Lynyrd Skynyrd, guitarist Stevie Ray Vaughan, and Buddy

Guy, the Chicago bluesman. I have talked with Muhammad Ali about his conversion to Islam and about Vietnam.

Among the many talents I was privileged to meet, several have a special place in my heart. One of them is Sammy Davis Jr. In the mid-1970s, I attended a reunion of Medal of Honor recipients in Lakeland, Florida, a small town between Tampa and Orlando. I was sitting at the hotel bar having a drink with several fellow recipients. A very tall man walked in the bar. He ordered a beer, and we started talking. After a bit, he told us he was Sammy Davis Jr.'s bodyguard. The Rat Pack entertainer was giving a concert in the area and was staying in the same hotel.

"Really?" I said. "That's strange. My name is also Sammy Davis!"

"Nah," said the bodyguard. "Get out of here!"

I took out my ID and showed him that my name really was Sammy Davis. "You can't imagine the ribbing I've taken because of my name," I told him. Most of my life, I had been asked to sing and dance or had to listen to bad jokes about eye patches.

"Well," said the bodyguard, "meet me in twenty minutes in room 2010."

A little while later, I went up and knocked on a large double door. The doors flew open onto a suite, and this little bitty guy came running out and jumped at me, straddling his legs and arms around me. Before I knew it, I was holding Sammy Davis Jr. in my arms. He patted me on the back.

"I've always wanted to meet you!" he exclaimed. "You don't realize the ribbing I've taken all my life because of your name!"

I laughed. When he was back on his feet, I came in and was offered a glass of wine. We talked for a while. After that day, Peggy

Jo and I always went to see him perform if we happened to be in the same area. We were on the road a lot, and our paths crossed several times in Las Vegas and New York City. Whenever Sammy Davis Jr. saw us sitting in the front row, he'd always invite us backstage. He introduced me to Frank Sinatra and Dean Martin following one of his shows. I also met Burt Lancaster and Jerry Lewis a couple times. My namesake was a real gentleman—and an awesome character— and it is a privilege to have known him.

One of my funniest memories on the road was with Martha Raye, the singer and comic actress. I had met her on many different occasions, because she was always ready to perform for our soldiers and did a lot of work with the USO, the outfit that organizes entertainment for service members. On one occasion, we were flying in a C-130—a turboprop military aircraft—to talk to the troops in Illinois. We were approaching Chicago Midway Airport, and for some reason we couldn't land immediately and had to make another approach. Martha Raye had to go to the bathroom real bad, but the C-130 wasn't equipped for ladies. All it had was a relief tube with a little curtain around it. To make things worse, the flight was kind of bumpy. But that didn't discourage Martha Raye. "Well, guys," she said, "I'm sorry but I've got to go use it." She went in the little bitty curtained room. We could hear her in there, giggling and laughing as she carried on. Then she threw the curtains open. "I've got a ring around my ploony!" she announced. I'd never heard of a "ploony," but I took it that she meant her private parts. We all laughed so hard. And from that moment on, every time Martha Raye and I were together, we'd laugh about how she'd peed over Chicago. Years later, she claimed she still had that ring mark. God bless her. It still just kills me every time I think of it.

Besides the good laughs, there were also tears. Over the years, I've visited many wounded veterans, but I will never forget one particular young man I met in Tampa, Florida. He had just gone through surgery, and he was still dozing off when we got into his room. As I stood by his side, his eyes popped open. "Sergeant Davis!" he exclaimed. "Do you have your harmonica with you?" I almost fell over. How did this kid know who I was? He explained that, when he was a small boy, his grandpa had taken him to the Kokomo veterans reunion. He'd heard me talk about Johnston Dunlop and how "Shenandoah" had helped him rest and heal his soul. I'd played it on my harp for the vets who were there, and it had made a big impression on him. "Sergeant Davis," the young man then said, "I really need to rest. Would you please play 'Shenandoah' for me?" I took my harmonica from my pocket. I kept playing until he fell asleep.

Most people face a different kind of loss. On October 19, 1987, I was invited to speak at the New York Stock Exchange. This turned out to be one of the darkest days in the history of the stock market. On that day, which is remembered as "Black Monday," the Dow Jones Industrial Average fell by over 20 percent—far worse than the historic decline of 1929. Panic seized the market, and trading volume hit the roof. It was financial carnage, and nobody knew what lay ahead. As I walked on the trading floor, I saw shock and despair on the faces of traders whose lives were being upended. What could I possibly tell them to make it better? I told them about Cudgel, and how when everything seems lost, there is always hope as long as we stand together.

Memorable as they were, these encounters pale when tallied against far more personal ones. In May 1988, I was speaking at a veterans event in Florida. When I came back to my hotel, I found a message from Peggy Jo, who'd stayed home. She said she'd received a phone call from someone by the name of Jim Deister, who claimed to be the man who was shot in the head and who I had brought across the canal at Cudgel. I was sure this was a cruel prank. When I'd carried that soldier on November 18, 1967, I knew he was dead. His chest wound looked real bad, and I had pushed his brain back into his skull. But Peggy said the man had left a phone number, and could I please call him back at work the next day? He worked as a rehabilitation counselor for veterans in Kansas. I was more than a bit skeptical, but I thought I might as well call.

The next day, I picked up the phone. Jim Deister answered, and I asked him which unit he'd served with. He told me he'd been a combat engineer attached to the Fifth/Sixtieth Infantry, and that he'd been with the infantry recon platoon across a large canal from Fire Support Base Cudgel. He told me why he thought he'd been one of the three soldiers I'd seen across the canal. I was silent for a moment. A hundred thoughts were running through my mind, and I didn't know what to make of this. "It could be. I want to meet with you," I told him. "The closest place I will be to you this summer is at the Nebraska Vietnam Veterans Reunion." We agreed to meet there. I still believed this was a hoax. How could the man I'd ferried across be alive? Yet I couldn't help but hope.

In August, Peggy Jo and I drove out to North Platte, Nebraska. Once at the Holiday Inn, I heard the reception desk page me. I went to the lobby, looked around, and saw a man sitting in the corner, waiting. Although he had suffered serious injuries, I immediately recognized him. He was one of the soldiers I'd found on the other side of that canal. I couldn't believe it, and tears streamed down my face as I hugged him. How was this possible? I took Jim Deister to my room, sat on the bed as he pulled up a chair, and we talked for a long while, trying to fill in the blanks. At a reunion of his unit, the infantry medic had told him that after he was back across the canal, he was first put in "a pile with the dead guys." Then someone saw him moving, and they worked on him and did what they could, probably shooting him up with morphine. They must have thought he was lost, because when the Dustoff choppers came in, Jim was loaded in a body bag. And that's when, apparently, he tried to get out of the bag and was flown to a hospital. Jim—who had a 9mm bullet removed from his midbrain—miraculously survived his wounds but lost most of his hearing.

A few months before, he'd come across a book about Medal of Honor recipients that I was featured in. Looking through the table of contents, he noticed that I'd been awarded the medal for actions at Fire Support Base Cudgel on November 18, 1967—the exact battle where he'd been injured. He'd read the chapter about me. When he came upon the description of the three men across the canal, Jim's heart jumped to his throat: he realized he probably was one of them. A big chunk of the blank had just been filled in. He had very truncated memories of what had happened that night after he'd been injured. But he remembered seeing my face through the tall grass as I came upon the three of them, and then later looking at flares illuminating the night sky as he laid on the air mattress. Unaware of where he was, he kept thinking, "Turn off the damn lights! They are going to see us!" After twenty-one years, he finally knew how he'd come across the canal, and he knew my name. When the Moving Wall came to his hometown of Salina, Kansas, he'd gone to see it. One rainy night during the Moving Wall's weeklong stay in Salina,

Jim met the fellow who drove the replica around the country in his truck, a man who went by the name of Michael Widawall. He asked Michael if he might know me, since I was a Medal of Honor recipient, and explained why he was looking for me.

I'd often been invited to speak at events organized around the Moving Wall all over the United States, so I'd met Michael many times, and we'd become real good friends. Michael knew everything about my story, so when Jim Deister approached him, he knew this was big. He brought Jim to the nearest phone and immediately called my home. They'd talked to Peggy Jo, who then left me that message in Florida.

That evening in North Platte, Nebraska, Jim and I sat very close so he could hear me. Our wives later told us—and then teased us for years to come—that we held hands for a good couple of hours. It was a miraculous encounter. A few months later, Peggy Jo and I visited Jim and his family in Kansas and went pheasant hunting. Jim's daughter had given birth to a beautiful baby girl the month before—she was Jim's first grandbaby—and I got to hold her in my arms. There I was, holding this tiny baby, brand-new to the world. And I thought of Jim by the canal at Cudgel all those years before. My heart almost burst, and I had a lump in my throat. If I hadn't done my job that night, that beautiful baby wouldn't be here.

Jim and I became like family, and over the years, we have attended countless veterans events together. I was honored to have him by my side at the Sammy L. Davis Federal Building dedication. At one time or another, he noticed the fléchette that I carried around my neck as a necklace. I had another one made, and when we next met at the Freedom Fest in Skidmore, Missouri, I gave it to him. I believe he still wears it, and he has promised his grandson—who is also named Jim and knows everything about our bond—that when he passes on, it will be his. It warms my heart to know that, even when Jim and I are no longer alive, somebody will carry that memento and remember what happened at Fire Support Base Cudgel all those years ago.

About twenty years after I came back from Vietnam, I was speaking at Kokomo, Indiana, the oldest—and probably the largest—annual veterans reunion in America. I was onstage, addressing thousands of brothers. At the far back of the crowd was a garrison flag suspended from a telephone pole, and I noticed the crowd parting over there. I kept speaking. Then I saw a short black man with white hair walking toward the stage. He kept getting closer, and at first, I didn't recognize him. I kept talking. As he came by the stage, he called my name. Hearing the sound of his voice, I immediately knew who he was: Sergeant Gant. The man who had made us polish our bullets night after night and set time fuses blindfolded in a hundred-degree heat. The man who still visits me at night as I keep polishing those bullets in my dreams. The man who had prepared us so well for the worst night of our lives.

I was stunned into silence. First, I'd thought Sergeant Gant was dead. Last I'd seen him, I had taped a piece of my poncho on his open chest wound and held his hand during what felt like his last moments on earth. And there he was, standing in front of me. Second, the Sergeant Gant I remembered was eight feet tall and four hundred pounds. He was so intimidating to us privates that he seemed larger than life and invincible. But the man in front of me was actually quite short. I jumped down to greet him. He had heard from a friend that I had spoken at the Kokomo reunion the year before, and he decided to go the following year to see me.

"I threw the M60 in the canal!" I blurted out. Twenty years after I'd last seen him, that was the first thing that came to my mind. I had gotten rid of the weapon that night at Cudgel so the enemy wouldn't take it, and I'd never had a chance to tell him.

There were more blessings to come. In March 1993, the Moving Wall traveled to Manteca, California, and I was invited to speak at my old high school. A stage had been set up on the same football field where I'd once played for the Buffaloes, and thousands of students and guests filled the bleachers. I was onstage addressing everyone when Harry Nagy, the retired Manteca High teacher and fellow veteran who'd organized the whole thing, brought someone up on my left. I looked over to see what was happening, and there stood a man wearing original camouflage fatigues and a boonie hat. I would have recognized him anywhere. It was Gwyndell Holloway. I hadn't seen him in twenty-six years, since the Third Field Hospital in Saigon, and he was dressed exactly like he had been that night at Cudgel. We both burst into tears and hugged each other.

I had no idea he was going to be there. For some reason, I'd thought he was from the East Coast, and I didn't know what had happened to him after Vietnam. As it turned out, he was from Stockton, California, and he still lived there—just a few miles from where I'd lived in French Camp. Harry Nagy knew me well, and when he heard some story about Gwyndell from another guy who knew him, he put two and two together and organized the surprise reunion. After a little while, Gwyndell and I recovered from the shock and were able to speak, and we explained to the crowd why this was a very special moment for us. Everybody cheered and clapped. "All this bull about prejudice and racism is just what I said. Bull," I explained. Gwyndell will always be my brother, and I will never forget that day. It still brings tears to my eyes every time I think about it.

Billy Ray Crawford, the third man I'd found on the other side of the canal at Cudgel, survived Vietnam as well, but he did not survive life back home. After Jim Deister gave me his name—Billy Ray, like Jim, had been a combat engineer—I looked him up. That night at Cudgel, I'd immediately known he was from southern Texas: I'd spent enough time there as a kid to recognize that twang anywhere. I found his phone number in Alvin, Texas, just south of Houston, and would call him maybe once or twice a year. He always told me that everything was peachy. One day, he stopped answering the phone. I was told he'd shot himself in the chest, but I'm not sure what exactly happened. I didn't get to be there for his funeral, but I went down to Alvin later on to try to find his family and friends. That's when I found out that he'd never recovered from Vietnam, and that life in rural Texas hadn't been kind to a black man who had lost a leg. He'd been talking a good story. I went down to the local veterans association, and they told me they'd met him a few times, but he hadn't wanted to be a part of anything. He'd lived in isolation and self-medicated by drinking heavily. It broke my heart, and I wished I'd come down to see him when he was still alive. I never got to know Billy Ray that well, but I felt that Cudgel had created an invisible bond between us. To me he was a brother. I mourned his loss.

Over the years, veterans events have brought many other brothers back into my life. After scattering and wanting to forget, we sought one another's company. So many years after Vietnam, a good number of us from Battery C found our way back to one another again. And I believe it was at the Kokomo reunion that I met a relative of Johnston Dunlop's. He was dressed in full Scottish gear and carried a bagpipe. We tried to play "Shenandoah" for Johnston, me with my harmonica and him with his bagpipe. The harmonica and the bagpipe are tuned in different keys though, and it didn't work out too well. But I don't think Johnston would have minded.

After all these years, I think I understand now why I didn't die in Vietnam. Maybe the Big Man upstairs had another plan for me. I was ready to die for my brothers in arms and for my country. Instead, I got to live for them. Until my very last breath, I will do whatever I can to serve my country and to serve my brothers.

I still see them in my sleep, those men who died in Vietnam or because of it. The Johnston Dunlops and the Billy Ray Crawfords. They keep me company, and I like to think that they watch over me, as do the loved ones that have left me too soon.

★ 12 ★

NEW BEGINNINGS

By 1999, Peggy Jo was not feeling well. She went to consult our family doctor in Robinson, Illinois, and after a battery of tests, the verdict came down. My wife had cancer. She had surgery and radiation, but the disease kept spreading. Then came chemotherapy. We lived in Indianapolis for a while so she could get treated in a big hospital, and we traveled to Minnesota and Florida to consult cutting-edge specialists.

With the kids all grown up, we'd been spending a lot more time together. No longer tied by school holidays, she'd been traveling with me across the country whenever I was speaking or attending veterans events. Her disease brought us even closer. All those hours traveling and sitting in doctors' waiting rooms, we spoke of our life together. We left nothing unsaid.

I knew that Tim "Doc" Holiday Taylor, the Vietnam vet and musician who'd started the Last Patrol walks across the country, had been battling cancer as well. We'd often met at reunions and other veterans events over the years, and I was real sad to hear that Agent Orange had caught up with him. It must have been extra hard for a talented singer like him to have throat cancer and gradually lose his voice. He'd been diagnosed several years before Peggy Jo, so I e-mailed his wife, Dixie, for some advice. She was real helpful and gave me some tips about nutrition.

Peggy Jo battled on for five years—several more than the doctors had initially predicted. She hung on to life the best she could with all the grace, love, and courage that defined her, but cancer eventually spread to her lungs and her brain. It broke my heart to feel that she was going, but it also broke my heart to see her suffer the way she did. I was by her side holding her hand as we walked that last stretch together, and not being able to make it right for her was killing me. In March 2004, I brought her to the hospital in Robinson, Illinois—the very same hospital where two of our three babies had been born. After a few days, our physician and friend took me aside.

"Sam," he said, "she's not going to make it. She'd down to just a few more hours now."

I picked her up, carried her out to the car, and drove her home. She rested on a bed set up in our living room, and our kids and grandkids came over. She lasted another day and a half. Grandbabies played and giggled on the floor by her side, and I was right there tickling them. That was the very last sound she heard. On March 12, 2004, after thirty-five years of happy marriage, cancer stole Peggy from me. She passed at home with her family around her, the way she'd wanted it.

That day, I lost my wife, my best friend, and my rock. We'd had a wonderful life and raised three children together. Until she got sick, I'd never imagined that she would be the first to go. She had watched me flirt with death and brought me back. Her love had saved me and carried me through the years. She'd held me during my darkest hours. She'd taught me to let go of the hurt, anger, and bitterness I'd brought back from Vietnam, and filled my heart with love and compassion again. Even though I knew that day was coming, for she had been very sick for a while, I was caught helpless by the grief that gripped my chest and clouded my soul. She was only fifty-three years old, and I'd hoped we still had a lot of life ahead of us. At the same time, I was grateful she no longer had to suffer. I was all mixed up, caught in a jumble of feelings that pulled me in all directions.

When she was sick, my ever-loving wife had said she wanted me to find someone else after she was gone. She wanted me to be happy and to keep living life to the fullest. At that moment, it was real hard for me to wrap my head around anything like that, but I humored her and jokingly asked her how long I should wait. "At least thirty days," she retorted with her dazzling smile. That was Peggy Jo. With her gone, I was left with a big gaping hole in my heart. I feared nothing and no one could ever fill it.

Over the following months, I thought I would drown in loneliness. I felt a large part of my life was over. I imagined the years ahead stretching in front of me as I settled into being an old dad and grandpa, but no longer a husband. I didn't want to be alone. I kept speaking. I kept traveling. I kept busy to distract myself as much as I could. When I was home, I spent as much time as I could with friends and with the kids. It kept me going for those first few months. One day at a time. Some of those days were diamonds and some were hard, cold stone.

But once again, when the bottom fell out, I was thrown another lifeline.

A few months after Peggy was laid to rest, I was going through the piles of papers cluttering my desk, trying to clear my office—and my mind. Out of a daily planner fell a yellow sticky note in Peggy's handwriting. "Call Dixie," it read, with a phone number.

Tim had lost his own battle with cancer a few years before, and I hadn't seen Dixie in ages. I'd e-mailed her a while before to see how she was doing, but we hadn't talked. I picked up the phone. She still lived in Texas, and I was in Illinois. We reconnected over phone and e-mail, sharing our sense of grief and deepening our friendship. I convinced her to meet me at Freedom Fest—an annual celebration of veterans in Skidmore, Missouri—in September 2004.

Skidmore is a little bitty town of three hundred people in Missouri's northwestern corner. But every year since 1988, it had hosted a festival celebrating America's freedom and its veterans with good music, simple food, heartfelt speeches, and a generally grand old time. Every September since its inception, I'd enjoyed heading to Skidmore to gather with hundreds of people who'd come from all over the country and stayed in campers or tents to spend a few days enjoying the simple pleasure of being together. That year, I was looking forward to the festival even more. After several months of e-mail correspondence, I wondered what it would be like to see Dixie again after fifteen years.

I saw her in the distance on the festival grounds. The years hadn't altered her beauty and spark. The moment we hugged, I knew I no longer loved her like a sister. She had become a lot more. It took me by surprise. Maybe that part of my life wasn't over yet after all. We spent several wonderful days together in Missouri, and the festival closed with a tree-planting ceremony for loved ones who'd left us that year. I planted a tree for Peggy Jo. In my heart I thanked her for watching over me, and I knew she was smiling down on me as my life was starting again on a new course.

I continued my romance with Dixie via e-mail. Through our correspondence, we got to know each other pretty well. We'd often talked about Tim and Peggy Jo, how blessed we'd been, and how lucky we were to have found love again. We met again a few times in the following couple months, and it became clear to me real quick that this felt right. The more we were together, the more alive I felt. Colors were brighter and the sun was shinier.

There was one thing weighing heavy on Dixie's mind. Although I'd been trying to cut down on my smoking over the years, I'd never managed to quit completely. Dixie had lost Tim to throat cancer, and she couldn't face losing someone else. One day as we were driving, she opened up her heart and told me how difficult it was for her to see me smoke. I took my pack of cigarettes and threw it out of the window. I haven't smoked since.

In December, we went to Vermont for a Saint Barbara ball. Every year, the Order of Saint Barbara—named after the patron saint of artillerymen—is presented to outstanding servicemen. It was organized in a beautiful old inn that year, and there was snow everywhere. There were lots of kids back from Iraq and families of those who didn't make it home. I had also invited a few of Dixie's friends who lived in the area. I went up to speak to those assembled for the ceremony, and before I finished, I talked about Tim and Peggy Jo, and how we have to accept what life gives us and takes away and keep going the best we can. I usually don't talk about personal matters at these type of events, and I could see that Dixie was surprised, wondering what on earth was going on. When I finished talking, I reached into my pocket and took out a real pretty Fabergé-type crystal egg I'd found in a shop not too long before. I opened it so everyone could see the engagement ring inside. "Dixie, will you marry me?" I asked. She was speechless. So I walked back to our table, tucked the microphone under my arm, went down on one knee, and asked her again. I was real nervous, but fortunately, Dixie said yes. I felt like the luckiest man on earth. Everyone was cheering and clapping.

As we got to spend more time and travel to my speaking engagements together, Dixie became increasingly uncomfortable though. She felt she was not setting a good example for the grandkids. If she was going to travel with me, we needed to be husband and wife. So on March 29, 2005, the two of us went to a church in Olney, Illinois, and got married. Just us. We celebrated with hot dogs and a big ice cream at the local Dairy Queen, me in my suit and Dixie in her sparkly jacket. She went back to Texas to tie up some loose ends, and by the summer, she'd moved to Illinois with me.

On September 10, 2005—exactly one year after we'd met again—we were back at Skidmore, Missouri, for the annual veterans event. Many friends were there—people who knew me and Peggy Jo, and lots of people dear to Tim and Dixie as well. It seemed the most appropriate place to have a proper ceremony. Reverend John Steer, another Vietnam veteran, had been a close friend to all four of us, and he'd agreed to officiate. The ceremony took place on the main stage. We were all dressed up in red, white, and blue, and Colonel

Earl Hopper, who had lost a son in Vietnam, gave Dixie away. He was real close to Dixie, and she and Tim used to call him Colonel Dad. He walked her down the aisle, or rather he wheeled her to the steps in his chair, for he could no longer walk by then. He was a hoot, and he carried a shotgun across his lap—his take on the speed at which we'd proceeded with our nuptials, I suppose. There was a lot of music and big lights, and it was a beautiful summer night. Except for the bugs that buzzed all around us: a moth went straight into one of the singers' mouth, and a big old june bug hit Dixie in the eye. But in front of hundreds of friends and fellow veterans, we tied the knot. We laughed. We cried. At fifty-eight years old, I was once again newlywed. I never expected I'd feel so young and ready for a new beginning.

There was another reason to be emotional. That night, I met Dennis Schaible again. He'd been my captain at Tan Tru, and I hadn't seen him in over thirty-five years. As a present, he gave me a piece of metal mounted on a tray. It was a fragment of the howitzer that I had fired at Fire Support Base Cudgel. That fragment was a piece of the gun's shield, which protects the crew from harm.

Today I keep crisscrossing America, with Dixie by my side. After more than ten years of marriage, we never miss a chance to spend time together, hold hands, and waltz in the aisle of the grocery store.

I have once again been given another chance. How lucky can one man get? I don't know why I have been so blessed. I don't know why I am still alive, when so many others died in Vietnam. I don't know why I am still here, when so many are not: Peggy Jo, my

Epilogue

THE PROMISE

The Medal of Honor changed my life in ways I never expected. Wearing it comes with duties and obligations, and I have strived to become a better person because of it. I have tried to live my life honoring what it represents and refraining from anything that would tarnish what it stands for. For that medal around my neck does not belong to me. It belongs to all those men who fought at Fire Support Base Cudgel the night of November 18, 1967. If any of us had failed to do our jobs, none of us would be alive. The medal belongs to all the men who earned it and didn't receive it, and to those who didn't get to come home. My name is on the back of it, but that doesn't mean it is mine. I'm just the caretaker. I have never forgotten what Jimmy Doolittle told me the very first time we met. I had just been awarded the Medal of Honor, and to me he was a war hero and a giant. "Son, you have to always remember," he said. "Don't let the sound of your own motor drive you crazy."

Since I haven't died for my country, I've chosen to live for it, and I will continue to do so for as long as the Big Guy above thinks I am still fit for the job. Living for my country means serving my fellow man and standing for what is right. I could spend my time fishing and hunting, having a good old time. Instead, I'm on the road, speaking to whoever will listen. It's part of the obligation I feel I have to the medal.

I speak to veterans and soldiers, businesspeople or schoolchildren. I listen to their stories, I answer their questions, and every day it warms my heart to meet so many good people. I share what's in my heart and what I've learned in life, and I talk about what I believe in: duty, honor, and country. And of course, I often get to talk about Forrest Gump. Everyone seems to relate to that movie, and many people know me as the "real" Forrest Gump. Like Forrest, I try to stay true to my heart and be a good man. And as I like to tell school kids, I too was shot in the buttocks.

After more than forty years, I'm humbled that so many people still want to hear what I have to say. I still get nervous every time I'm on a stage, and then I remember what my mama told me all these years ago. "Open up your heart, son, and just let them look in." This is what I try to do. I hope others will find something in what I say that is useful to them. If there is just one person in that audience who finds comfort or hope in my story, if there is one single person encouraged to stand for what they feel is right, then my work is done.

I don't preach politics. But I believe that we, the people—old or young, rich or poor, man or woman, Democrat or Republican—have an obligation to shape our country and fulfill America's promise of freedom and justice for all. Freedom doesn't come free. Justice doesn't happen by itself. Much remains to be done to fulfill that promise, and our work is cut out for us.

It is up to us. This is our community; this is our country.

And we won't lose 'til we quit trying.

Acknowledgments

Many people have contributed to this book. By sharing their memories with Caroline, they have refreshed mine and made this book far better than it would otherwise have been. The men who were brave enough to revisit their recollections of Tan Tru and Cudgel for this book deserve very special thanks, particularly Jim Deister, Bill Few, Frank Gage, Joe Moore, Gary Powell, Steve Rogers, Dennis Schaible, and Larry Zimmerman. You all are and will forever be my brothers. Thank you also to Bob Gibson for his contribution to the section on Australia; Michael Letton, for clarifying how Jim Deister found me again; Jim Newman for talking about his dad; Paul Sutton for providing valuable details about Agent Orange, the Pointman Project, and my medical condition; Tom Cottone and Alan Jones, who filled in many details on the theft of the Medal of Honor; Gary Wetzel, for his memories of the White House and of the infamous cheese fight; Don Kelby, without whom there would be no Sammy L. Davis Federal Building; and Richard Grasso, our New York friend. Thank you also to my daughter, Nikki Johnson, for sharing memories of her childhood: you, your brothers, and the wonderful families you've created mean the world to me.

Acknowledgments

Several people were kind and generous enough to read the manuscript and provide valuable comments. Thank you Jack Jacobs, Major General USAF (Ret.) Perry M. Smith, Bob Hamer, and Jimmy and Bruce Guider. I am also grateful to Bob Jerome for his legal advice.

A most special thank-you goes to my co-writer, Caroline Lambert. Without her, this book would never have been written. She quickly captured my voice and my feelings on the page, and her diligent research and in-depth interviews uncovered details and events that I had forgotten—or in some cases didn't even know about. Her willingness and ability to dig deeper unearthed long-buried emotions, which not only helped this book but also resulted in additional healing for me. Dixie and I love her like family.

To every brother with whom I served in Vietnam, thank you. I wouldn't be here without you. I wouldn't be here either without my wife, Dixie, whose love and constant encouragement have filled my once-broken heart with hope, strength, and laughter.

—Sammy L. Davis

Working on this book has been an immense joy and privilege. I am forever grateful to Sammy and his wife, Dixie, for opening their hearts, their lives, and their home to me, and for making me part of this adventure. Thank you for answering my many questions with such patience and grace. You are both an inspiration, and getting to know you has made me a better person and a better writer.

I am also grateful to the many people who agreed to be interviewed for this book. Our conversations were inspiring, heartwarming,

Acknowledgments

sometimes heartbreaking, and always a great help to me. Your generosity and dedication to Sammy are humbling. I also wish to thank the Lyndon Baines Johnson Presidential Library and the Vietnam Veterans Memorial Fund for their assistance.

Special thanks to the wonderful Ivan Kronenfeld and Jack Jacobs for introducing me to Sammy, and for believing in this book and trusting me with it; Nathalie Casthely for her support throughout; Frank Weimann and Dado Derviskadic at Folio Literary Management for steering us through the publishing world; and Thomas Colgan and his team at Berkley Caliber for bringing Sammy's story to the bookstores.

None of this would have been possible without the unwavering love, support, and encouragement of my husband, David, and daughter, Zoe—who, thanks to Sammy, is well on her way to becoming one mean harmonica player.

—Caroline Lambert